AUDIOVISUAL EQUI

AND MATERIALS

A Basic Repair and Maintenance Manual

by

DON SCHROEDER
and
GARY LARE

The Scarecrow Press, Inc.
Metuchen, N.J. & London
1979

Manufactured in the United States of America

Library of Congress Cataloging in Publication Data

Schroeder, Don, 1931-
Audiovisual equipment and materials.

Bibliography: p.
Includes index.
1. Audio-visual equipment--Maintenance and repair.
I. Lare, Gary, joint author. II. Title.
TS2301.A7S35 621.38 79-384
ISBN 0-8108-1206-1

FOREWORD

This book is intended to provide help and procedures for in-house maintenance and servicing of audiovisual equipment and materials. The content is one step beyond the how-to-use content of courses and texts in the audiovisual field and the specific operating instructions that come with most equipment when it is purchased. It makes no attempt to make a full service technician of the reader. In fact, it will frequently suggest that some types of problems are the clear domain of well-trained and equipped service personnel.

However, better than half of the problems encountered in the operation of audiovisual equipment can be handled without recourse to a service technician or agency. The problems fall into three degrees of severity:

1. Operator error or ignorance;
2. Minor problems with cords, lamps, needles, and the soft-ware materials;
3. Circuit component failure requiring competent diagnosis and repair.

Corresponding solutions to the problems include:

1. In-service training programs and personal assistance;
2. Establishment of a small service bench with a small set of tools and this book;
3. Sending the equipment to a dealer or other service agency.

This book has been written on a practical level for school administrators, librarians and media specialists, teachers and students who are charged with, or become involved with, the equipment aspect of the audiovisual program. It might also prove useful to the industrial training person who wants some background in making minor equipment adjustments and repairs.

The ultimate aim of anyone working with audiovisual equipment should be to minimize problems and obstacles that interfere with effective delivery of the intended communication. Actual use of this book in a local service program should contribute considerably to that goal by reducing service time (and costs) and keeping audiovisual equipment ready for use.

CONTENTS

PART I

SERVICE CONCEPTS

SERVICE CONCEPTS

Service Logic

The key to diagnosis of an audiovisual equipment problem is application of a service logic, which is really the scientific method applied to mundane equipment failure. All service work is done this way, either consciously or subconsciously. The steps are:

DEFINE THE PROBLEM, usually by asking or being told what the equipment is, or is not, doing. It is probably best then to confirm the problem yourself. This will reveal operator errors or controls that have been left in some abnormal position by a previous user. Having established that a technical problem exists...

MAKE OBSERVATIONS, using all your senses, in an effort to localize the problem. This also requires a sound knowledge of "normal" operation, or access to the original operating instructions that came with the equipment Try to get a clear idea in your mind of what is working and what is not. Then...

MAKE A HYPOTHESIS as to what might cause the malfunction you have observed.

TEST THE HYPOTHESIS by taking some kind of corrective action or making a further test or measurement. If your first guess isn't right (you should be so lucky), make another hypothesis and test it.

If your test shows you are correct, and you are able to do it, MAKE THE REPAIR.

If your tests all prove inconclusive, or you fear the repair is beyond you, SEND THE EQUIPMENT OUT FOR REPAIR.

Service Knowledge

The knowledge of electronics and mechanics required for efficient service work is unique. It usually does not need to be as theoretical, and certainly not as mathematical, as the knowledge required for engineering design. An aptitude for understanding things mechanical is an asset, but such aptitude comes in a very long scale, and most people can understand basic principles of the type taught in General Science courses. It is the application of those principles to Service Logic that makes Service Knowledge unique.

While it is impossible to anticipate everything you might need to know, the authors have distilled years of experience as media specialists to provide the essentials that they believe would be helpful in maintaining audiovisual equipment.

This book contains several appendices. Your attention is particularly directed to "How We Use Magnetism" and "How We Control Light." An understanding of these basic discussions will prove invaluable in formulation of the hypotheses required in the application of Service Logic. This is especially true if you want to go beyond the check-list type of information provided under each type of equipment.

In the discussion of observations under Service Logic, "a sound knowledge of normal operation" was mentioned. This can not be overstressed. How can you hope to find malfunction if you do not know proper operation when you see it? The best time to gain this knowledge is when the equipment is new and the instruction booklet is available. All new equipment should be checked for proper operation upon receipt anyway, and that's a great time to try all the knobs, buttons, levers, switches, etc. The knowledge gained at this time can be useful in helping staff learn proper use, in running routine performance checks, and is essential when malfunction is reported. You will know you are getting on top of operational knowledge when you can say to the person on the phone:

Client - "I got the cassette recorder but it doesn't run."
You - "Have you checked that the switch on the microphone is ON?"

Client - "The filmstrip projector is showing halves of two pictures but I can't find the lever that makes it show one."
You - "On that projector there is a button in the middle of the advance knob. Push that in and turn until you have one full picture and release the button. Call me back if that doesn't clear up the problem."

Client - "I've used this video tape equipment before, but I can't get a picture from the camera."
You - "Does the recorder play back an older tape?"
Client - "Yes, that's working fine."
You - "Are you sure there is power on the camera? Do you have a picture on the finder screen?"
Client - "The little orange (green, red) light is on, so I must have power, but there is no picture on the finder."
You - "OK, that's probably the f-stop ring out on the lens. It's the ring closest to the camera body. Turn that ring and see if you don't get a picture."
Client - "Hold on a minute... Hey, that did it. Phew, I'm sure glad we didn't break something."
You - "That doesn't happen very often, but sometimes when the camera is moved that ring accidentally gets turned. Remember, that's the ring we usually adjust to get the best modeling of the cheek-bones."

Client - "I can't get the dry mount press to stick the pictures."
You - "Do you think it's hot enough?"

Client - "I've got it set over 200 and it's been on for 20 minutes."

You - "What color is the dry mount tissue you are using?"

Client - "Kind of pink looking."

You - "Oh my gosh! (Straining to suppress convulsive laughter.) You're using the separator sheets. You throw those away. Try using the yellow sheets and I'm sure you'll be ok."

Look what a great service day you are having. All that help and not one really technical problem in the lot. But all your help is founded on secure knowledge of how the equipment operates. Most of the audiovisual problems aren't any more difficult than these, but use of this book will make it possible for you to be even more helpful in keeping things going.

One final word. Remember the old adage, "A little knowledge is a dangerous thing." The kind of help shown above will get you the respect of your colleagues. It will not make you an expert in all aspects of educational technology. Remember the other word in this heading--SERVICE. Service is rendered humbly, without involved technical explanation. It's the client's show. Don't expect more than an occasional "thank you" and a lot more demand for even more service. Remember, it's the little bit of grease that keeps the big wheels turning smoothly. Service is not the prima donna role, but is nonetheless essential to the enterprise. To know that your work is useful and necessary is one of life's greatest internal satisfactions.

Service Skills

Fortunately, the majority of audiovisual equipment does not require a high order of mechanical or electronic skill in order to make adequate repairs. (Exceptions include motion picture projectors and videotape equipment, where specialized knowledge and tools make it practically foolish to remove any covers at all.)

The manufacturers of the equipment may have had to machine parts to very close (thousandths of an inch) tolerance to assure proper operation. Service procedures rarely get involved with these built-in tolerances. Electronic components are made with values and ratings stated by the manufacturer. Replacement parts are bought with the same or better ratings, and soldered into the circuit. As long as the soldering is skillfully done, the accuracy is a characteristic of the component.

Because of the extremely wide range of skills ability expected among the intended readers of this book, a short appendix also contains a list of basic tools necessary to perform the service procedures described. Those with tools available and experience in using them should just skip the Tools appendix.

Only experience can teach you how much to tighten, how hot to solder, how tight to grip. A little practice with old equipment might help to build the confidence that seems to be the attitudinal requisite to good use of hand tools. Knowing when to give up also helps, because some tough cases just have to be referred to more skilled hands.

An Example of Service Logic, Knowledge, and Skill

A stereo record player is returned with the complaint that the right channel doesn't play. You plug the unit into power, plug in the two speakers, put on a record, and confirm the complaint (L). You turn the balance control full right (K), and almost all sound fades away. Because cables are so troublesome (K), you hypothesize that one cable may have a broken wire (L). Returning the balance control to mid-setting (K), you switch the speaker plugs to test the hypothesis (L). Sure enough, the right channel is now playing but the left is dead. You move the wire back and forth with a slight into-the-plug pressure and suddenly the channel plays, goes silent, plays, and goes silent (K, S). You cut the wire just above the plug, strip the insulation, and prepare the wire for connection to the plug (S). Before attaching the wires, you put the replacement plug in the jack and very carefully touch one wire to each contact of the connector (S), while the record is playing. Quickly, but carefully, you reverse the wires, listening for which combination is loudest. (This is called "phasing" the speakers, and the loudest combination is the right one--K.) Solder the wires to the plug contacts (S). If you forgot to put the plastic or metal shell (the part we use to grip the plug when inserting or removing) over the wires before soldering, welcome to the club. You'll just have to unsolder (S), add the shell (K), and resolder (S). These little errors fall into a category known as "common sense"--and that is beyond the scope of this book.

A Few Words about Electrical Safety

Most audiovisual equipment operates off 117-volt line power. While the Occupational Safety and Health Administration (OSHA) rules and enforcement are generally viewed as expensive nuisances by both manufacturers and consumers alike, their intent to provide improved safety from accidental shock, fire and even death can hardly be disputed.

Throughout this book there are frequent references to electrical "ground." In power distribution in the United States this refers to a reference potential of 0 volts when measured to an earth ground (a metal stake driven about 4 ft. into the earth). One wire of the power distribution system is actually grounded. The other wire, referred to as the "hot" wire, is then 117 volts "above ground." It is thus possible to get a lethal shock just by touching one wire (the hot one) when you stand on a wet floor in your bare feet (not as far out as it seems when you consider the use of video equipment for swimming stroke or diving analysis). The metal rim of a sink top or plumbing fixture connected to a water pipe (ground) can also complete a shocking circuit. (Also not far-fetched, considering that media preparation areas often have electrical equipment on a cabinet top that includes a sink.)

Most equipment is quite safe when functioning normally. But wires become frayed with use, and careless or unskilled individuals sometimes make sloppy repairs, leaving tiny strands of wire touching metal frames or casings. To provide a measure of protection the three-wire power cord has been offered in recent years. The round prong of a three-prong plug should actually make a true ground connection between any metal frame or cabinet and an earth ground, independent of the grounding of the power distribution system. A circuit short within the equipment may then blow a fuse or circuit breaker, but it should stay safe for the operator. Use of two-prong adapters, without grounding the green wire or lug, subverts this whole protection system.

Do not rely on asphalt tile as an insulator from electrical shock. It would probably prevent lethal current levels, but it does pass some voltage when laid on concrete floors, especially on the ground level of buildings (where AV departments so often seem to be located for ease of moving equipment).

Take time to unplug equipment before removing the case. You can always plug it in again when you are past the danger of a finger slipping into an exposed terminal with line voltage on it. Since so many of our repairs are cord and plug replacements, take time to do them right and carefully. If possible, try to wire the new wires to the same plug prongs as the original ones were. Before closing a plug or recasing a unit, inspect your work for any little loose strands of wire and cut off any you find.

If you are unsure of these procedures, seek a demonstration from someone who does this kind of work. Anyone in this society should be able to replace a power plug, but we all have to learn how to do it right.

Don't go probing around in the amplifiers and motors with screwdrivers, pieces of wire, or soldering aids. Unless you know what you are doing, this will almost invariably cause even more trouble and a higher repair bill than you had in the first place. Experience at this level should be gained in courses or supervised apprenticeship.

Remember, there are two levels of the electrical safety problem--your own, and all the rest of us. Since audiovisual equipment is almost always used in some sort of institutional setting, it entails a degree of public responsibility beyond that of fixing your own home appliances. When we do the work ourselves, we don't want future charges of endangering others because of our lack of knowledge or skill. And if we take a supervisory role, we must see to it that people who take the work seriously are doing the repairs.

PART II

EQUIPMENT MAINTENANCE AND REPAIR

INTRODUCTION

Part II covers specific types of equipment, listing most common problems, suggesting what you may be able to do to correct them, and offering some preventive maintenance checks.

This is a generic section, deliberately written and photographed without reference to any specific brand of equipment. Where a manufacturer or model of equipment is identifiable, neither endorsement nor indictment should be inferred. Certainly some designs and constructions have proven more serviceable than others and anyone involved with the maintenance of any kind of mechanical or electronic equipment develops preferences.

Overall, the experience of the authors is that audiovisual equipment performs better than the general run of consumer devices and appliances. We tend to buy larger quantities and institutional-quality equipment. The quantities increase our chances of getting a few "dogs," but this is offset by the more durable nature of many of the designs. We also often have multiple users of a single piece of equipment, a situation widely recognized by technicians as particularly hard on mechanical and adjustable electronic components.

If you need help with criteria for selection of equipment, Dugan Laird's AV Buyer's Guide; A User's Look At the Audio-Visual World, published by the National Audiovisual Association (see bibliography) is recommended.

MOTION PICTURE
PROJECTORS

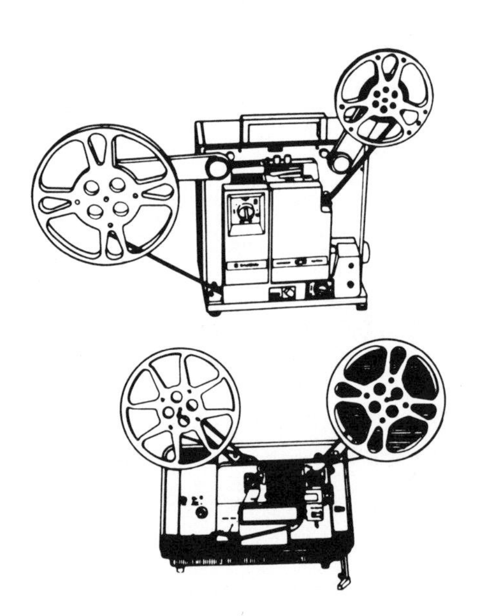

Function: The illusion of motion is produced by showing a sequence of slightly different still pictures in rapid succession. The projector provides a shuttle claw that precisely advances the film, one frame at a time, at a rate of 18 frames per second (fps.) for Super 8, or 24 fps. for 16mm sound. A shutter interrupts the light during each advance to prevent blur, and once or twice between advances to reduce flicker. A system of reel arms and spindles and sprocket wheels feed film into the intermittent shuttle and pull it out and wind it onto the take-up reel.

Sound projectors include a sound drum and speed stabilizers, plus a photo-electric or magnetic tape system, that reads the sound recorded on the film. Speed at the point of sound take-off must be as uniform as possible (in spite of the jerky motion of the shuttle where the picture is projected) to avoid wow and flutter in the sound. The electrical signals of the "reading" system are amplified and connected to a speaker to reproduce the sound.

Problems: Mechanical

Film does not feed evenly from supply reel

Projector does not hold shuttle loops, causing rapid vertical blur on screen

Sound reproduction is fluttery

Film does not wind onto take-up reel fast enough, or tightly enough

Rewind is sluggish or incomplete

Various odd squeaks, chatters, or other mechanical noises from the projector itself (not the sound system)

Optical

Low light level on screen

Hole burned in film when stop motion is used

No sound or poor definition of sound (optical cause)

Electronic

Lamp or motor control switch failure

Motor tries to run but is slow or fails to gain full speed rapidly

New exciter lamp fails to light in sound system

No sound or distorted sound from sound system (electronic cause)

General statement about motion picture projectors

These audiovisual devices are second only to video tape recorders in complexity and electro/mechanical design sophistication. They require an array of specialized lubricants and indiscriminate oiling can cause damage that will raise a subsequent repair bill. Equipped service dealers use special gauges and shims to adjust the projector mechanism, and keep abreast of factory recommended changes and service techniques through service bulletins. Often, adjustments that seem to restore operation are in fact two wrongs to make a right, and result in excessive wear and otherwise unnecessary replacement of parts.

Only the most superficial things are recommended for checking and repair at the level of this book. Almost all adjustment and complex repair should be left to technicians in a company-recommended service shop or dealership.

Mechanical Repair

Film feed problems are rarely caused at the first sprocket wheel. They can be caused by a bent reel, a sloppy film wind, or a lack of pressure in the system that retards "free-wheeling" of the reel when film is being pulled off. This last and most probable cause can quickly lead down to a system of clutches in the drive and/or rewind mechanism. Adjustment is not recommended, because replacement of a clutch part may be the real need.

If the claw in the film gate becomes excessively dirty with a gummy accumulation of lint and oil, the projector may not be able to maintain a loop. Such accumulations should be carefully scraped out with a toothpick. NEVER USE A METAL TOOL OR IMPLEMENT IN THE GATE AREA. (One slight slip can cause a scratch which turns up a burr and can scratch hundreds of dollars worth of film in a single showing.) Also, open the gate and check the pressure plate for free movement. The plate is spring-loaded to rest firmly but gently in the film channel of the gate. Slight cleaning of the plate support system may be needed to maintain constant pressure. Gates should always

16mm. film gate with pressure plate

be kept clean, but changes in the air-flow pattern make this less a problem with new projectors than with older ones.

If the sound is present but less than good, try to spin the sound drum with your fingers. It has a flywheel inside the projector that will make it hard to turn, but which should keep it turning a few moments after you remove your fingers. If it is not turning easily the flywheel must be removed, the drum shaft slid out, cleaned, relubricated with light oil, and the wheel re-attached. DO NOT TRY TO OIL THE BACK OF THE SOUND DRUM. There is an optical system here that does not need a film of oil. Some modern slot loading projectors require that the threading procedure be followed explicitly, or the film will not seat in the guides and rollers in the sound area. If the film is pulled off the feed reel as it is slid into the slot, the problem is solved. Old-timers who try to push the film into the slot as they did when threading older machines often have trouble getting clear sound from these newer projectors.

16mm. sound drum and flywheel assembly

16mm. sound drum detail

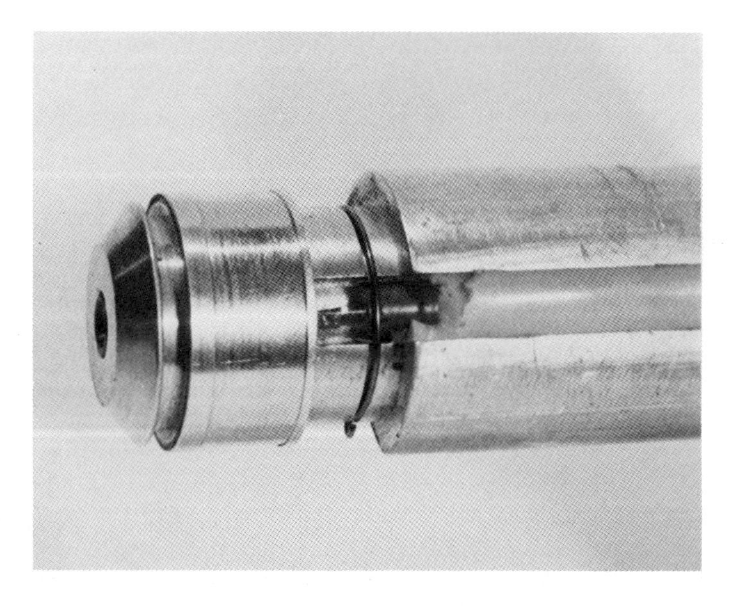

Poor wind on the take-up reel is usually a clutch problem. If the projector has an external belt to the take-up spindle, you should try replacing it. Anything beyond this should be done by a trained service technician. Many of these clutch drives use felt or fiber pads and washers. Like any clutch, they tend to wear. They can also pick up lubricant from other parts of the assembly, causing slippage beyond the design limits. Adjustment is rarely an adequate answer for these problems.

Rewind difficulties are also commonly clutch problems, or the result of failure of the high-speed shift system. Once again, try replacement of the external arm belt to the feed reel, if there is one. If that doesn't fix it, send it out to someone equipped to make adjustments and replacements as needed.

Annoying noises can sometimes be located and remedied with a little lubricant carefully applied. Most current projectors use a series of belts in the mechanism and some of these have guides (little metal sleeves rotating on bent wire shafts) that can squeak. The procedure is to remove the back of the projector and move your head around while the projector is running to try to locate the area of the squeak or whistle. This is usually about as successful as trying to find a squeak or rattle in a car. Then carefully push a fingernail against one after another of these small moving parts. Any disturbance of the normal pressure or speed will change the sound. If you find the problem, put just a very small drop of oil on the shaft, run the projector a few seconds, turn it off, and wipe off any excess oil with a tissue. NEVER OIL ANY CLUTCH MECHANISM OR ANYTHING THAT LOOKS LIKE A FELT PAD. These all require special lubricants and oil will destroy their function. The special cleaner/lubricants containing silicone can be equally damaging in these areas.

This whole clutch business in projectors may be worth a few lines of explanation. Any device that spools film or tape while maintaining a constant speed somewhere in the mechanism requires some kind of clutching action. The reason is that very little tape or film is wound with each revolution of the spool or reel when the diameter is small, but a great deal more is wound per revolution when the spool or reel is full. Think about that! Since the basic speed of the mechanism is constant, the design revolves the spindle fast enough to wind the film or tape at the smallest diameter on the reel. As the diameter gets greater (more material on the reel) the reel turns more slowly to wind the same amount of film or tape. This speed difference is handled by a clutch. The clutch also must compensate for the amount of torque (turning force) required to get a tight wind without overloading the drive mechanism. Obviously, this is a quite complex function, requiring precise adjustment. A little lubricant in the wrong place (or lack of it) can change all the design relationships and cause malfunction of the device.

Optical Repair

If there is a low light level on the screen, turn off the projector and remove the lamp house cover. First, check that the lamp is the right one for the projector (the model and serial number plate often gives the correct ANSI Code). Next, check for operation of the heat-absorbing glass and screen if the projector has a still picture feature. This small device is located at the front of the lamp house. It should be up if the film is moving through the projector. If a heat screen is not staying up, it is a service shop repair. It could be wired up for the duration of a showing, but should not be kept in service this way since any attempt to show a single frame will burn a hole in the film. If the projector does not have this system, and the lamp is correct, either the optics (condenser and projection lenses) are dirty or missing (some newer lamp systems use only one, or no, condensers), or there is an electronic problem in the voltage going to the lamp.

Heat screen in light path

No sound is most frequently the result of an "exciter lamp" failure. This small lamp sends light through a slit optical system and the sound track to a photo-electric cell. Once again, the correct lamp must be used. Several will fit the socket, but only the right one will have the filament properly positioned to focus on the sound track.

If the light is lit, is the right one, and the sound is poor, look for an obstruction or general dirt on the small lens barrel in front of the exciter lamp, or, in some models, dirt on the mirror behind the sound drum. Adjustment of the small lens is not recommended since it must be both in focus and with the slit in the proper direction. Just wipe the area out with a lightly wadded lens cleaning tissue. If the sound does not improve, try another film. If both sound bad, send the projector out for service.

16mm. sound reading area

Electronic Repair

Switch failure is a service agency repair because most modern projectors use special sets of switches or rotary switches that are not available through normal parts channels (the selection at your local hardware or discount store).

Projectors that fail to run, or run at full speed, are either overloading the motors, or have some kind of motor problem. A slipping main drive-belt can also be the cause. But there is nothing that can be done about these other than a trained technician with a supply of parts.

Sound system problems are often power supply failures. Any fairly sharp electronics technician may be able to diagnose and repair these malfunctions. The exciter lamp is either lit by direct current or a complex oscillator circuit. In either case, inability to get an exciter lamp lit can be symptomatic of amplifier difficulty far beyond the simple lighting of a lamp by an AC circuit common to most technician's experience.

Preventive Maintenance

Keep a service record on motion picture projectors to determine accumulated maintenance costs. If a projector is only requiring service once a year or less, let the service agency do a general cleaning and lubrication whenever specific repairs are made.

On your own service bench:

Keep all gates and sprockets clean.

Keep a few new empty reels of various sizes on hand and throw away any that become dented or distorted beyond straightening.

Keep optics clean, using lens cleaning fluid and tissues. Be particularly careful to blow off the surfaces first and not to grind grit into the lens surface.

Consider a dealer summer maintenance program. These always seem a needless expense, but may pay better service dividends in the long run.

If you are really concerned about motion picture projection quality, buy a print of the SMPTE Jiffy Test Film (see Bibliography). This film is good for evaluation of new projectors and a quick quality control check of either on-going performance, or performance right after repair.

FILMSTRIP PROJECTORS

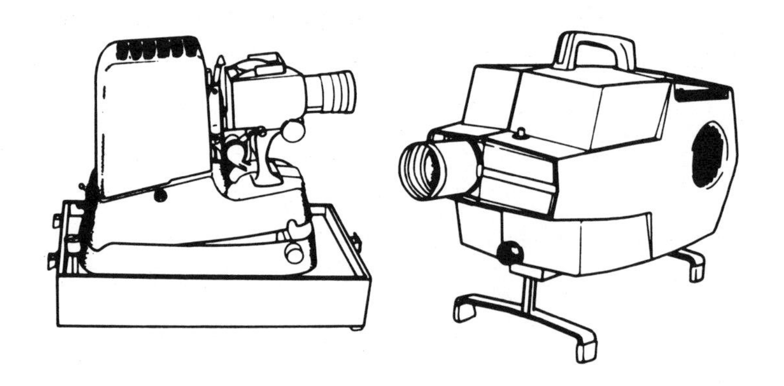

Function: Filmstrip projectors provide intense, even illumination of the filmstrip frame, an optical system for projection of the image on a screen, including some focusing scheme, and an adjustable mechanism for advancing the filmstrip frame by frame. Fan or blower cooling is usually provided.

Problems: Mechanical

Film gate does not hold film flat
Advance mechanism does not engage film sprockets for consistent film advance
Advance mechanism will not adjust for exactly one-frame projection
Blower or fan runs slowly, causing hot odor and early lamp failure

Optical

Uneven or weak illumination
Uneven focus over the whole picture on the screen
Spots in the picture area, even when no filmstrip is inserted

Electrical

Lamp or fan switch is intermittent or fails to work at all

Mechanical Repair

Failure to hold the film flat will appear as non-uniform focus of the image on the screen. This is indicative of missing or improperly inserted gate glass, or, in the case of glassless gates, a problem with the pressure springs or misalignment of the pressure plate with the film channel.

If the filmstrip advance mechanism and gate assembly can be removed from the projector, take it out, insert a filmstrip, and very slowly advance a filmstrip through the mechanism, watching for causes of the problem. The glass is held in by very thin spring clips. These may need to be bent slightly to alter the gate pressure. If the assembly is held together with screws, go over them to be sure they are all tight.

Some projectors have a hinged lens housing and locking catch. If the hinge has been forced and is bent, the pressure plate does not seat in the film channel properly. Similarly, if the catch is not tight, gate pressure can vary, affecting the focus. Bent hinges should be removed for straightening, if possible. Be very careful when applying counter pressure to bend things back because of the brittle metal or plastic lens housing to which the hinge is attached.

If you determine that the sprockets are not engaging the film enough for reliable advance, it will be necessary either to shim the advance shaft bearing slightly forward (if possible) or to bend the filmstrip guide to permit the sprocket teeth to protrude further.

When working in the gate area, be very careful with any tools. Great care must be exercised to prevent scoring or burring the film track in order to avoid scratching all subsequent filmstrips.

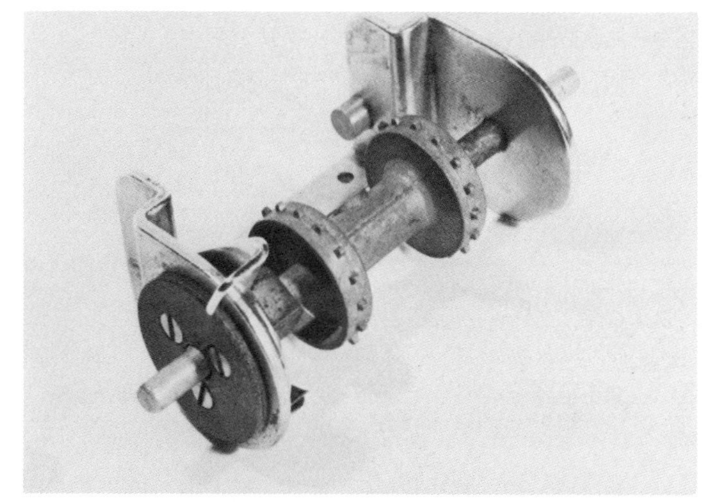

Filmstrip sprocket assembly (above)

Replacement gate glass should be ordered through the dealer from whom a projector was bought. Not many glass shops can grind the curve at the leading and trailing edges of the glass, and those glass plates with metal slide tracks are definitely beyond local fabrication.

Frame adjustment failure is remedied by disassembly of the sprocket advance mechanism, cleaning, and reassembly. Before doing all this, try a little WD-40 on the sprocket shaft and framing mechanism, working it in by moving the adjustment knob or lever back and forth several times. Some of these framing devices are amazingly complicated, largely because of the springs that set the advance distance. If it looks too complicated, give up before it all flies apart and you lose some of the parts.

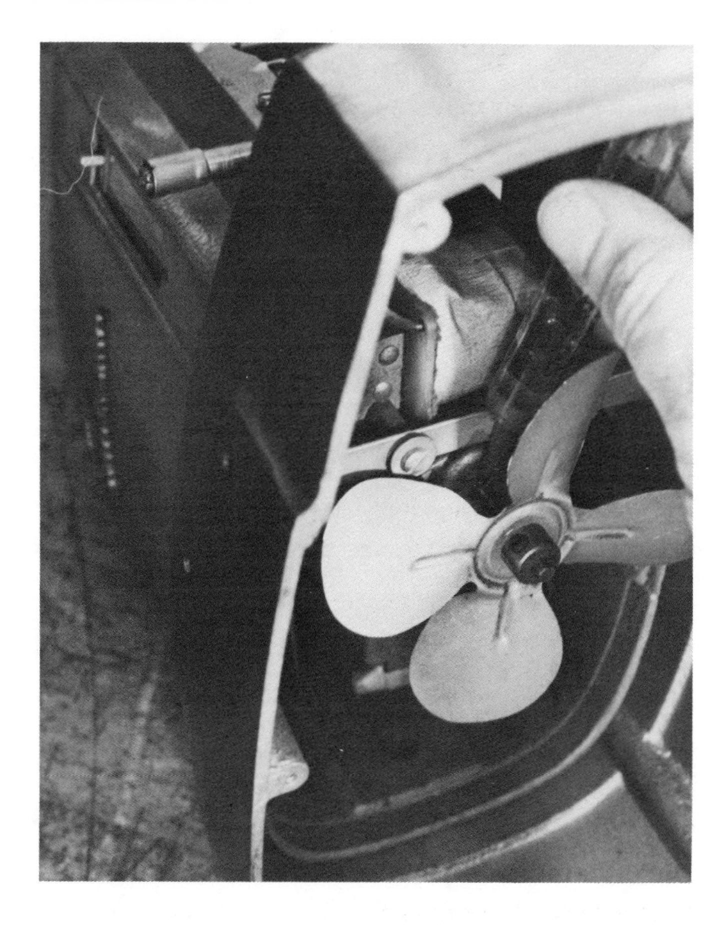

Blower fans get up to full speed rapidly (a few seconds) and sound like they are moving a rush of air when they are operating properly. Cleaning and oiling the fan motor bearings will normally bring a fan back up to speed. Access is gained from the top after removal of the lamp, and from the bottom after removal of any protective screen or grille.

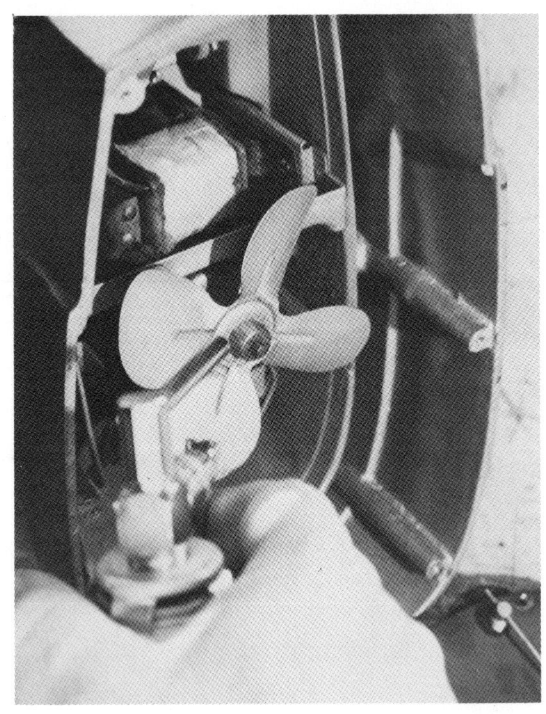

Wipe off the fan blades and blow or wipe dust off the motor whenever you are down in this section of a projector. If the motor fails to respond to cleaning and oiling, you will have to remove it and follow the complete procedure given in the How We Use Magnetism (Motors) appendix.

Optical Repair

Check for proper lamp, and proper insertion of the lamp, if the illumination is uneven. Be especially sure that the lamp is fully seated in the socket. Check the condenser lenses to be sure they are all there (not as easy these days, since the number and types of condensers varies with the type of lamp employed) and that they are in the right order, with convex and flat sides facing properly. (The only rule of thumb is that convex sides face one-another. See illustrations in How We Control Light appendix.)

Uneven focus over the entire picture can be caused by the gate pressure problems discussed above, or in some cases it results from improper assembly of the projection lens. (Not a factory problem, but one created by people who have to take everything apart.) A reversed lens element usually causes sharp center and blurry sides, or vice-versa. Sharp on one side and blurry on the other would more likely be a gate pressure problem.

If the whole frame is sharp, then jumps out of focus, suspect insufficient cooling and oil the fan motor, or check the gate pressure plate system. Advancing the film will sometimes unseat the pressure plate, which then has some problem dropping back into place, usually because it is hung on some dirt or corrosion.

Black spots or dark areas that turn when the lens is turned are caused by dirt in the lens. This dirt should be blown away and/or the lens cleaned with Lens Cleaning Tissue and fluid. Dirty gate glass is a more common cause of black spots on the screen. The gate must be taken apart, the glass cleaned with lens tissue and fluid, and the whole thing carefully reassembled to avoid focus and advance problems.

Electrical Repair

About the only electrical repair you can make is replacement of the fan and lamp switches, and the power cord and plug. When replacing the switches, be sure to ask for one with a high enough current rating (at least 5 amps at 115 volts AC, for a 500-watt projector). And of course it must be small enough to fit in the space available. Switches of this type are stocked by most appliance repair shops.

The lamp sockets and cooling motors are not at all common and would require return to a dealer for replacement.

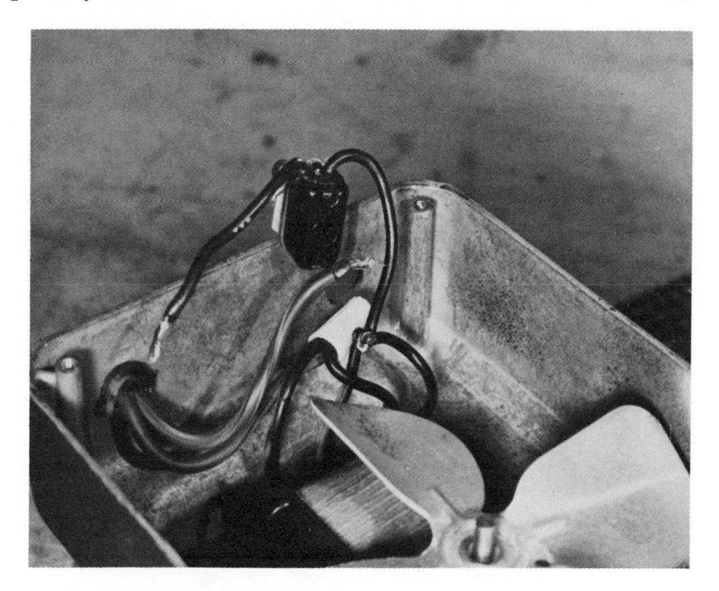

Switch removed for replacement

Preventive Maintenance

At least once each year:

Clean the fan and put a small drop of light oil on each end of the motor shaft at the bearing

Clean all optics with lens cleaning fluid and tissues. This includes the gate glass, which should also be cleaned each time a lamp is replaced.

Put a filmstrip in the projector and check for normal frame and advance operation. Check the elevation system and lubricate if it seems hard to work. Look at the power cord and plug for cracks or fraying. Replace the cord if there is any doubt about its condition.

SLIDE
PROJECTORS

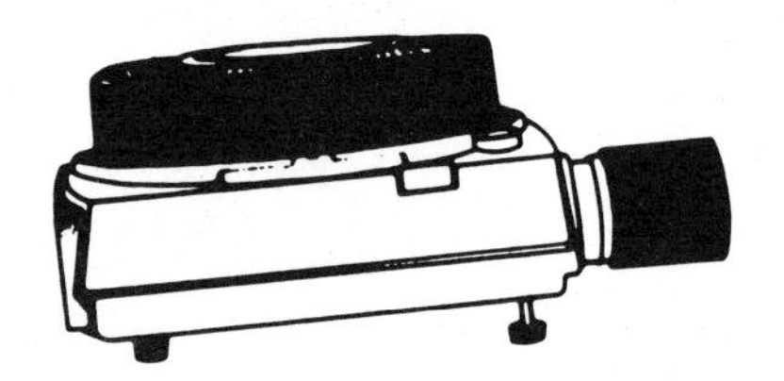

Function: Slide projectors evenly illuminate the area of the slide for which they were designed (24mm X 36mm in a 2" x 2" mount is standard) and provide a lens system to focus the image on a screen. Blower cooling is part of the design of most modern slide projectors. The key component of projectors exclusively for slides is the slide change mechanism. Even so-called manual projectors (loaded one slide at a time) usually have a slide carrier that masks the light during slide change and provides for discharge of the last slide projected while positioning the next slide in the gate. Mechanical change projectors use an array of "magazines," some requiring special individual slide frames, to contain the slides in the projection sequence and to re-store them after projection in the same order.

Problems: Mechanical

Overheating due to some blower problem
Slides jam or fail to insert
Loss of synchronization of shutter system, resulting in partial picture on screen, or no picture
Slide change is visible on screen

Optical

Non-uniform brightness on screen
Inability to focus whole image simultaneously
Zoom lens will not focus at all

Electrical

Nothing works
Remote change control will not work, or works in one direction only
Overheating due to over-wattage bulb

Mechanical Repair

Blowers in slide projectors not only cool the lamp, but some of the air is directed through the gate area to cool the slide. Most projectors will also include a pre-warming system to heat the next slide prior to projection in order to reduce a shift in focus if the film buckles in the gate because of heat absorption from the light of projection.

Slide projector blower motors may have gummy bearings, which will require cleaning with a little lighter fluid and relubrication with a light oil. A single blast of WD-40 in each bearing may do both cleaning and lubrication simultaneously. Some models have belt-driven blowers and these belts may slip or break. As with all projectors, care must be taken to avoid script pages, books, etc. from getting in the way of air intakes or outflows, reducing the volume of air required by the specific design.

Jamming and change failure is almost always a slide failure. Cardboard mounts fray with use. Some tend to bend because of the heat in the gate, especially if a slide is held on-screen too long (about 60 seconds is considered a safe limit). One brand of plastic mounts has a black side which, in some projectors, may absorb enough heat, if used on the side facing the lamp, to warp the mount. Slides that are determined to be the cause of jamming should be remounted.

Some of the simpler slide changers are like a card trick. If the springs don't engage the slide properly, the change fails to take place. Fixing these is a matter of analysis and bending gently, but repeatedly, until operation is restored.

Some mechanical change systems handle one slide at a time, either letting it fall into the gate by gravity, or sliding it in with a pushing mechanism. Failure in these systems is usually a matter of alignment, and the magazines or trays should not be overlooked as possible causes of problems. Each slide chamber must align precisely with the gate and/or insertion mechanism. Bent or broken slide container elements can prevent proper alignment. So can a partially gummed advance wheel or lever. The track through which the holder moves must also be clean and smooth.

The other most common mechanical change is accomplished by shuffling the slides off the bottom of the deck. This system is particularly vulnerable to bent slides, or problems with slides mounted in varying thicknesses of cardboard or plastic. The change mechanism itself must be dry (free of any gummy or wet lubricant) because of its contact with the slide mounts.

There are a number of shutter problems. An out-of-synch shutter is the hardest to correct mechanically, and will probably have to be sent to a service agency. Usually this problem shows up as part of the picture fully illuminated, though possibly out of focus. The rest is obscured by dark areas, either at top and bottom, or at the sides. Failure of slides to seat fully in the gate can also cause this kind of problem, but that in turn can be a synchronization problem. The key is whether the problem occurs with all slides, or just some slides. If it appears that slides are causing the problem, try either substituting freshly mounted slides, or re-mounting the suspect slides.

When the slide change is visible on the screen, the shutter mechanism is probably stuck. Removal of the projection lens will give somewhat better access in some models. Try to figure out the linkage that works the shutter and try spraying connecting points and bearings with a minute squirt of WD-40. (Because of the optics in this area, we want to avoid getting WD-40 all over everything.) Never force a shutter part, but try nudging elements with a finger or screwdriver in an effort to free the stuck component. If you can get it free, work the mechanism several times to work the lubricant into the sticking area.

Optical Repair

A number of things might cause non-uniform brightness on the screen. Super-slides might tend to have light fall-off in the corners if used in a regular projector. You either have to find a projector with wider illumination of the slide, or live with the problem. Wrong lamp is a not uncommon problem, causing the lamp elements to block some of the light, or the filament not to align with the projection axis. Sometimes the lamp has not been fully inserted into the socket, again causing alignment problems.

One of the most difficult causes of uneven illumination to identify is mis-insertion of, or missing, condenser lenses. Unless you really know the projector, or can find another like it for comparison, you will just have to use trial and error, exchanging and turning lenses around until the screen evens out.

Focus problems are either caused by buckling of the slide itself, or by something wrong with the projection lens. A projector that runs hot will cause more slide warp than a cooler one. Some slide mounts grip the film so tightly that they do not allow for expansion, and this increases the tendency to buckle the film in the mount.

Changes within the projection lens can cause focus problems if the lens was disassembled and not reassembled in the right order. There is only one right order for the spacers, glass elements, and direction of curve of the lenses. This leaves a fantastic margin for error. Most projection lenses are sealed, but this never seems sufficient to deter the determined.

One brand of zoom lenses is particularly vulnerable to this kind of problem. Some know-it-all will invariably try to focus the lens by turning the zoom ring. When the lens fails to focus, unbelievable power is applied, breaking the seals and opening the lens barrel. All of this usually happens in the dark, and the tiny pins that control the zoom element are lost. Repair is just about impossible for use in general service, although a good technician may be able to cut and file some new pins and restore the lens for use within an area of adequate supervision. If the zoom element is installed backward, the lens will not focus at all.

Electrical Repair

When nothing works, a power problem is the usual cause. If the cord is permanently attached to the projector, suspect the power plug. If the cord plugs into the projector, it may be necessary to bend the projector pins slightly, or to dig into the soft rubber connector and close the metal sleeves slightly for a tighter fit. Also, don't overlook the possibility of a bad outlet at the wall.

Next, consider the power switch. Either there are two switches for lamp and blower, or there is one complex slide switch that turns things on and off in sequence. A lamp switch won't work unless the blower switch is also on. The lugs of these switches can be shorted momentarily with an insulated-handle screwdriver to try to restore operation. Single switches are usually common types and can be replaced. Special rotary and slide switches should be replaced by a repair agency. They can get the switch, and they might as well put it in because access is always very limited and it's pretty hard to get all those wires onto the right switch lugs.

The remote controls have rather fine wires that may break on either the plug or the control end. Try another control if one is available. Broken wires at the control end can be fixed by cutting the cable about an inch back from the control, stripping the small color-coded wires, and soldering them back to the appropriate colored wire point in the control. (It is best to remove one and resolder one at a time to prevent confusion.) Plug ends are molded to the cord and are virtually impossible to repair, requiring ordering a replacement control from the manufacturer. Sometimes a remote control works intermittently because it fails to make good contact when the change button is pressed. Opening the control will reveal the contacts. With the unit unplugged (either the projector or the control) put some coarse bond or construction paper between the contacts, press the movable one down, and slide the paper back and forth to clean the contact. Also, analyze the movement required and try to bend the element(s) slightly to assure easier contact when the button is pressed. There is a tendency for some people to be brutal with this sort of control, and overpressing the button may have bent something, making light contact impossible.

Designs demand the wattage for which their cooling, be it convection or blower, is rated. Use of over-wattage lamps, either by accident or to increase brightness, will result in overheating, with resultant damage to the projector and shortened slide life.

Preventive Maintenance

Use of slide projectors is widely variable. In elementary schools use may be infrequent, whereas in some exhibit modes of use the projectors may run 10 to 12 hours a day. Maintenance depends upon use.

Projectors that are rarely used need only an occasional check after use. Clean the front element of the projection lens if it shows finger smears. Attach the remote control, insert a slide magazine, and test forward, reverse, focus and zoom (all may not be available). Try to determine if a normal amount of air is being circulated by the blower. One way to check this is to sniff the outflow air. If it smells like a hot toaster, the cooling may not be sufficient. While it's a subjective test, outflow air should feel only slightly warm about one foot from the projector when a hand is placed in the air stream.

Projectors that are in almost constant use should be cleaned at least once a week. Condenser lenses, heat absorbing glass, and projection lenses should all be cleaned. The track in which the magazine rides should be wiped out with a cloth moistened with WD-40, which will leave a slight dry lubricant when it evaporates. Check all operating controls for normal function. Remote controls may not be used because exhibit machines are usually changed by some tape-cue device. Above all, try to keep a log of running time on projectors in this kind of service. Manufacturers have a recommended life for their machines. Trouble can be saved by honoring the time limit and replacing projectors when they have run the recommended time.

FILMSTRIP AND
SLIDE VIEWERS

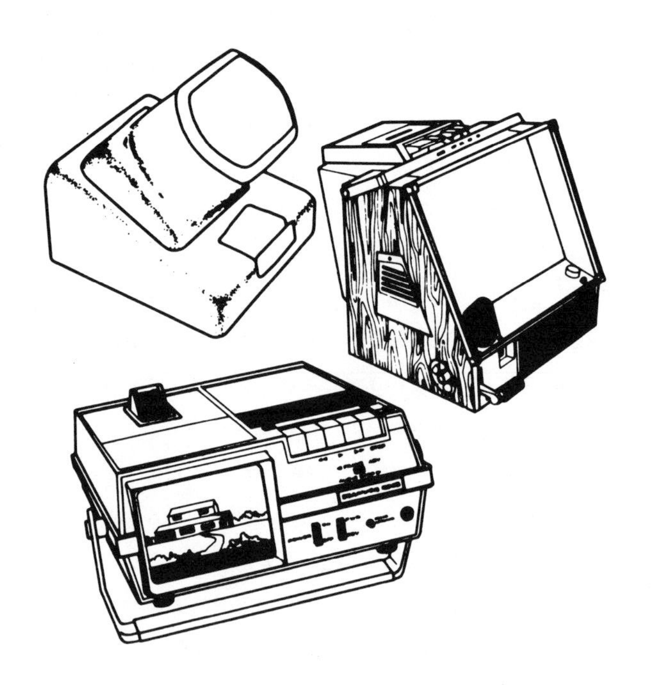

Function: In their early form these devices consisted of a magnifying lens, a light diffusing screen, and sometimes a source of artificial illumination rather than use of a window and daylight to light the image. More recently viewers are actually mini-projectors, using bright but low-wattage lamps and an optical system to project the slide or filmstrip image on a relatively small, self-contained rear projection screen. Many of the most recent viewers also incorporate cassette players to audibly describe the visuals and automatically advance the slides or frames.

Problems: Difficult to categorize in sound units; a list includes:

Short lamp life
Failure to advance manually
Failure to advance automatically
Image slightly out of focus
Jammed slides
Shutter not opening all the way, slides not in clear focus
Sound missing, weak or distorted

Repair Notes

Short lamp life is not uncommon in viewers. Convection-cooled BLC lamps are notoriously short-lived. Rated at only 30 watts, they must burn brightly to produce the white light required for good color rendition. While it is not recommended, if lamp life is an overwhelming consideration and quality is less important, a 25-watt double-contact bayonet-base lamp used in vacuum cleaners can be used in place of the BLC and will give comparatively infinite service. BE ABSOLUTELY SURE THAT ANY SUBSTITUTE LAMP IS RATED AT LEAST 110 VOLTS AND HAS TWO SOLDER CONTACTS AT THE BOTTOM OF THE LAMP BASE.

Viewers that have cooling fans or blowers will usually smell hot if the cooling system is not moving enough air. Any odor complaint should be checked quickly, before permanent damage is done. Slipping or broken belts are a common cause of this overheating, which will also shorten lamp life. If these viewers are used in carrels, be sure not to push them against wooden carrel sides or back; this impedes the free flow of air. Users should also be cautioned not to let notes or other paper block air intakes.

Manual advance systems range from small rubber sleeves on an exposed shaft, in early magnifying viewers, to almost magical slide changers, and ratchet and pawl levers in some of the newer viewers. The rubber sleeve units are easily adjustable by loosening the spring screws, pushing the rollers into contact, and retightening the screws. Faulty slide changers are usually the result of spring fatigue. Work the mechanism slowly and try to figure out how it should work. This will usually reveal something that needs just a slight bit of bending to restore the original spring force. If a spring system has been forced and the metal distorted, repair may not be possible without fabricating a new piece of metal.

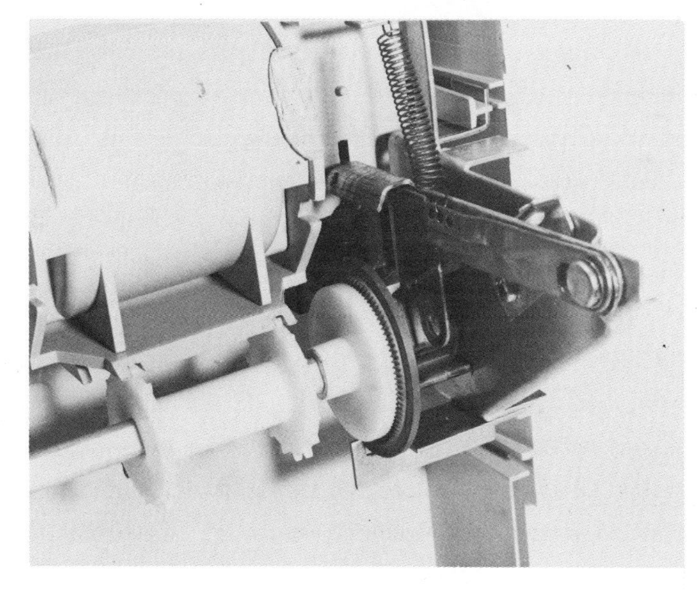

Watch mechanism operate slowly . . .

. . . to analyze reason for failure

Ratchet pawl systems either get gummy (free them with a very light touch of WD-40) or the springs break or slip off. Inspection will usually show what the problem is, but repair may be beyond your local shop, especially if springs or parts are required.

Automatic advance failure can be caused by anything from a stuck advance magnet mechanism, through a broken or slipped linkage, to some complex failure of the cassette player electronics that detect, amplify, and transmit the advance signal. It can also be the result of something as simple as insertion of the cassette with the audible, rather than automatic cue side up. Always try a known cassette before deciding that the unit, and not the cassette, is at fault. Aside from making a visual inspection and possibly repairing a malfunction of the advance linkage, automatic advance problems require attention of a capable and equipped technician.

All of the projection-type viewers using rear projection screen panels have some means of focusing the tiny projection lens. These are usually secured with some sort of screw which must be loosened before the lens will move. It may require more than one attempt to restore prime focus because tightening the locking screw can move the lens enough to take it out of focus again.

Automatic slide viewers may have a series of troubles related to the slide gate. If slides tend to jam, the most likely source of trouble is the slide frame itself, especially if it is cardboard. Slides that have been bent or creased should be opened and the film remounted in a fresh cardboard or plastic mount.

Most slide change mechanisms include some light shutter arrangement that cuts off the light during the slide changes. This mechanism can also include parts that lock the slide in the correct plane so that it is in focus during projection. While it is not a common problem, this whole related group of gate parts can get completely out of synchronization. Such a failure requires retiming of the mechanism--definitely a job for an experienced technician with access to a service manual.

Viewers that include sound can have the same kinds of problems that are associated with any cassette recorder. Access to the circuit board and mechanism can be complicated by their inclusion within the viewer housing. If the unit has provision for an earphone, it is always worth trying a headset to be sure the problem is not simply with the contact in the earphone jack. Also be sure to try another cassette that is known to have something recorded on it. If you can get access and want to pursue the problem, consider the problems listed in Part II, Cassette Recorders.

Preventive Maintenance

If viewers are in almost daily service, as is often the case where they are installed in carrels or study areas, an every 3-month maintenance schedule would not be too often.

Turn the unit on and look at the screen. If there are an annoying number of black spots, clean the optical system, particularly any glass in the gate area.

If the unit includes a cassette player with automatic advance, establish a seldom used but known-good cassette for test purposes and play at least part of it to check the advance system.

Blow off with canned compressed air and/or wipe off the cooling fan and put a drop of oil on the motor bearings.

Visually inspect any belts for evidence of wear (look also for small piles of black dirt near belt pulleys as evidence of belt slippage and grinding). Lightly pull on belts with a finger to check tension. They are never very tight, but should not slop or seem too large for the run they make. Stretched belts should either be replaced, or at least replacements ordered.

Exteriors of viewers should be cleaned with a damp cloth rubbed first on a bar of Lava soap. Rinse off any soap residue with a cloth lightly wetted with clear water. Marks on the screen surface may also be removed. Use only petroleum-based solvents on these screens. If all else fails, try rubbing lightly with a cloth that has been rubbed on a bar of Lava soap. Do not attempt to clean the large mirror behind the screen unless it is very cloudy. (See How We Control Light (Mirrors) appendix.)

OVERHEAD PROJECTORS

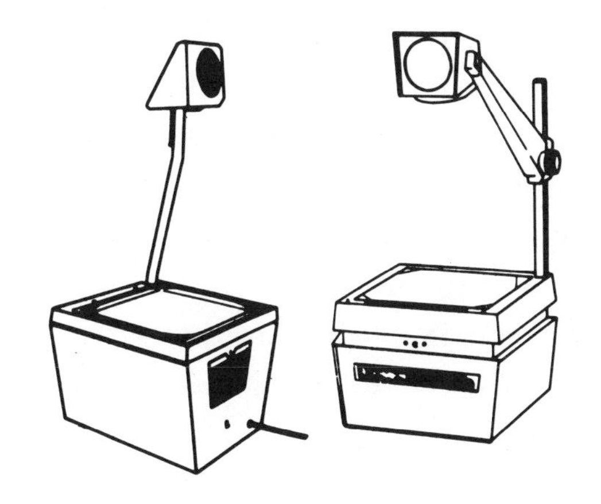

Function: Overhead projectors, so named because they were originally used to project images above the chalk boards in large lecture halls, project a transparency up to 10" x 10" from a convenient horizontal "stage" onto a projection screen or other good reflective surface. Only the overhead projector allows development of an impromptu visual idea during a presentation. Because of the extremely high projection efficiency, relatively little room darkening is required, except when critically color-coded materials are projected.

Problems: Optical

Focus not uniform over entire screen area
Illumination not uniform over entire screen area
Red or blue discoloration at corners of image

Mechanical

Overheating because of poor fan ventilation
Tilt of lens head will not hold
Focus control too stiff or too loose
Blurring of image because of vibration from cooling system

Optical

Failure to maintain uniform focus is usually not a projector fault, but rather results from the up-tilt angle required of overhead projectors. Depending upon projector height, this can result in a wide range of distance from lens to top of screen and lens to bottom of screen. The degree of keystoning of the overall image is some indication of the amount of tilt. The solution is to angle the screen sufficiently to make the sides of the pro-

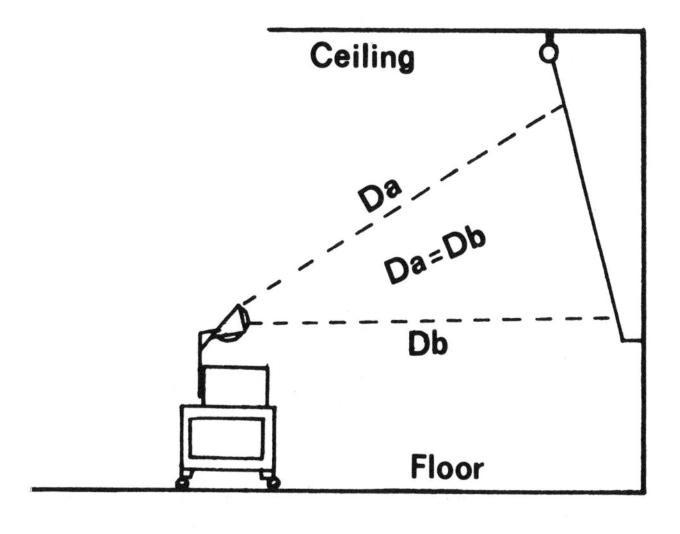

jected light area as nearly parallel as practicable. When this is not possible, users should be told to check the screen occasionally and adjust focus to make the section of the transparency being discussed most clearly in-focus.

All other optical problems are related to alignment of elements along the optical axis of the projector. Some are further related to distances between elements of the system. Non-uniform illumination could be as simple as a dirty stage glass or fresnel lens, but is more likely a heat-warped fresnel lens (dark spot in center) resulting from insufficient cooling now or at some previous time. Or, the fresnel lens may be installed upside down, causing a bright spot in the center of the image. If you put a fresnel lens on a page of print you will be able to see it all when the top side of the lens is up ... only the center part is clear if the top is against the type.

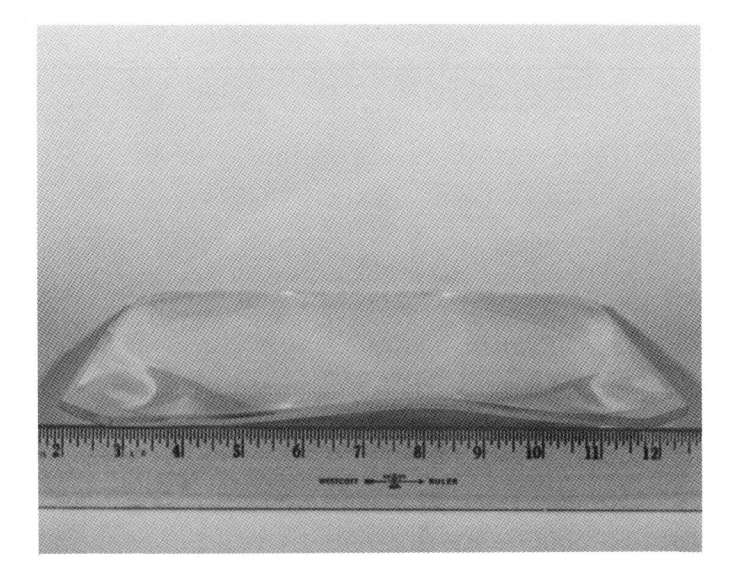

Straightedge shows lens warp

The lens head should be centered over the center of the fresnel lens. A quick check of the entire alignment is made as follows:

Place the projector to produce a screen-filling image of the size most commonly expected

Put something on the stage of the projector and focus it on the screen

Being sure that the projector axis is centered with the screen, adjust the head tilt for a slight upward angle.

Check the bottom of the image for parallelism with the bottom of the screen. If it is not parallel, adjust the lens head for lateral tilt if adjusting screws are provided. If not, proceed with the next step before attempting adjustment.

Look up at the lower lens. All of the light from the stage should be going into the lens and none should hit the rim. If the bottom of the image was not parallel to the bottom of the screen, and light is hitting the lens housing, the whole lens support system is sprung and must be returned to alignment. Have someone hold the base of the projector firmly and just as firmly, but slowly, apply enough twisting force to the lens support bracket and column to get all the light from the stage into the lower lens when you release the head. If the image bottom was parallel to the bottom of the screen, but light was hitting the lens housing, the lamp is not centered beneath the fresnel lens, or the fresnel lens is not properly centered. Fresnel lens centering can be checked by turning off the projector and holding a piece of string diagonally from corner to corner of the stage glass, first one diagonal, then the other. The string should pass over the center point of the fresnel lens, but you will have to get your eye over the center point to be sure of the alignment.

Finally, hold a piece of white paper in contact with the lower lens and check the size of the illuminated area. Now hold the paper in contact with the front lens and again check the illuminated area. They should be about the same size. If they are not, the height of the lamp should be adjusted. There are screws that hold the whole lamp housing in place and these permit adjustment of the lamp to fresnel lens distance.

This adjustment is also made to reduce or eliminate corner discoloration. Raise the lamp if color is red, lower if blue. Turn all height screws about two turns, check image for color, and turn more if necessary. The correct lamp-to-lens distance is related to the screen image size. Projectors used consistently with auditorium screens may require a different adjustment from those used with classroom-size screens.

Mechanical

Overheating can be an expensive problem because of the cost of lamps and replacement fresnel lenses. The volume of air required by various models of overhead projectors varies and is hard to estimate by listening or feeling the "draft." A fan is probably operating at speed if you can spin the fan blade with your finger and it turns freely. You should also feel no resistance when you very gently try to turn the blade. If the blade does not turn freely, put a drop of oil on each end of the motor shaft, work it in by pushing the shaft back and forth, and try spinning it again. Very bad cases may require the full motor treatment described in the How We Use Magnetism (Motors) appendix.

Another possible cause of overheating could be use of the wrong lamp. Projectors have been made in a number of wattages over the years, with cooling designed for the intended lamp heat. Unfortunately, it is possible to insert another, higher wattage lamp in the same socket, producing more heat than the fan can cope with.

Lens heads that will not hold tilt need tightening of the head bolt or nut. If they will not tighten, a thin fiber washer between head and bracket will add enough friction to make the adjustment hold.

Focus systems vary, but cleaning, lubrication and/or adjustment when possible will make focusing smooth. This is important if users are to maintain highest image quality.

Vibration blur can be confirmed by steadying the lens head with a hand, or firmly pressing down on the whole projector with both hands, watching for the image to sharpen. The most common source of vibration is fan blade imbalance. Slowly rotate the fan by hand and look for one or more blades that appear bent. Bend such blades back in line and to the same twist as the other blades. Since some vibration can be expected, look also for loose lens head support screws, missing rubber feet, or a shaky lamp filament. Any of these could cause unstable screen image.

Preventive Maintenance

Once each year, or whenever lamps are replaced, each overhead projector should be given a quick optical alignment check as described in this section.

Projectors that are in daily use should get a little oil on the fan motor shaft bearings every three months. Twice a year is recommended for less frequently used projectors.

Since most overhead projectors use quartz lamps, be careful not to touch the glass when replacing lamps.

At least once a year, clean the lenses with lens tissues and a cleaning solution. Wipe off both surfaces of the fresnel lens with a moist soft cloth. Clean the stage glass as often as necessary on top, but both sides at least once a year. The heat and motor oil, and in some cases smoky rooms in which the projectors are used, leave a film on the optical surfaces that must be removed if full light efficiency is to be maintained.

Check power switch, line cord, and thermal switch for normal operation.

SPECIAL NOTE: Just because they are relatively simple devices, overhead projectors are usually taken for granted. Only corrective repair is performed and full operational checks are rarely made. This is bad practice. The lens head support system is subject to abusive handling and the stages get very dirty from handling and their horizontal, dust-catching surface. Viewers deserve the same image quality from an overhead projector as from any other projector.

OPAQUE PROJECTORS

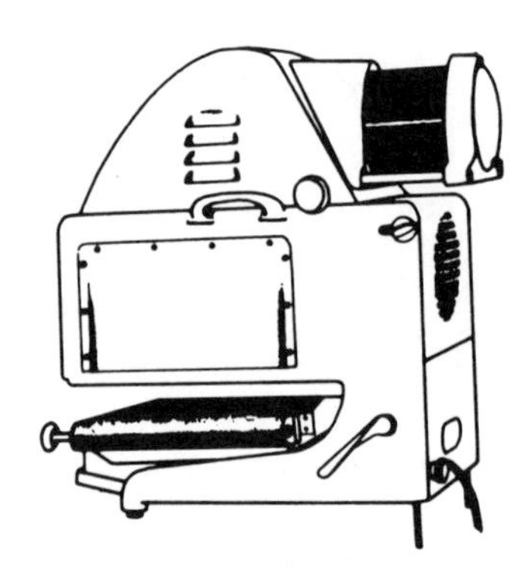

Function: Opaque projectors use a very large lens and mirror to focus printed material or a small object onto a screen for viewing by a whole class or group. The material is illuminated by a very bright (usually 1000 watts) lamp whose efficiency is further increased by a system of mirrors. Since the high wattage generates a lot of heat, a fan or blower is provided to keep things as cool as possible. Current models use heat-absorbing glass, spring-loaded stages, and conveyor-belt designs to position and hold the material being projected. Some models include a projected light spot or arrow for use as a pointer.

Problems: Mechanical

Stage system(s) not working properly

Elevation legs do not work

Focus mechanism difficult to work

Pointer system inoperative

Electrical

Lamp will not light, either because it is burned out, cable or plug is faulty, or power switch is burned out. If cooling fan operates, cord, plug and switch are ok.

Lamp lights, but cooling fan is slow or inoperative.

Optical

Illumination uneven. Check for broken or missing mirror.

Projector will not focus ... caused by its being either too close or too far away from the screen; or the lens barrel needs to be re-set in the focusing mechanism.

Picture lacks good definition and contrast ... usually because of too much ambient light in the room, or the material being projected also lacks good contrast.

Mechanical Repair

STAGE SYSTEM failures are usually the result of screws that are missing, are loose, or have become too tight (this seeming contradiction results from the needs of various parts of the mechanism). A touch of lubrication may also be needed at the various pivots.

If the belt has become so stretched that normal adjustments will not restore normal feed, lift or slide the belt feed system off the stage elevator and dismantle it. Lightly spray the rollers (only) with Scotch Spray Mount Adhesive. Give them at least 15 minutes to dry, then reassemble the belt feed system and re-install it in the projector. The best solution would be to order a new belt, but this method will keep the belt operating until a replacement can be obtained.

Because these designs vary, you have to look at the mechanism, figure out what does what, and then tighten, loosen, and lubricate in an effort to restore proper operation.

ELEVATION control is usually by means of spring-loaded legs at the front of the projector. BE VERY CAREFUL WHEN WORKING WITH THESE LEGS. Because of the weight of the projector, the springs that extend the legs have considerable force. Normally the weight of the projector will retard the speed and a stop on the internal end of the leg will prevent its coming out completely. But if things were normal, you wouldn't be working on this part of the projector. The common problem is a stuck leg. You must release the holding screw and then attempt to pry the leg out. But if you suddenly free it, it is likely to come flying out with all the force of the spring, possibly even breaking the stop and shooting out of the projector. Just be sure it's aimed at something other than a person, in case this should happen. There is a tendency to try to make this repair by pulling the front of the projector over the edge of a cart. In this case look out for your feet.

The reason for jammed legs is usually a missing foot, which has allowed the leg to get up into the sheet metal of the projector and get stuck. Threading a screw into the hole in the bottom of the leg (if there is one) gives something to grip with a pair of pliers in an effort to work it loose. Any well-stocked discount or hardware store should have some kind of chair glider or leg tip that can be made to fit the projector leg. Since the legs work independently, it is not necessary that both feet be replaced if the other one is ok, but do whatever it takes to prevent wobble of the whole projector.

FOCUS MECHANISMS may need to be wiped out thoroughly with a cloth wetted with a little WD-40. Spray just a little in the bearings of the focusing knob and along the rack gear area, if you can get at it. These steps should restore smooth operation.

If the focus knob doesn't work the lens at all, either the knob has come loose (tighten the set-screw in the knob), the pinion gear teeth are stripped (a service shop repair), or the lens has been forced beyond the limits of the rack teeth--requiring forcing back over the pinion gear. This last step would take more nerve than most of us have, and perhaps should be left to a service facility, rather than damage the focusing gears even more. If the knob is missing, either find a set-screw knob from a junked piece of equipment, or pick one up from a radio shop or electronics parts jobber. The knob should be no smaller than 1-1/2" diameter to give sufficient leverage.

POINTERS may have mechanical or electrical problems. The control knob may have come loose, making operation tough to control. Tighten it. Loose linkages in the system are harder to find and fix because access is very limited. Do what you can, but remember that these devices are rarely so necessary as to be worth spending a lot of time trying to fix them. Some of them have separate small lamps, and if that lamp is burned out it will have to be replaced to restore the indicator.

Electrical Repair

The circuit of an opaque projector is very simple. Power goes from plug through cord to a single switch, which controls both the lamp and the cooling fan. Because of the high wattage of the lamp and the heat in the projector, switch failure is not uncommon. Be sure to replace with a switch rated at least 15 amps at 120 volts AC. Because of access problems, it is easier to splice a new cord to a stub of the old cord just inside the projector than it is to try to run the cord all the way up to the switch. If the insulation on the stub of cord is at all dried out, you must replace the whole cord. Don't take chances!

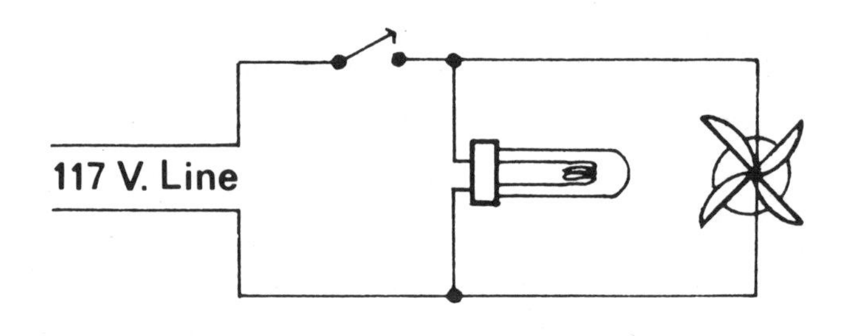

Like all COOLING FANS, these tend to gather quite a lot of dirt. Try to blow it out with compressed air, wiping with a rag if you can get at the fan blades. Then put two drops of oil on each end of the motor shaft, turn on the projector to let it run in, turn it off, let it cool, and wipe off the excess. If the fan did not come up to speed, you may have to do a complete motor overhaul as described in the How We Use Magnetism (Motors) appendix.

Optical Repair

If illumination is uneven, open the access door and check for presence and condition of the small mirrors that surround the stage area. Also, look beyond the lamp at the large concave reflector behind the lamp. Sometimes these crack from the heat, and if this is the case, a replacement will have to be ordered from the dealer who sold the projector to you.

(A problem related to this area, but one that is fortunately very rare, is a lamp that was mis-inserted in the socket, became welded in, and can not be removed when it burns out. If you encounter this rarity, either give up first, or reconcile yourself to a very long and intricate job of replacing the whole socket ... which is not a common item itself. Old projectors or stage lights are the only source of these sockets other than ordering a new one from the manufacturer.)

Complete FAILURE TO FOCUS, other than the mechanical type of problem described above, is usually the result of the instructor trying to use an opaque projector from the back of the room, or of the lens barrel slipping in the focusing mount. One model has a screw in the metal collar that tightens around the lens barrel. To reset the focus mechanism, place the projector 12 feet from a screen with printed material on the stage. Loosen the collar screw, turn the focusing knob until the travel of the collar is at mid-point (half-way forward and half-way back). Now move the lens in the collar (if it won't move, loosen the collar screw more) until the image is in focus on the screen. Re-tighten the locking screw in the collar. This adjustment is not necessary or possible with projectors that focus by rotating the lens.

Preventive Maintenance

At least once each year:

Check for proper operation of elevation, focus, and stage

Turn on projector and try to determine if fan or blower gets up to full speed fairly quickly (5 to 10 seconds)

Remove lamp and clean all mirrors (see procedure under mirrors in How We Control Light appendix). Small light-reflecting mirrors are not as critical as the large first-surface mirror that reflects material or object from stage to lens. Clean lens front and rear elements with several lens tissues and lens cleaning fluid. (These are large lenses and the tissue used should be proportional.)

Examine cord and plug for drying and cracking of insulation. Replace if deemed advisable.

Wipe dust from fan blades and lubricate motor shaft and bearings

Check pointer or spot for smooth operation (if included in projector)

Extend legs fully and wipe off thoroughly with cloth wetted with WD-40 or light oil

PROJECTION
SCREENS

Function: The projection screen provides a surface that reflects light (or transmits it, in the case of rear projection screens) with greater efficiency than ordinarily available light-colored materials. The screen should not contribute to or detract from the color of the projected media. Screens at this time (1978) work for the best compromise between high reflectivity and widest angle of light dispersion. Some screens deliberately sacrifice wide angle to give high brightness along a narrow path near the projection axis, especially with projected color television. Many screens include mechanical support and storage systems, permitting them to be put out of the way when not in use.

Problems: Screen surface

Fabric ripped
Reflective surface discolored or marked
Transmission surface marked, stained, or cracked

Mechanical

Screen roller failure
Tripod legs or riser wobbly; parts missing
Screen housing follows fabric as screen is raised

Surface Repair

In general, it is a safe statement that any screen surface problem is going to result ultimately in replacement. This creates a "nothing to lose" situation ... the kind in which it is safe to dare more, often with surprisingly good, if temporary, results. So, with that in mind:

Ripped fabric should be repaired from the back by applying some kind of fabric adhesive tape along the rip while the two rip edges are held closely butted together. Suitable tapes include Utility (Duct) Tape, binding repair tape, and, somewhat harder to get, Gaffer's Tape, used in photo and TV studios to tape wires to the floor.

Prepare the back of the screen by cleaning the taping area with a cloth moistened with lighter fluid or other petroleum solvent. (Do not use anything that smells like acetone, or is a known plastic solvent. Many screen bases and surfaces are plastic.) If possible, take the screen down and lay it out face-down on a table. If the repair must be made in place, get an assistant to hold a board against the front surface so you can get enough pressure on the tape to make it bind. Since rips are usually from the side of the screen, it is best to have a little too much tape and cut off the excess at the screen edge.

Matte surface and lenticular screens can be washed with warm water and liquid detergent to remove routine dirt. Beaded screens should not be subjected to any surface treatment since anything will remove beads and cause an area of non-uniform reflectance. Yellowing that is unsightly does not appreciably degrade the projected image.

Crayon marks can often be removed by many wipings with Q-Tips or clean cloth, moistened with a petroleum solvent, followed by a general washing with warm water and detergent.

Rear projection screens are subject to pencil and crayon doodling, as well as soft-drink and coffee splashes, etc. The key here is to avoid both gross abrasives and plastic solvents. Most of these screens are installed with the image surface away from the viewer. Start with a little warm water with detergent added. This is usually sufficient. You may need to dry the surface to prevent water marks from air-drying. If water hasn't removed the marks, go next to some petroleum-based solvent on a cloth, working only on the specific marked area. If it works, follow with warm water and detergent rinse and dry for uniformity. The last resort is a lather of Lava soap on a soft cloth. Don't get all carried away with the rubbing, especially if you are working on the image surface of the screen. After using the soap lather, rinse several times in clear water and dry.

These treatments, if used successively, will restore most screen surfaces to usefulness, if not their original transmission or reflectance and clarity.

Cracked surfaces of plastic rear screens can be treated by very gently putting acetone or film cement at the edge of the material and flexing it slightly to induce a capillary flow of solvent into the crack. Do not use so much as to have solvent run onto the surfaces. At best this only retards lengthening of the crack. Screens that are cracked into pieces must be replaced.

Mechanical Repair

Mechanical problems with screens are almost as difficult as fabric problems. A screen roller with a broken spring must be replaced, and ordinary window shade rollers do not have the strength to roll the heavy screen fabric. Since replacements are difficult to order from most manufacturers, it is wise (if unsightly) practice to store broken screens behind a door somewhere, and to exchange torn fabric on good rollers with good fabric on broken rollers, etc.

One end of a roller has a simple center pin. The other end has a flat shaft and a detent pawl device that stops the roller when it is turning at slow speed in the winding direction. If the detent is not working well, a squirt of WD-40 at the end of the roller with the flat pin will often free the tiny mechanism and restore better operation.

Be very careful when opening screen cases. Most are odd shaped and do not rest firmly on a work surface. Once the smooth end-bells are removed, sharp sheet-metal corners are exposed. If the screen is rolled fully into the case, pull it out a little until the roller detent removes tension. Otherwise, the whole thing will try to unwind when the end-bell or insert (depending upon make and model) is removed. Be very careful of prying on the detent when the roller is out of the case because if it suddenly releases, the flat end pin will spin rapidly and may throw the tool you are using. A firm grip on the roller and a pair of Vise-Grip pliers on the flat end-pin, again firmly held in the other hand, is the best way to try to get this mechanism to work. Solvents and/or lubricants are your only hope for repair in this area.

Roller detent mechanism

Replacement of fabric may be done with a staple gun on wooden rollers. Do not use tiny office wire staples. If you do not have access to a staple gun, either use gummed tape or pry out the original staples or tacks and try to re-drive them with a hammer. Fabric must be taped to metal rollers, using the same tapes recommended above for fabric repair. Here the key is getting the fabric on straight. Many rollers will have a scribed line or seam that can be used as a guide. If this is not available, wind about a half-dozen wraps of fabric, not too tightly, get the ends to wind evenly, then very carefully unwind with the roller until the end can be taped or stapled.

Returning the whole fabric and roller assembly to the case is also a problem. Care must be exercised to prevent the sharp case edges from slitting the fabric. Both fabric wind and roller ends must be correct if the white side is going to face the room. (This revelation normally hits as the last end-bell screw is being tightened!) If the spring tension has been released, either it must be rewound with a Vise-Grip plier, or the screen must be partially reassembled, the fabric pulled down until a detent just prevents it from winding up (a light tension point), the roller and fabric removed and the fabric rewound by hand, and the fabric and roller re-inserted and the case assembled. This is a critical step. If the roller is pre-wound too far, the fabric will not pull down all the way. If, on the other hand, the roller was wound insufficiently prior to reassembly, the fabric will not wind fully into the case.

Electric roller screens are so expensive and usually so inaccessible that professional repair help is recommended. If some kid has tried to hoist his buddy with the screen and stripped a gear, or some out-of-it staff member has tried to pull it down with a window pole and messed up the mechanism, it will probably be a contract job anyway.

Tripod screens are rather loose arrangements when new, and they don't get any tighter with use. But the troubles fall into two broad categories, both easily remedied with stout rubber bands. That sounds like a cop-out, but some of the retainer schemes are so esoteric that they barely grip when new, and restoration may be more time-consuming than it's worth.

The first problem is that the legs won't stay together when the screen is folded in-line with the base. A rubber band around the legs will keep them together. The second problem is failure of the screen case holding system to keep it in line with the support rod when the screen is folded. Again, a heavy rubber band will keep it in line.

Replacement of the spring-loaded stop knobs is almost impossible. Solder won't hold, and there is no room for retainer nuts on the inside of the support column. Problems related to lost self-tapping sheet metal screws can be solved for a while by using the next larger screw, if you have an assortment available. (Look behind that door and see if you can rob some from another old screen.)

Another problem is failure of the screen case to hold at the level desired, so that it rises instead as the screen is raised. This results from some kind of mechanical failure in the area of the screen handle. Since this too would be difficult to repair, a hole can be drilled in the support column and a short but rather large-headed sheet metal screw can be turned in. Drill the hole at a good average use height, which would probably be about 18" above the "down" position of the case. Be sure the screw you use is short enough not to interfere with the center screen-holding rod.

The head of the screw will prevent the continued rise of the case, but still allow it to drop back to the normal position when closed.

When all else fails, pry the screen case off the broken tripod and hang it up somewhere as a wall screen. You may then discover that it has no stops and you have to put a hook under the chalk ledge and a small piece of rope on the screen handle to keep the fabric down. (You use two more small loops of that same rope, or some carefully formed coat hangers, at either end of the case, to make the hangers for the screen.)

Preventive Maintenance

If you have the time and staff for it, go around and check all wall screens for smooth operation once each year. Give each one a small shot of WD-40 on each end of the roller itself, but especially in the area of the detent mechanism on the end with the flat pin. Immediately after using the WD-40, pull the fabric down and wind it up again to work the solvent into the mechanism.

Check tripod screens for loose or missing screws each time you see one and tighten or replace as necessary. A little in-service instruction for all borrowers and users might also be in order, since the fastening systems change according to make and model.

Electric screens should be checked for proper limit operation, particularly that the fabric is winding just to the case edge, to reduce the danger of the fabric being pulled or pierced when it is wound up. There are limit switches under the case cover in these mechanisms and your plant maintenance staff should be able to reset them if necessary.

RECORD
PLAYERS

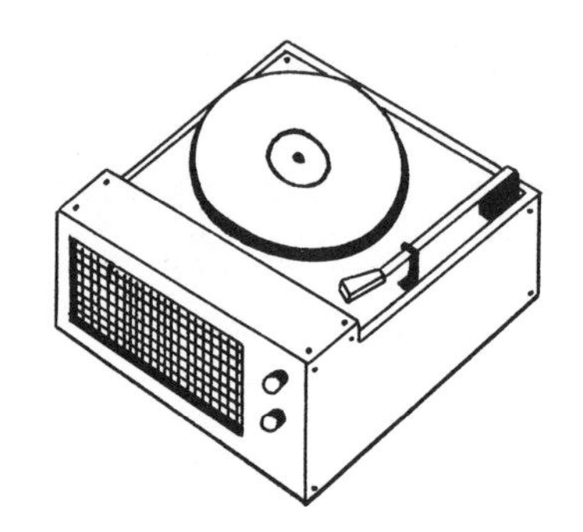

<u>Function:</u> The mechanical system of the record player rotates the record under the reproducing needle, maintaining a constant speed at the rate of the original recording and contributing as little mechanical vibration as possible (which is reproduced as "rumble").
The electronic system includes the needle and cartridge, which converts the mechanical motion of the needle in the groove to an electrical signal. The signal is then passed to an amplifier, where the feeble current from the cartridge is increased to a current sufficient to drive the speaker. The speaker reconverts the electrical signal to mechanical sound pressure in the room.

<u>Problems:</u> <u>Mechanical</u>

Turntable does not rotate at all (usually nothing else is working either, indicating a power or cord failure). If the amplifier is working (test by turning volume up a little and rubbing finger <u>lightly</u> under needle), the trouble is usually failure to understand how the "pause" system works, or failure of the speed selector system.

Turntable does not turn at constant speed, resulting in varying pitch. (Motor drive and/or turntable bearings are "gummy" with old oil and need re-lubrication.)

Tone arm skids across record, or stays in one groove and does not track record. (Wrong size needle, needle tip broken, damaged foot makes record player slant--anything other than level--[don't overlook the possibility that the building is settling, causing the floor to slope], "stiff" tone arm bearing or slanted support post, wires through tone arm not staying flexible throughout arc required to play a record.)

Rumble or howling heard in the speaker. (Turntable needs a more resilient pad--plastic foam is available; speaker sound vibration getting back to needle, especially when unit is played loud--try a cushion turntable pad, caution against playing the unit at full volume; check for worn-out tone arm support washers; replacement cartridge has higher output than original.)

<u>Electronic</u>

No power to amplifier or turntable. (No power at outlet, [changers only: automatic last-record switch is off, or malfunctioning]; power cord is broken in plug or plug prongs are too compressed to make contact in outlet; switch on equipment has failed [this failure can also prevent turning the equipment off, if it fails in the "on" position].)

No sound from record, but amplifier buzzes a little at full volume. (No cartridge in tone arm, tone arm wire broken, amplifier faulty [this requires a service technician], speaker missing.)

Distorted sound from record. (Wrong or broken needle tip, faulty cartridge, damaged or poorly pressed record, amplifier faulty [requires a service technician], speaker damaged.)

Mechanical Repair

RECORD SPEED problems are the most common. If the turntable is slow (assuming the correct speed setting) or sound pitch varies, indicating irregular speed, turn off the record player and unplug it. Carefully remove the washer or clip in the center of the turntable. Be sure to put a finger against the clip or washer to prevent flight. (Countless repair hours are spent searching for these airborne retainers.) Try to lift evenly at the rim of the turntable while pushing the center-pin down. The center-pins are usually tapered and fit rather tightly into the turntable. If you can not get the turntable to lift off, get someone else to rap the pin smartly with a plastic or wooden screwdriver handle while you are lifting and the turntable will break loose. Remove the turntable and set it aside in a secure place (if it falls on the floor and dents the rim, it will never run at really constant speed again). Now just follow the pictures, cleaning and oiling where shown. The unit you have may differ slightly, but you should be able to see the similarities. Be careful not to over-oil. Always wipe off any excess, whether you can see it or not.

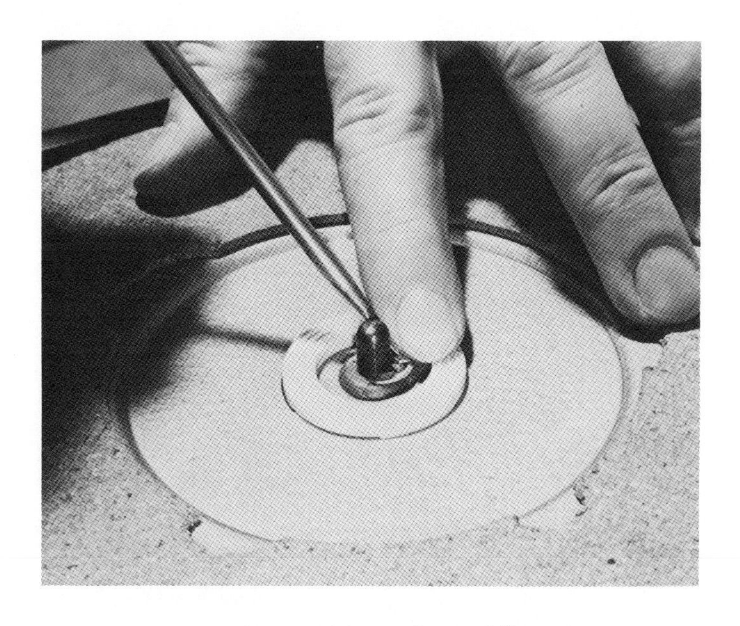

Remove turntable retainer clip

When the turntable is removed you are likely to see a lot of lint and dirt clinging to the oily surfaces.

Carefully remove the C-clip holding the idler wheel on its shaft.

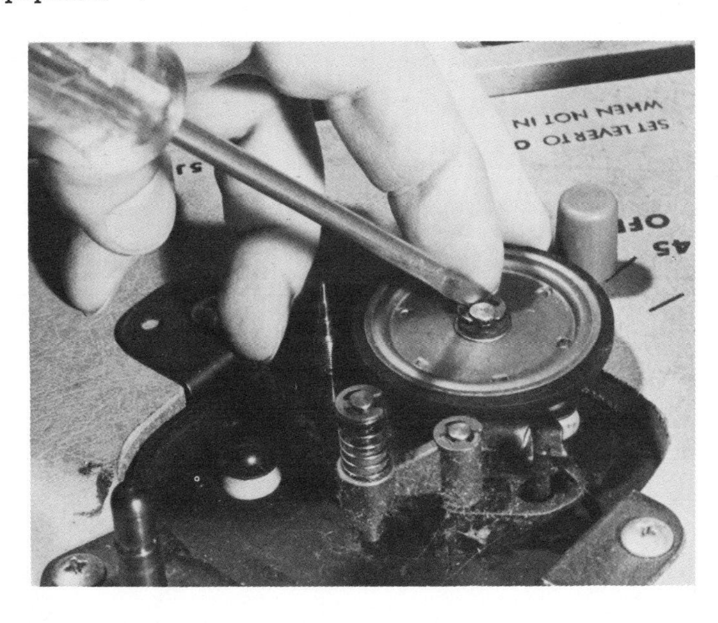

Remove the idler wheel and wash out the bearing with a Q-tip dipped in cleaning solvent. Blow and wipe the dirt off the assembly.

Spray slow-moving parts with WD-40 to clean and lubricate them.

Wipe off the idler shaft and apply fresh oil.

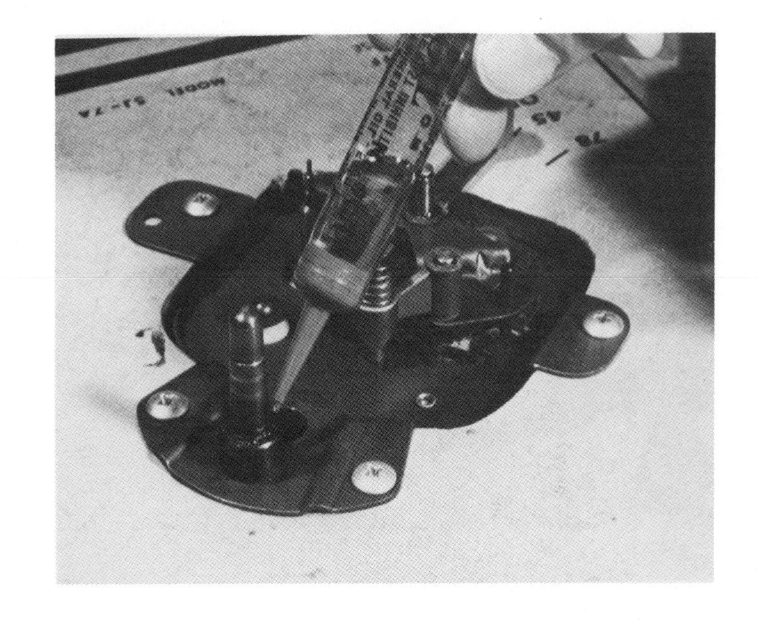

Wipe off the turntable center pin and apply several drops of oil to the large base bearing.

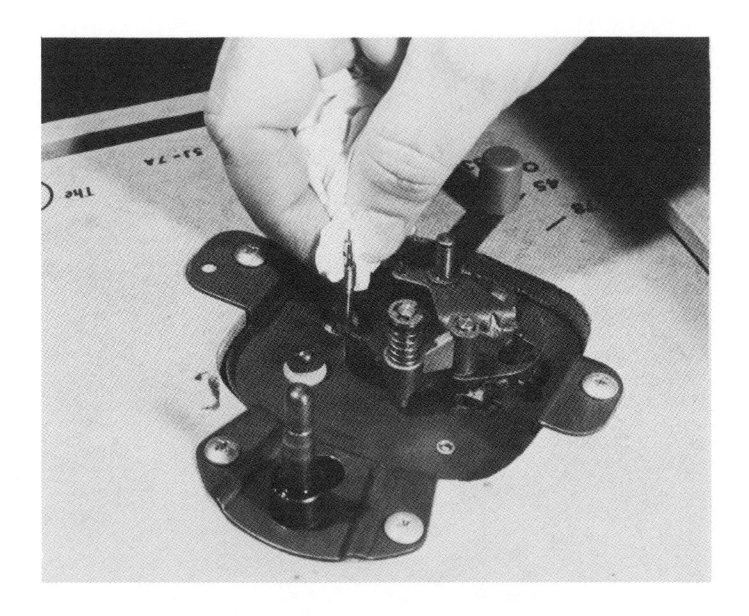

Oil the motor bearing at the base of the motor shaft. Wipe off any excess oil with a tissue.

Replace the idler wheel, being careful to keep the small washers in place. Squeeze the C-washer on the shaft with a pair of pliers and add one drop of oil.

Before replacing the turntable, there are several things that should be checked. Turn the speed selector knob and see that the idler wheel steps cleanly from step to step of the motor shaft. (This is also the thing to check if the complaint is that the record player seems to run at any speed other than the one selected.) The motor should be running during this check because it sometimes causes the armature (and the steps) to rise a little. Slight adjustment can be achieved by putting more or less washers above or below the idler wheel. The same caution applies to removal of the idler retaining clip or washer that applied to the one on the turntable. Be careful--they fly!

Next, spin the idler with your finger while keeping it from touching the motor shaft. It won't spin long, but it should spin freely. If it doesn't, remove, clean and re-oil (see How We

Use Magnetism [Motors] appendix). Wipe off all excess oil. Using a piece of rough toweling, press hard against the rubber tire of the idler wheel and thoroughly clean the tire rim. A little tape recorder head cleaner on the cloth might help. Finally, take this same cloth and roughly wipe out the inside of the turntable. Go around the rim several times.

Now gently drop the turntable back on the center-pin. Do not force it down. Find the idler wheel and tuck it under the turntable rim. Now push the turntable down on the center pin with your fingers. Place the retainer clip or washer against the center-pin and gently squeeze it into place with a pair of pliers. Once again, keep some fingers or a hand in the flight path. Sometimes the retainer turns under the plier and springs away. It's a skill area but even practice is no real assurance that one won't get away now and then.

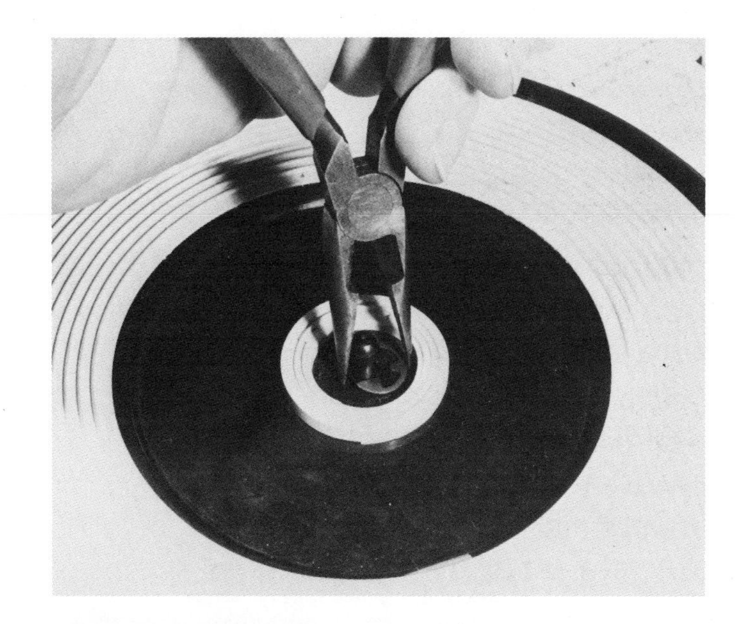

TONE ARM PIVOT BEARING can prevent free tracking of the record. Some models of record players have a foam washer at the base of the tone arm support. This washer loses its cushion with age. Either cut a new foam washer with a slash that permits installation without removal of the support, or tighten the nut on the bottom of the support. (This latter violates the mechanical design and isolation and is not recommended.) A drop of oil at the top of the support, worked-in by moving the tone arm back and forth a dozen or so times should free any bearing problem.

Do whatever you must to assure that the turntable is level in all directions. A lot of the movements depend on it.

Electronic Repair

POWER CORDS can often be wiggled at the plug to restore power momentarily; this indicates a broken wire. (See Cables and Connectors [Power] appendix for repair procedure.) Likewise, wiggling the whole plug in the receptacle, or trying another outlet, may indicate a bad plug or receptacle. Try the plug repair if you think it is the prongs failing to make contact. Faulty receptacles should be replaced only by qualified maintenance personnel.

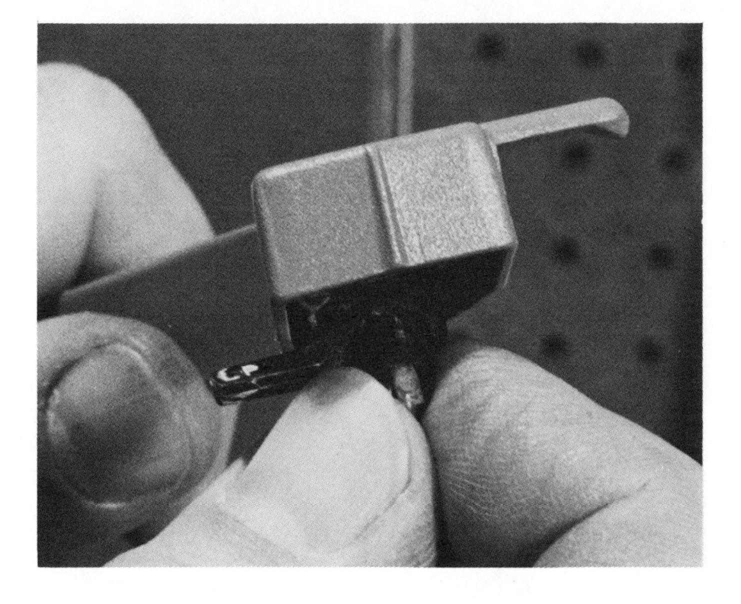

Grasp cartridge sides to remove

Note positioning rib (below)

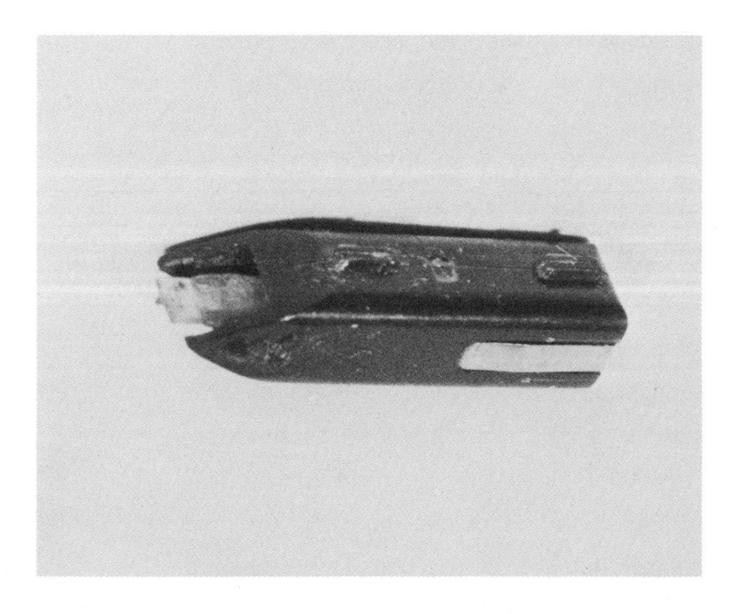

CARTRIDGES AND NEEDLES in most audiovisual record players are a complete unit and must be replaced together. Grasp the cartridge at the sides as shown and pull gently from the tone arm. The number of the cartridge is usually printed on one flat surface. Only an exact or equivalent cartridge should be used for replacement. There is a small rib on one side of the cartridge that must be aligned with a tiny groove in the socket to assure proper needle tip being down (according to the "turnover tab") and correct connection. Never force a cartridge, but do be sure that it is fully seated in the socket. Always be very careful of the needle tips and the movable plastic part on which they are mounted. Never use pressure on this part, or any tool, to remove or insert these cartridges.

If any of the cartridge problems are suspected, try a replacement cartridge before going to look for other things.

TONE ARM WIRES AND BEARINGS must be inspected visually and by very lightly swinging the tone arm above the turntable to feel for any stiffness or rough spots. Because of the turnover cartridge action, it is not uncommon for wires to break at the back of the cartridge socket. These wires are incredibly fine. A broken wire must have the insulation stripped very carefully, the wire tinned (see Soldering appendix), and the wire quickly tack-soldered to the socket terminal. The tiny stub of old wire is usually not removed, to prevent excessive heating. Try to free the wire just a little as it comes through the tone arm, to prevent further strain as the cartridge rotates (there is usually quite a lot of this wire going down through the tone-arm post and a little can be pulled up, carefully worked forward in the cement, clips, or foam used to hold the wire up, giving some relief at the cartridge). A record player that buzzes when the tone-arm is touched usually has the wires to the cartridge reversed, or for some other reason the tone-arm is not at circuit ground. If reversal is suspected, disconnect and resolder.

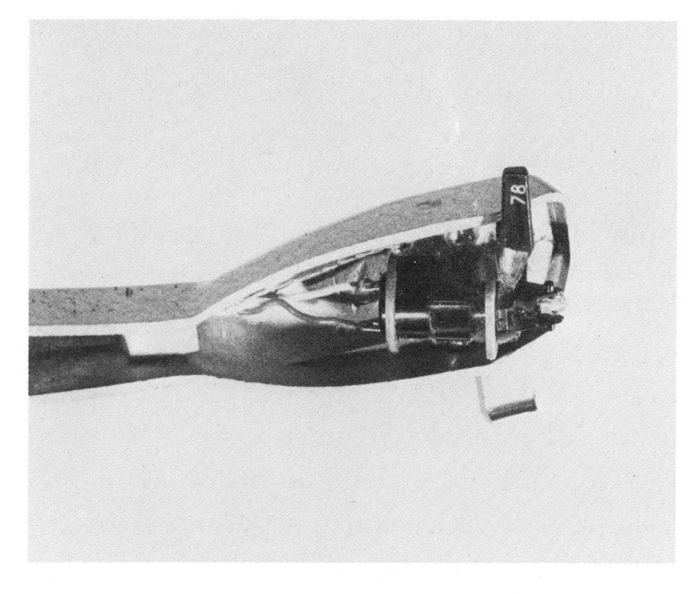

Fine wires connect cartridge

AMPLIFIER troubles require a service technician trained in electronic circuits and troubleshooting techniques. This is beyond the scope of this book.

SPEAKER problems can be checked by plugging another speaker or headset into the jack on the record player. If the sound is good through the plugged-in component, speaker trouble is indicated. Replacement is usually required (see How We Use Magnetism [Speakers] appendix).

Preventive Maintenance

Assuming at least once-a-week usage, at least once each year:

Run through the cleaning and oiling shown under Mechanical Repair.

Replace the cartridge and needle. This should be done two to four times a year if the record player is in almost daily use.

Thoroughly wipe off the top plate and the case with a wax/cleaning agent. (This psychs out the clients and often makes them claim the thing works better than when it was new.)

Check the power cord and plug by careful visual inspection. If anything looks frayed or broken, replace it.

Be sure that the speed selector is left on a neutral setting or the pause system is engaged prior to any long-term storage (as over the summer in a school). Failure to do this puts a dent in the idler tire from pressure on the motor shaft. Deep dents in old tires may not "run out," resulting in a bumping sound and uneven speed.

CASSETTE RECORDERS

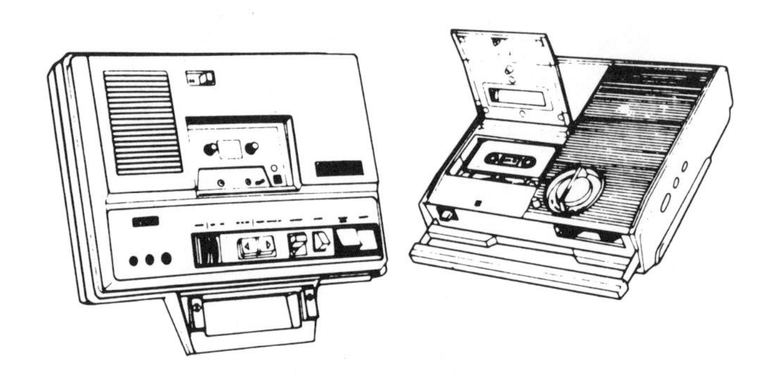

Function: A cassette recorder provides the drive mechanism that moves the tape in the cassette (but the cassette is part of that mechanical system, introducing a repair problem variable that must be considered apart from the recorder itself). The recorder also supplies electronic amplification and bias for recording and playing back the information content on the tape.

Problems: Mechanical

Tape wraps up on capstan or rubber pinch wheel, either because some sticky substance is on the tape or, more likely, because the take-up spindle is not pulling hard enough because of a clutch or belt problem.

Tape fails to move smoothly from left to right spindle, causing wowing sound from the tape. Most commonly due to a cassette fault, preventing free rotation of the tape hubs.

Recorder motor fails to run at all, usually due to battery or power circuit failure, or because one of the small lever switches actuated by the control buttons is not closing.

Record button will not depress, either because the left cassette "accidental erasure" tab has been removed, or the small finger that feels for this tab is bent slightly.

All cassettes have a wowing sound, probably caused either by the rubber pinch wheel needing cleaning, or a faulty motor governor, generally requiring replacement of the motor.

Electronic

Recorder plays ok, but will not record. Try a substitute microphone.

Recorder plays, but sound is not crisp and clear. Clean the heads. Try another cassette.

Tape moves, but recorder will not play. Turn volume control way up and play the machine with and without tape inserted in an effort to hear tape hiss. If not (no sound at all), try plugging in a headset. If the headset plays, there is something wrong with the switch in the headset jack that automatically shuts off the internal speaker, or the internal speaker is open. If you feel that you hear amplifier hiss but it doesn't change whether tape is running or not, either a head wire has come loose or the record/play switch needs cleaning, or the circuit board has some kind of problem like a hairline crack in the circuit foil.

Recorder plays (or records) at very low volume. This is an amplifier problem in most cases, probably faulty output transistors. Very distorted sound is a comparable symptom of problems with output transistors.

Momentary normal function when the buttons are depressed, followed by failure to record or play back, is evidence of some switch linkage or spring not working normally. Use a cleaning lubricant on the switch and adjust the linkage if you can trace it.

Mechanical Repair

Most mechanical problems in cassette recorders result from cassette faults, dirty heads and capstan and pinch roller drive elements, or slipping belts, in that order. Certainly the easiest thing to do is to try another cassette. Of course, we do not want machines that are so temperamental that they only work with the very costliest cassettes, but most name-brand cassettes should work in any recorder (allowing for that occasional bad cassette that will be found in almost any brand). The next simplest thing you can do, and it should be done routinely anyway, is to clean the heads and drive rollers with a head cleaner sold for that express purpose. It is easiest to clean the rollers when they are rotating, but be very careful to do this on the "out-feed" side so as to avoid the cleaning cloth or Q-Tip being drawn into the rollers.

Clean pinch roller (above)

Hold spindle to check drive force

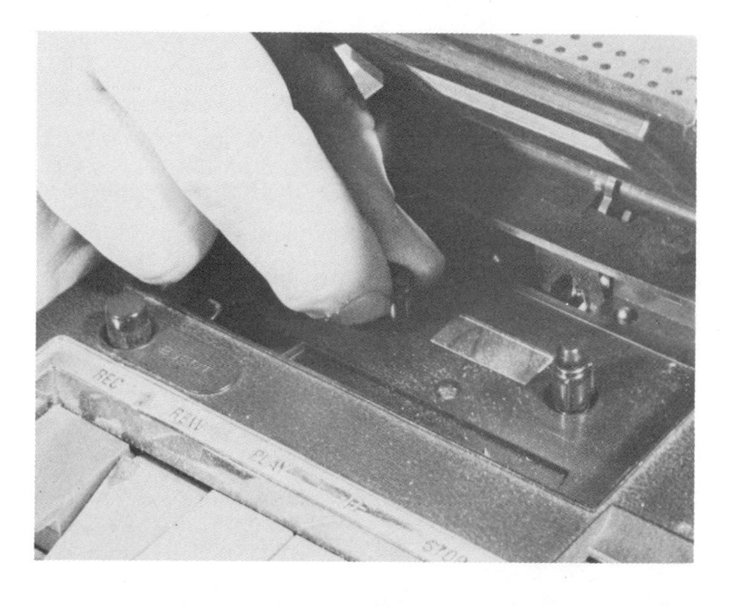

Only experience can tell you about the rubber drive belts. With the cassette door open and no cassette in the machine, depress the play button and try to hold the right, or take-up spindle, with your thumb and forefinger. Do this with about six fairly new recorders and you will get a good idea how much pressure you need to stop the spindle, or how hard it pulls to get free. If, after this experience, you find a recorder with jammed-up tape and seemingly little torque on the take-up spindle, you have a slipping drive belt. Replacement of these belts runs from a relatively simple removal of the old and replacement with the new, to having to slightly spring support brackets and stretch the belt to snap it deftly over the end of a shaft and thence onto the pulleys, to difficult cases that require considerable disassembly to get the old belt out and a new one in. All of these drive belts stretch with time, whether the recorder is used or not. Substitutes, such as rubber bands, will not work because of excessive elasticity. A small supply of replacement belts for the various makes and models of recorders owned by an institution or company should be stocked in the repair department. A catalog and clever measuring device is available from Projector Recorder Belt Corporation (see bibliography for address).

Another reason for poor torque on the take-up spindle is loss of the spindle cap or retainer washer. The shaft on which the spindle rotates is slotted all around near the top. A tiny washer or plastic cap snaps into this groove, keeping the spindle in contact with the drive face of the clutch below it. If the retainer is lost, the spindle has little or no pressure against the drive and does not pull hard enough. A visual inspection will show if something is missing. There is no real substitute for the right washer or top, but a piece of fine, fairly springy wire, can be bent to snap into the groove and will keep the unit operating.

Spindles must have caps or washers

Power failure in cassette recorders can be anything from overlooking the on-off switch on the microphone, to weak batteries, through the usual power cord and connector problems, to a number of tricky little switches, some labeled (like Battery and AC) and others operated indirectly by inserting a power cord or pushing a control button. Substitution and elimination, visual inspection and comparison with a functioning unit of the same model, are about the best you can hope to do. Power failure can be evidence of complex problems in the rectifier or motor control circuits, and these require the services of a fully competent repair technician.

Failure of control buttons is not uncommon. Sometimes they won't go down, sometimes they don't release. It is easy to get in over your head with these problems because so much disas-

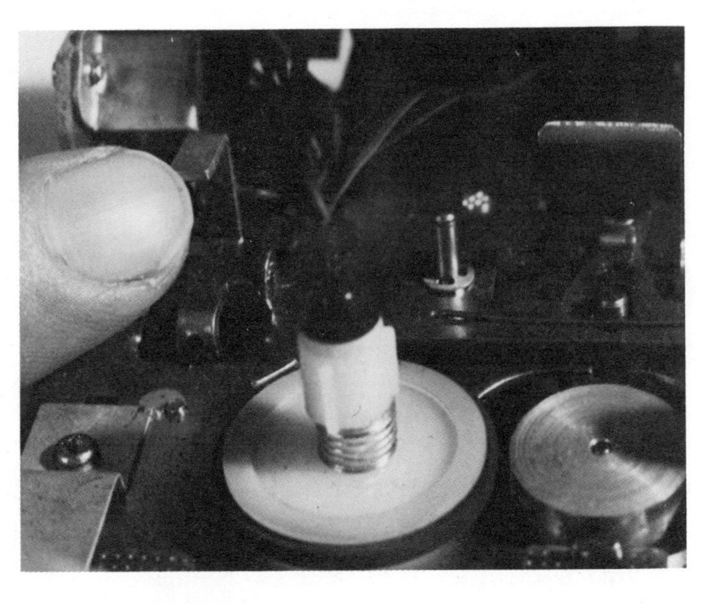

Feeler locks record button

sembly is usually necessary even to get an analytical look at the mechanism. The easiest one to correct is RECORD button failure. With no cassette in the machine, push your finger tip against the metal feeler finger at the back of the left side of the cassette compartment. While pushing the metal finger back with your finger, try to depress the RECORD (usually red) button. If it will go down when you do this, but not with a cassette inserted, very carefully try to pry it forward a little. (If you can get access to the levers worked by the metal finger, you might find another place in the linkage to do a little bending.) If you don't get it to work in two attempts, better get help before you break something.

Sometimes very small screws work loose, or other debris gets under the buttons and prevents full movement. Finding this kind of thing is a matter of getting lucky and solid knowledge of how things ought to look, or being able to compare a defective unit with a working one.

Electronic Repair

Generally the circuit board in a cassette recorder presents a difficult challenge, even for an experienced technician. The components are about the smallest available, and between wires, mounting screws, and mechanical linkages, access is extremely limited. There is relatively little you can expect to do at the level of this book, but there are a number of the usual peripherals that you can check. This also introduces the peculiar problem of cost of repair when you send one of these units out. If no replacement components are required to effect a repair, the technician will still need to make a minimum service charge. This rises rapidly when parts must be installed, not so much because of the parts cost, but because of the time for diagnosis and access. Because most cassette recorders are relatively inexpensive, a service charge could very legitimately approximate half or more of the original cost of the recorder. A service history might be helpful in making a repair decision. If this is a first repair, and the machine has been in service for a year, it might be worth a repair cost that is lower than replacement. If the recorder is several years old, or has been serviced twice before, replacement might be a better decision.

So what can you do?

First, there is the power problem. Weak batteries would show up in the motor drive before the amplifier, contributing to a "wowy" wound. Some recorders use odd systems of changing from battery to line (e.g., the power plug being pushed into the recorder switches the power source, and the plug must be fully inserted or there is a seeming line power failure).

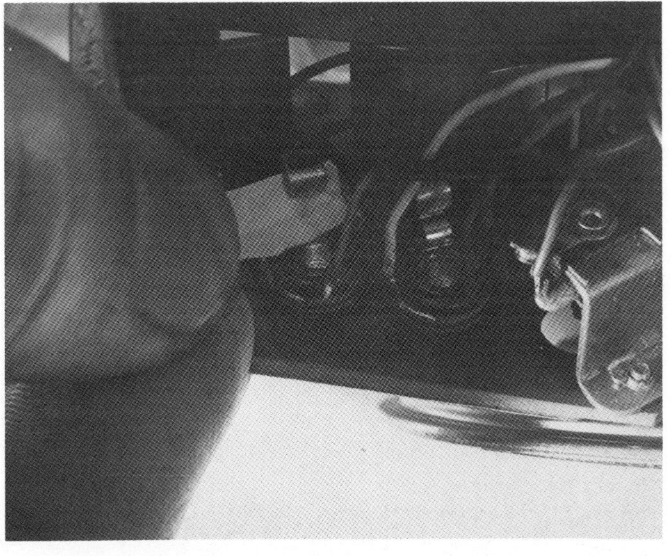

Clean jack with paper

If the motor runs and the tape moves, but there is no sound from the unit, put your ear close to the speaker grille and listen for anything at all. If there is no hum or buzz, try plugging in a headset or external speaker. If that plays, either the recorder's speaker is blown, or the small leaf switch on the speaker jack is not making contact when no plug is inserted. With the back of the recorder removed, it is usually possible to move the jack parts a little, or to burnish the contact area by rubbing a piece of paper back and forth between the contacts. Sometimes bending the contact leaf slightly with the tip of a screwdriver will restore amplification.

If you do hear a rushing sound but no tape content, try moving the wires attached to the head, if you can get to them. Heads are often connected with tiny push-on metal collars. If these come loose, or fail to make electrical contact, the tape will not play but the amplifier hiss can still be heard. Just twisting these collars a little on the head connector pins will re-establish connection and restore operation. Remember that the heads move in and out of the cassette and this movement can work the wires loose.

The final electronic problem you might hope to solve is one of intermittents. These are maddening because most of the time everything works fine, but sometimes it doesn't.

A common intermittent problem involves the long switch that changes the circuit from record to playback.

The record/play switch can be found by looking for a long straight row of solder points (on this board, just below the long wires, in the center).

The switch is a metal sleeve and can be cleaned by spraying at center and both ends.

In actual practice the whole assembly looks about like this. You have to try to get the solvent into the switch between the circuit board and the mechanism.

Sometimes this appears as a momentary sound of playback when the PLAY button is pressed, but it stops playing when the finger is removed from the button. Another form of the problem is failure of one function (play, record, erase), all other functions remaining normal. First try squirting a little contact cleaner/lubricant into the switch (see Cleaners and Solvents; Lubricants, appendices). Then work the buttons that make the switch slide back and forth. This should clean any contact that is failing to maintain connection. If this doesn't clear the problem, try to analyze the linkage that operates the switch. Sometimes bending a part of this linkage a little will adjust the switch travel and restore full function.

Look for hairline cracks . . .

. . . and bad solder joints

Intermittents also result frequently from a bad connection or hair-line crack on the circuit board. With the unit running, try to get it to play (or stop playing) by pressing or tapping lightly with the handle of a small screwdriver in various areas of the circuit board, listening for even a momentary restoration (or interruption) of sound. Also, very carefully inspect the board visually for any component or interconnecting wire that was not soldered well during manufacture. Suspect connections can be

tested by trying to bridge the metal with the tip of a small screwdriver. Resoldering components and flowing solder across foil cracks (foil is the metal circuit on the board) is the method of repair (see Soldering Appendix for specific techniques).

Preventive Maintenance

At least once a year, and following any repair procedure:

Clean heads. Put a very small drop of oil on the capstan bearing. Blow and/or wipe out the cassette well (where the cassette is inserted into the recorder).

Wipe any residual oil off capstan and clean the rubber pinch-roller.

Test the take-up spindle torque as described under the mechanical repair section. If weak, replace belt.

Make a test recording, lightly kinking the mic. wire while recording, to test for possible breaks.

Play back the test recording, listening for normal sound.

Operate all control buttons to test for proper function.

AUDIO CARD PLAYER/RECORDERS

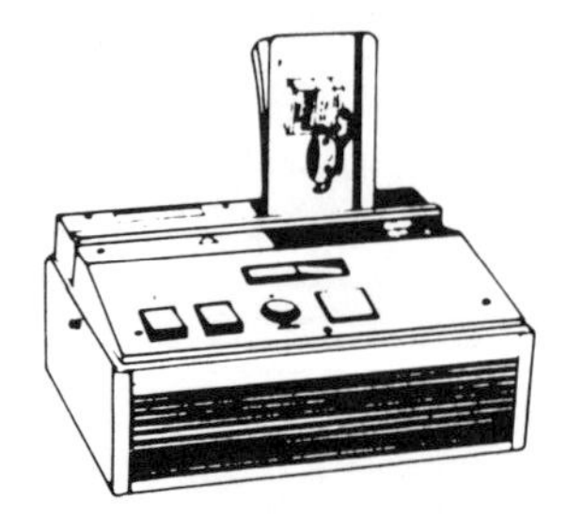

Function: These devices use the basic electronic technology of a tape recorder (or player) to record and/or play a magnetic stripe on a light-weight card. The range in sophistication of these machines is great. In the simplest form a special insert fits into the well of a specific model cassette recorder and electronic connection is made by a short cable. Earlier models operated in one direction only, at one speed, with the card either remaining stationary or moving through a slot in the machine. Current models offer repeat features, some operate at more than one speed, and fidelity is generally better than that of most early models.

Problems: Mechanical

Either card fails to feed through reading slot, or scanning head does not move across card

Card or head moves, but speed is not constant, causing a garbled sound

Cards are difficult to get started, but run ok

Electronic

Unit does not switch from Record to Play

Poor recording quality

Intermittent sound either during record or play, when headset and boom microphone are used

Mechanical Repair

Problems of failure, either of the card or of a head, to move properly are a combination of cleanliness, lubrication, and adjustment. Rarely is an actual motor failure experienced.

If the unit is one in which the card travels through the machine, both the guide channel itself and the guide and sensing rollers must be kept clean and free of any broken pieces of card or paper. Very light lubrication might also be in order on the rollers, but any excess should be wiped off immediately. As with tape recorders, it is essential to keep the rubber pinch wheel, capstan, and head surfaces clean. This is very easy to do if a piece of blotting paper is wetted with some tape recorder head cleaner and passed through the machine several times. (Blotters are not too available these days, but pieces of a desk blotter can be cut, about 3" x 7", and work just as well.)

Units that use the scanning head principle are equally vulnerable to accumulation of oxide on the head. Further, they need cleaning and re-lubrication of the head guide and drive system. This is usually just beneath the top cover.

Maintaining drive and head contact pressure is a matter of adjustment of the parts that control how tightly the rubber drive or the head is pressed against the card. Generally pressure can be added with a finger to restore proper operation. It is then a matter of figuring out which screws need to be loosened, which parts moved slightly, and which screws re-tightened.

Some of the small insert-type drive units are not easy to disassemble and must be returned to the manufacturer for adjustment.

If speed is not constant, start by trying the cleaning described above. If this fails to remedy the problem, try the pressure adjustments of the last paragraphs. If all of this fails, the machine should be removed from the case, and all bearings accessible, from the motor to the card, should be cleaned and re-lubricated.

Cards that do not start well have become frayed with use. The usual remedy is to cut about 1/4" off the leading edge of the card. Be sure to restore the rounded corner since this retards breakdown of the card stock.

Electronic Repair

There are a number of switches in these units. Some have a light pressure switch that senses the inserted card and starts the motor. If a unit fails to operate at all, look for a switch along the card path and try operating it with a small screwdriver by pressing on the sensing spot.

If the motor fails to run, a new switch may be necessary (assuming that's the actual problem), but the power cord and plug should also be carefully checked before sending the machine out for repair.

Like the related tape recorders, there are switches that convert the unit from record to play. If the linkages that operate these switches fail to move freely, conversion may not happen. Try to locate the switch (usually on the circuit board) and lubricate it with an electronic switch cleaner/lubricant. Also try to trace the linkage between the operating control and the switch. Lubrication with light oil at hinge pin points and/or slight bending may be necessary to restore switch operation.

Poor recording quality can be almost anything from a bad microphone through malfunctioning electronics, to a dirty head. First try cleaning the head with a blotter wetted with tape head cleaner. Try playing a commercially recorded card for comparison. If there is a separate boom microphone, plug it in and try it, or vice-versa with the unit's built-in mic. This would isolate a bad microphone. If these simple cures don't work, it is probably a circuit component failure and the machine will have to be sent out for repair.

Intermittent problems when using headsets and/or boom microphones are almost always cable problems. Very careful bending of the cables can often reveal the area of the break or short. Plug end problems can be solved with cut-back and replacement. (See [Audio] Cables and Connectors appendix.) Cable problems at the headsets or microphones can require replacement of the whole cable and the services of a very careful technician to get it all apart, repaired, and back together without destroying something.

All in all, these seemingly simple devices can be quite complex. Adjustments can require several tries to "get it right." The related switches can be confusing logically, often making one problem appear as quite another. It is certainly no indictment to have to send these out for service.

Preventive Maintenance

Try to keep the cards in good condition.

If machines are in very heavy use, run a blotter wetted with tape head cleaner through the machine several times, doing this at least once a month.

Use compressed air to blow out the card slot two or three times a year.

Clean and lubricate card guides at least once each year.

Expect problems after a summer of non-use, particularly related to card feed. If these seasonal problems occur, try to run a card through at least half-a-dozen times to loosen up the mechanism before concluding that the machine needs service.

VIDEO TAPE RECORDERS, CAMERAS AND MONITORS

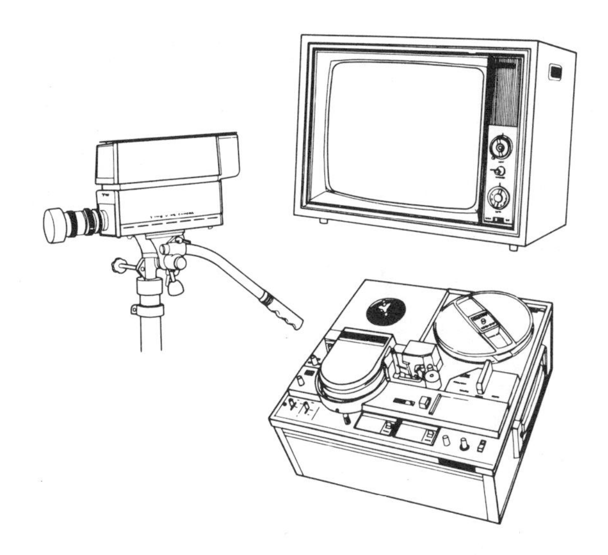

Function: Video equipment is used to display visual information in real time, or to store visual and sound information for playback at a later time. The camera and monitor are required for real time demonstrations. A video tape recorder of reel-to-reel, cassette, or cartridge format is added if storage and retrieval of the information is required.

The video signal is a composite of picture and synchronization waveforms. Coaxial cable is used for its transmission, and special circuit connections (other than the antenna terminals) must be provided. The actual voltage is about 1.5 volts maximum ... not enough to be felt at all if the wire is touched.

If sound is used, it is not combined with the video signal, but is carried on a separate wire with separate connectors (except in the case of the standard 8-pin video plug, whose cable and pins carry the separate video and audio signals in a common cable and plug housing). Cabling systems that use the antenna terminals of the monitor do combine sound and video on a locally unused VHF channel which must be selected on the front of the monitor/receiver.

Special Exception: Since there is little you can do with this equipment in the way of service, we are going to depart from the "problem" format to give a logic procedure that should enable you to isolate a specific defective unit, or to identify and repair cable problems.

The best place to begin is to ascertain that you have power on all units: the camera, tape recorder, and monitor or TV receiver. Each of these units has some kind of power indicator light that

Spread plug prongs to assure contact

should be lit when the switch is in the "on" position. Power failures are usually either broken switches, or, if you're lucky, the prongs of the power plug need spreading to restore socket contact. The power cables themselves are heavy and rarely break, even at the plugs.

The wide variety of types of video equipment, particularly the recorders, make it difficult to give specific steps, but the following procedure should work with almost all equipment.

Assuming you have no picture, start at the end, with the monitor. Since most monitors are also television receivers, switch from "Monitor" or "VTR" to "TV." Turn to an active channel and try to get a TV picture and sound. If the screen is dark but you have sound, check the contrast control and the brightness control. Also look at the back of color receivers for a small red circuit breaker and it should be pushed in and held only momentarily. If all of these steps failed to produce a picture, it is reasonable to suspect an internal circuit problem in the TV/monitor and another unit should be substituted, if available, and/or a TV service technician called.

If you have been able to get a TV broadcast picture, the link between camera and monitor, including the tape unit, is suspect. Let's consider systems using video connections first. Switch from "TV" to "Monitor" or "VTR."

Since the camera is your source of picture, now is a good time

to be sure the f/stop on the lens is at a low number (f. 1.9, 2.5, etc.) and the lens cap is removed.

Now check the settings of various switches on the recorder. If you are using a multi-wire camera cable, is the input selector switch on "Camera"? If you use a single piece of coaxial cable from camera to "Video IN" on the recorder, is the selector on "Line" or "Video IN," etc.?

Finally, is the equipment in "Record"? Particularly, is the red safety switch depressed? Still no picture?

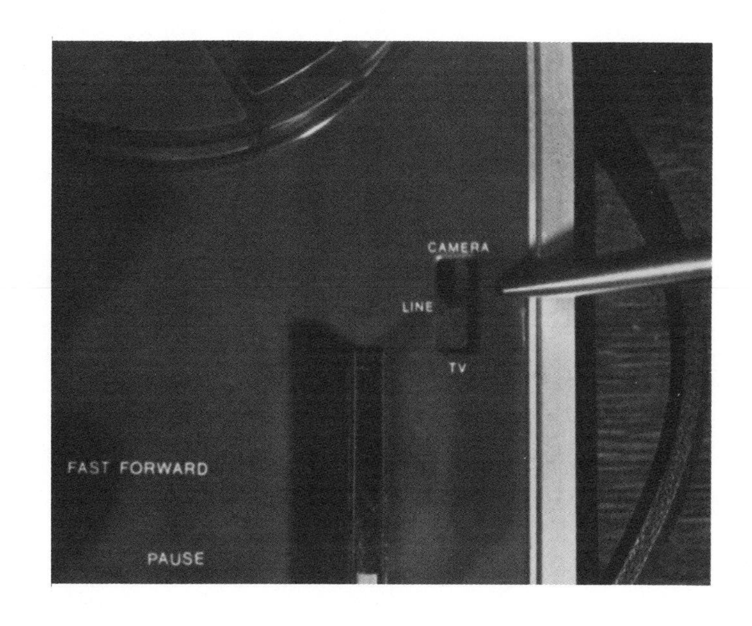

Find a cable with ends that will permit direct connection of the camera to the monitor "Video In." If you don't have the right wire, improvise. We are not interested in picture quality at this point ... just anything that looks like a picture. Even ordinary

power-type zip-cord would do to make a temporary connection between connector centers and outer shells for test purposes. Also check to be sure that any camera "Video/RF" switch is in the "Video" position. (Not all cameras have this switch.)

If you get a picture with a different cable, either there is a faulty cable or the recorder is not working. Cables can be checked with an ohmmeter (see Tools appendix) for both shorts or broken (open) wires. Visual inspection is also valid to find broken wires in multi-wire camera and monitor cables. You will have to look very closely though ... the wires are extremely fine.

The camera and monitor cable can usually be repaired at least one time without cutting all the wires back and redoing the whole thing. The wire can be stripped with a Xacto knife and tinned

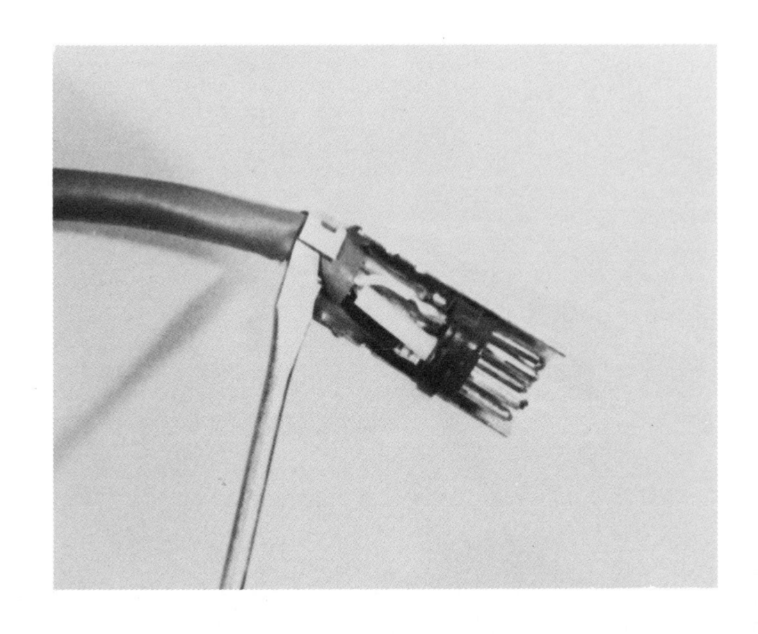

(see Soldering appendix). Use a tweezer or forceps to put the wire in line with the pin and quickly join the wire and pin with a drop of solder on a fine-pointed iron. Releasing the cable clamp allows you to push the wires closer to the pins, making connection a little easier. Re-tighten the clamp.

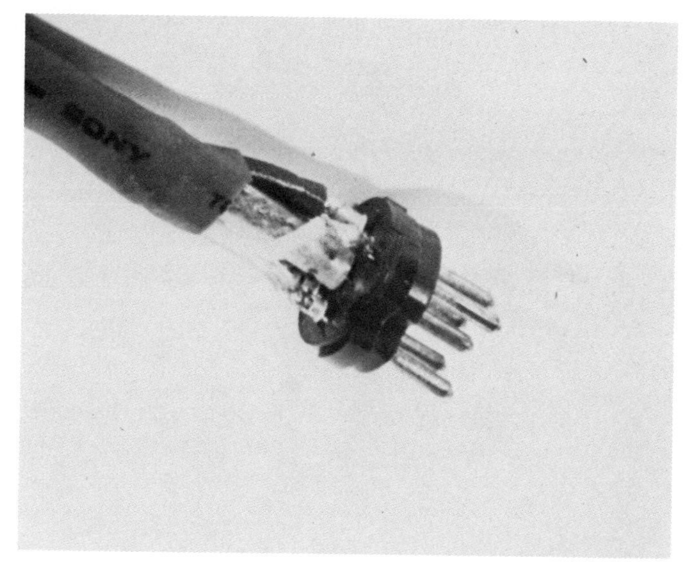

If all cable tests prove negative, either the camera is not producing a picture or the video tape recorder is not working. The earlier direct connection between camera and monitor should also check out the camera. If you got picture by direct connection, either there is a recorder failure or the switches still are not set right. Settings can be double checked in the instruction manual.

Two more conditions are possible. Some institutions use RF (Radio Frequency) connection to TV antenna terminals for the monitor and playback functions. Tuning failure is most common with this system. Either the wrong channel has been selected, or the fine tuning on the correct channel is not at the best tuning. Both picture and sound are carried by the same cable to the antenna terminals. The channel is indicated on the RF converter, plugged into the back of the recorder. After this channel is selected on the receiver tuner, the same fine-tuning is required as would be necessary for a broadcast channel.

Finally, you may have monitor function during recording, but only half a picture, or snow when the tape is played back. If these conditions are accompanied by normal sound, the problem is a dirty video head. Detailed instructions for cleaning these heads can be found in the recorder instruction book. Always use only a head cleaner approved for video heads, on a similarly approved applicator. Follow the manufacturer's instructions implicitly.

Preventive Maintenance

It is good practice to clean the heads before any major videotaping. ("Major" is a guest speaker, as opposed to start-stop classroom interaction analysis recording.)

Always keep an eye on the cables. Insulation pulled back from connectors, or evidence of severe kinks along the cable, can be indicators that repairs are in order before an actual failure needs to be reported.

If equipment is in fairly heavy service (running several hours each week) it should be sent to a service agency once a year for routine cleaning and lubrication.

Check the picture quality occasionally, looking for any increase in snow between a tape playback and the monitor function while recording. In a new machine there is virtually no difference between the monitored and the recorded picture. As heads wear, snow increases. Get the heads replaced before even light snow begins to fall. But try a thorough head cleaning with lighter fluid as a last-ditch effort to prevent ordering replacement of a dirty head.

Don't reuse tape forever. Cut off wrinkled and creased ends ... no one will miss the two or three feet you remove. Watch the picture for drop-out (short black streaks that appear only momentarily here and there on the screen). If you can count more than ten in 30 seconds, the tape is due for replacement. Dropout is some indication of the condition of the oxide on the tape, and tape with high dropout can be associated with excessive head clogging.

Let people know you are particular about the video equipment. Replace any missing knobs and keep all controls in good working order. Deny reuse to borrowers who abuse the equipment.

PUBLIC ADDRESS SYSTEMS AND SOUND LECTERNS

Function: Both PA Systems and Sound Lecterns are electronic devices used primarily to amplify speech and project it with enhanced volume in the room in which the speech originates. PA Systems may also be connected to other rooms or spaces to handle extended or overflow crowds. In this latter application, a service request may also include closed-circuit TV coverage, permitting people out of range of vision to see the speaker and/or any visuals that may be used.

Problems: Acoustical

System delivers poor intelligibility, either because of poor judgment in control settings, widely dispersed speaker locations, or difficult room acoustics.

Amplification never seems enough to avoid complaints that some people couldn't hear, and...

When volume is increased to level approaching "loud enough," the whole thing begins to whistle or have a trace of an "echo"-like sound.

Electronic

Speaker produces sporadic static noise

Hums when microphone or stand are touched

Hum or buzz in system all the time, but disappears if microphone lines are turned down

Severe distortion with general lack of power

Occasional pick-up of radio station or CB operator

Acoustical Treatments

Often a system fails to deliver fullest possible output because of improperly set tone controls. In most cases, the best setting is with the bass control only about 1/3 turn up from minimum bass, and the treble control 1/3 to 1/2 down from maximum. This is not the most flattering setting for the voice, but it does provide a clarity that aids projection into the room. Intelligibility is the goal ... not stentorian quality.

Current installation practice favors speakers concentrated in a single cluster, as opposed to one on the wall on either side of a stage (probably the worst place from the standpoint of acoustical "feedback"), or on the four corners of a basketball court gallery, etc. This makes sense since the sound waves move out from the speaker with uniform delay, rather than arriving with varied delay, depending upon the distance of any listener from the various speaker "sources." In very large auditoriums excellent quality speakers are suspended from the ceiling on a platform above the proscenium at the center of the stage. Sports arenas use clusters of speakers over center court, sending sound in all directions at a uniform delay rate.

Often a room presents problems because of its proportions or wall material. A solid masonry wall at the back of an auditorium can be especially deadly to sound clarity, as it reflects the last wave into the field of the next one. Often sound-tile can be decoratively cemented to such surfaces. A more thorough treatment is possible with the pleated burlap-like sound wall used in many modern movie theaters. Your local theater owner can put you in touch with companies specializing in installing this material.

If complaints come consistently from the same persons, try suggesting tactfully that they get their hearing checked. Depending upon their level in the organization, that should either send you looking for a better job somewhere else, or lose friends and discourage people. But really, most of the American public has been on a volume binge for the past 30 years. There is no acoustical limit to how loud the TV can blare, or the rock can roll (forth). You can simply not expect to offer that volume level when microphones are in the same sound field as the speakers. Once in a while you get lucky enough to handle an invocation, a dedicated politician, or a professional singer of the old school ... one who could reach the corners of the hall without electronics. The operator of a PA system today is caught in the middle between a public that can not pay attention and make the effort to hear, and orators and club singers who can not project. A bigger miracle is expected than 1978 electronics can deliver.

But there is one more gambit you can try, if you can get some money. Buy some microphones that are more directional than the ones you have (assuming yours aren't very directional). Or, if you are always using a rostrum, buy a "baby boom" for the microphone stand, making it possible to get that mic. within 3" of the speaker's mouth. If your system is particularly difficult, try to tell all platform guests that they simply must attempt to speak to the back corners of the room, and not rely on the PA system.

All of this should make it possible to operate the system somewhat below the feedback point ... that setting where the microphone "hears" the sound from the system's own speakers and an electronic/acoustical cycle is set up, causing the howl.

This above all: Don't buy a new amplifier in an effort to get "more power." If a 25-watt amplifier produces a feed-back level at a 1/2-volume setting (probably around 12 to 18 watts), a 50-watt amplifier will produce feedback at about a 1/3-volume setting (probably around 12 to 18 watts). Unless you can reach full volume setting without feedback, and the amplifier isn't faulty, the amplifier is not your problem. You must either get a lot greater separation physically between the speakers and the microphone(s), or you must improve the directional characteristics of either the microphone(s), speaker(s), or both.

Electronic Repair

Static is usually caused by a cable wire opening or shorting, or the amplifier is noisy. Try to localize your problem. Try one mic. at a time. Try turning the volume down when the static is occurring (one mic. at a time, to localize an amplifier). Wiggle cables at connectors and microphones to see if you can "make it do it." If it turns out to be a cable problem, see (Audio) Cables and Connectors Appendix. If you think it's the amplifier, get an electronics repairman to check it.

A constant hum that disappears when a mic. line is turned down and hums that occur when the mic. is touched are evidence of bad grounding. This is almost invariably a cable problem. Sometimes a neophyte solders the wrong wires to the right pins. Most times the wire has broken through use. Make a routine cut-back and resolder of the cable at both ends, as described in the (Audio) Cables and Connectors Appendix.

Severe distortion with lack of power is symptomatic of either a destroyed microphone (try another, if you have one), or, more frequently, trouble in the amplifier output. In these days of widespread stereo component ownership, everyone seems to think that he or she is a hook-up expert. After all, what is there to it? Can't anyone connect a speaker to an amplifier? Well, no, they really can't! Home systems usually have 4-, 8- and 16-ohm speaker connections, if they even offer all of these. PA systems are often wired for 70.7-volt distribution, or other odd sounding voltages. These systems are based on the wattage calculated to be needed from each speaker, the total equalling the full rated watt-output of the amplifier. Lines leading to speakers wired for this system can not be attached to 4-, 8- or 16-ohm terminals and transfer power efficiently. Worst of all, once done, this can burn out output transistors, which also results in no, or weak and distorted, sound.

Unwanted music and voice pickup from radio transmission is not uncommon, but it sure is tough to cure. Causes can include poorly grounded or wholly unshielded wires to speakers, broken ground wires in mic. cables, open mic. lines without microphones attached but with volume turned up (unused lines should always be kept turned down all the way), failure to include microphone input transformers in the amplifier--on the grounds that it is already low-impedance because it is transistorized, or parts in the amplifier acting as radio detectors.

If you have much of this problem, get professional help from the installing company. And bear with them. The intermittent nature of this type of problem makes it very difficult to correct, often requiring several attempts.

Preventive Maintenance

If the PA System or Sound Lectern is used with any frequency at all, cut all cables about 1" from connectors and resolder them as described in the (Audio) Cables and Connectors Appendix. Do this once each year.

If Sound Lecterns are supplied with batteries, check the battery condition after each use. Keep one set of spares on hand. Also check that all cables and parts are returned immediately after each use. A check-list in the lid is helpful.

Whenever PA System is set up with more than one mic., speak into each mic. with amplifier volume controls set about the same to get a comparison of microphone quality and sensitivity. If fairly expensive mics. are used, consider sending defective microphones back to the manufacturer (if domestic) for reconditioning rather than buying new ones all the time. Always switch mic. cables on seemingly defective units, to be sure the problem is not a locally repairable cable fault.

Where single amplifiers are moved about and plugged into several speaker installations, cut output cables about 1" from connectors and resolder the connectors about every two years. These cables are less fragile and moved less than mic. cables, but reliability demands that they be kept in good condition. Be careful not to switch wires when resoldering ... some systems have odd grounds, etc. that must be maintained for good operation.

PART III

MATERIALS MAINTENANCE AND REPAIR

INTRODUCTION

The techniques shown in this section are of a basic and emergency nature. They assume that you are not doing enough of this kind of repair to make investment in a tape or film splicer, special pre-perforated splicing tape, or a mechanical slide mounter worthwhile. All of these devices and materials include instruction for use. If your repairs of any single material classification are exceeding one or two per month, you should consider buying a commercial device or material.

If your primary problem is just keeping the show on the road once in a while, the techniques illustrated should prove helpful.

16 MM SOUND FILM

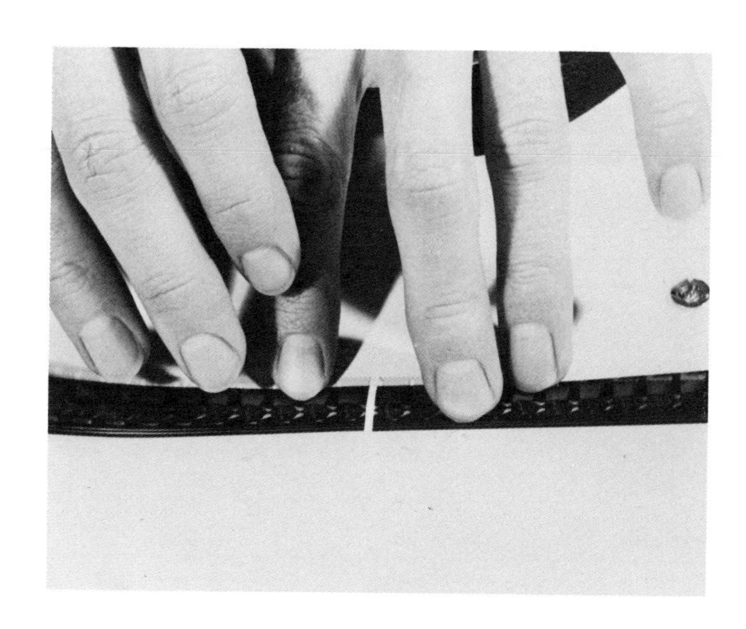

Hold the two broken ends down on a clean, dry surface, preferably Formica or other smooth non-adhering material.

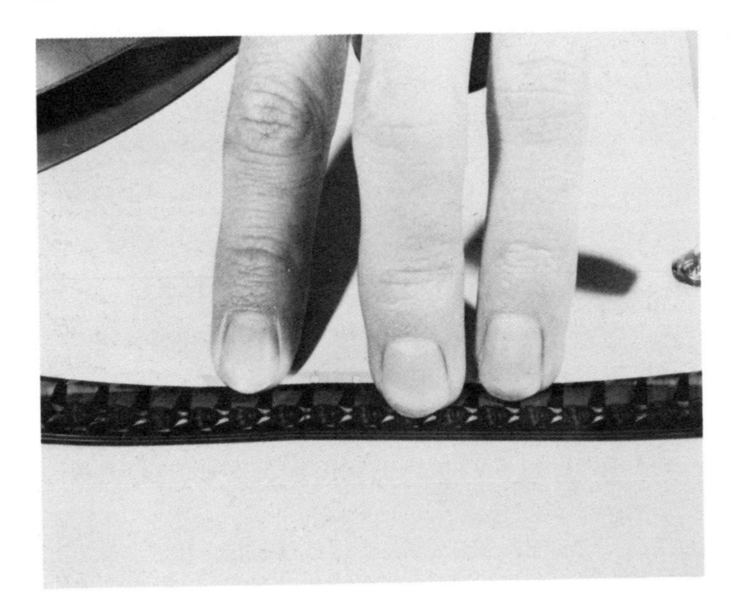

Butt the two sides of the break together as perfectly as possible.

Apply transparent tape across the break, first on one side, then in the same spot on the other side. Always go across the film, never with the length dimension.

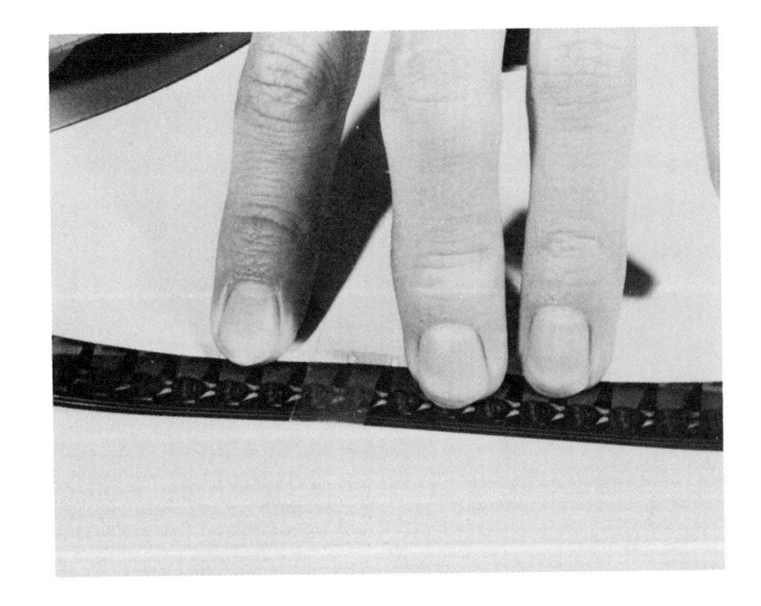

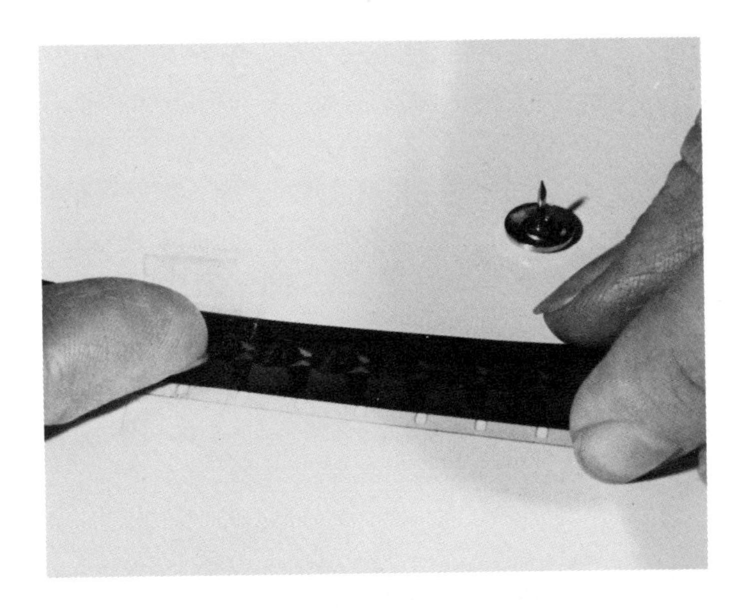

Burnish the tape and try to work out any air bubbles, using the flat side of a fingernail.

Very carefully cut the excess tape, cutting very slightly into the film to prevent tape gum from getting into the projector mechanism.

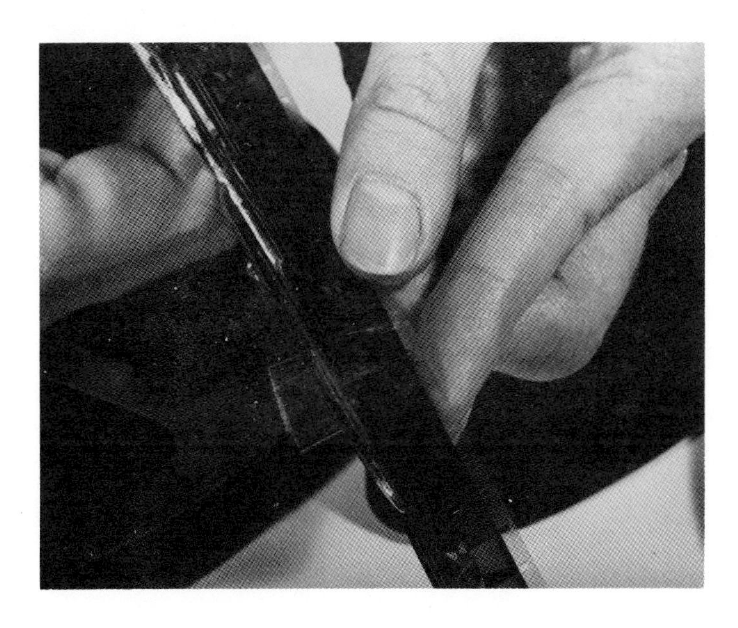

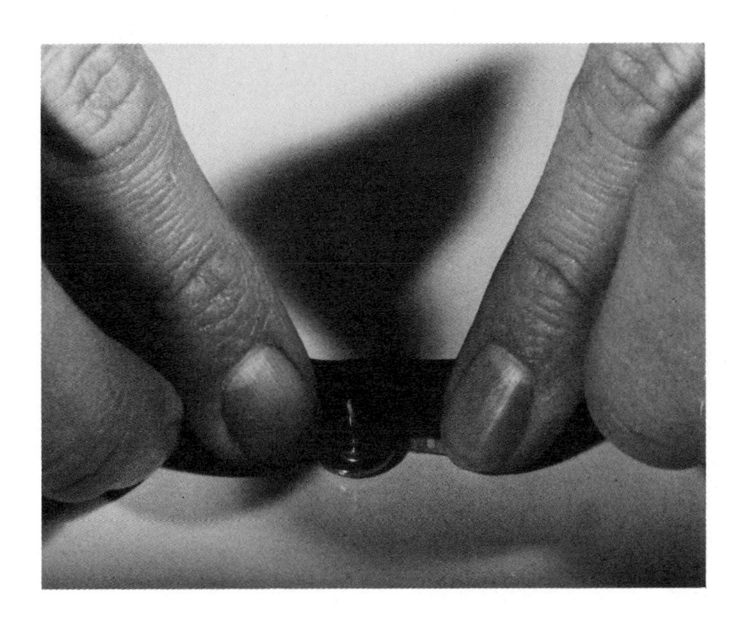

Press the film down on a thumb tack where the hole should be to perforate the tape. This completes the splice.

FILMSTRIPS

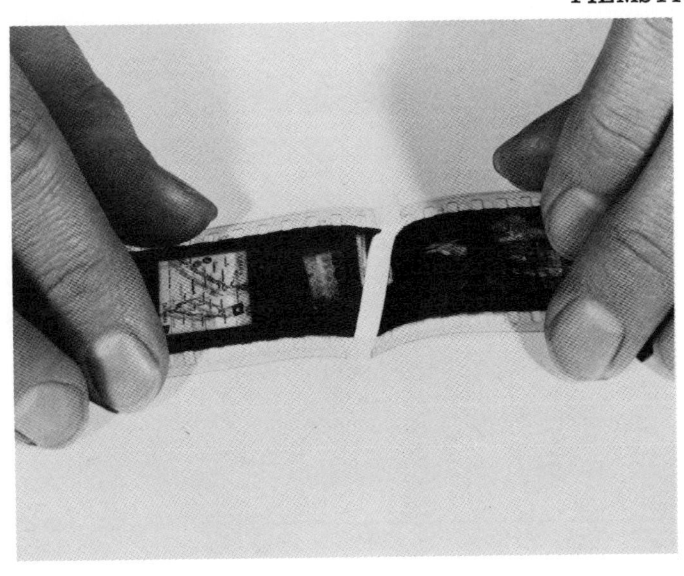

Unlike the motion picture film, each frame of the filmstrip is different. Nothing can be removed.

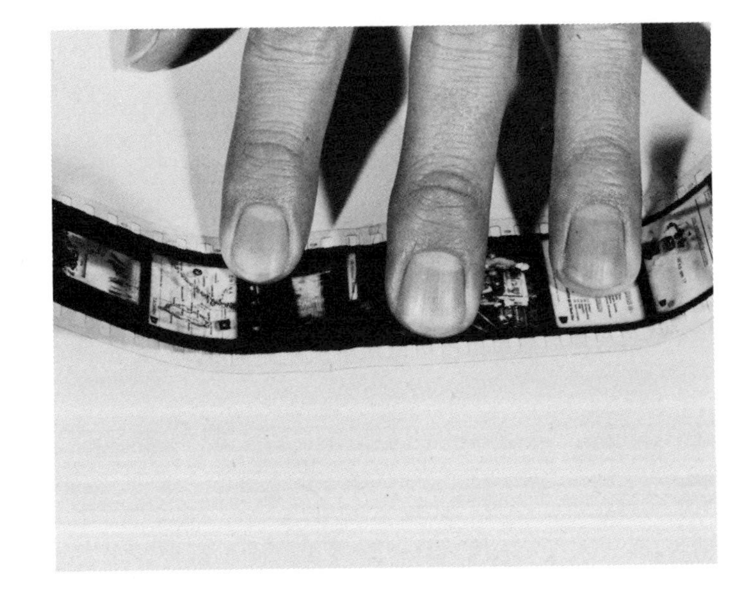

Butt the two sides of the break together ...

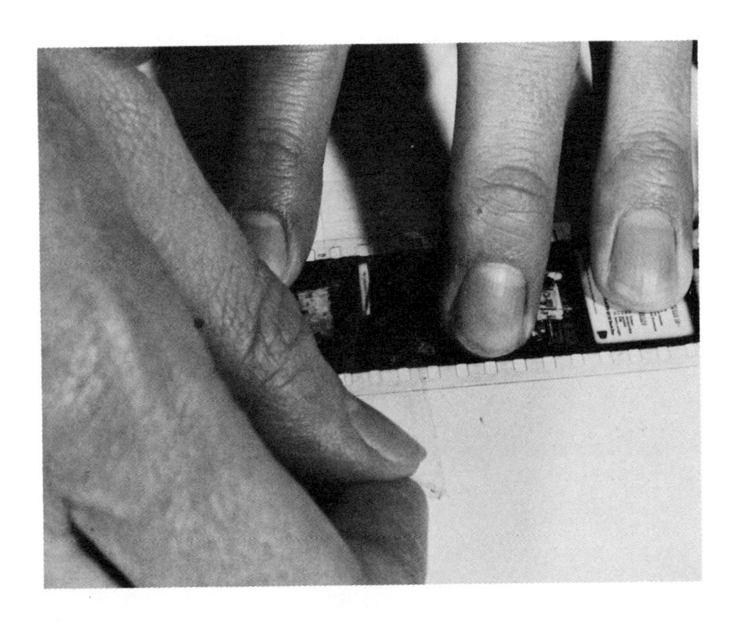

... and carefully tape the break, first on one side, then in the same spot on the other. If you can find some, transparent tape is better than translucent.

Burnish the tape with a fingernail to assure good adhesion and remove any bubbles.

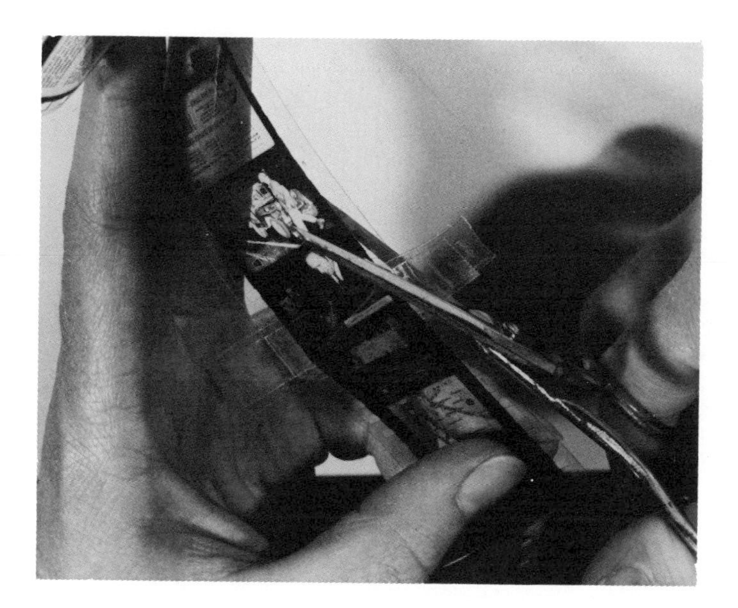

Cut off excess tape, trying to cut very slightly into the film.

Re-perforate the holes with a thumb tack. This repair should not be considered permanent, but only a temporary measure until a replacement can be obtained.

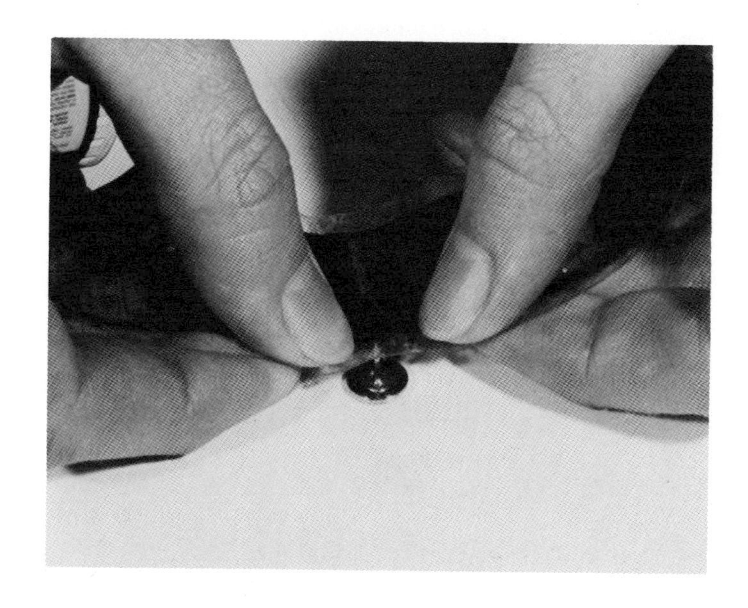

SLIDES

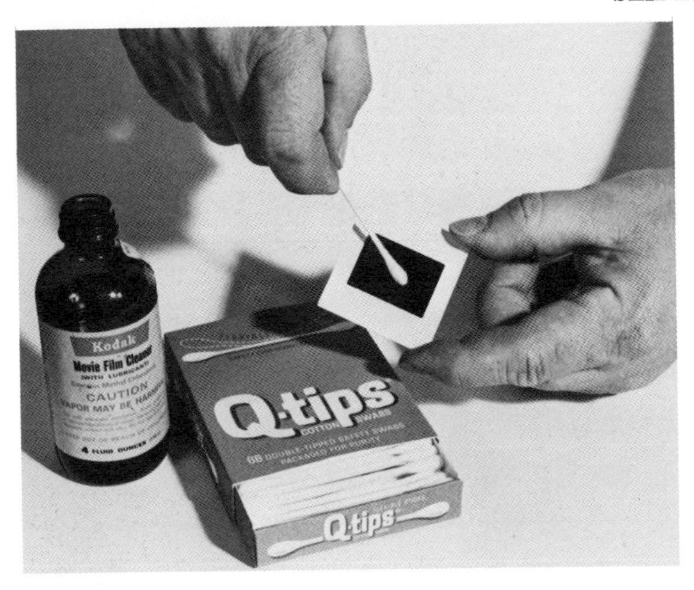

Handling marks can be removed from slides by use of a Q-tip moistened with a film cleaner. Twist the tip as you clean to present a fresh surface to the film and remove any residue.

Slides that are damaged can be split open by cutting from a corner with a utility knife. Remove the film ...

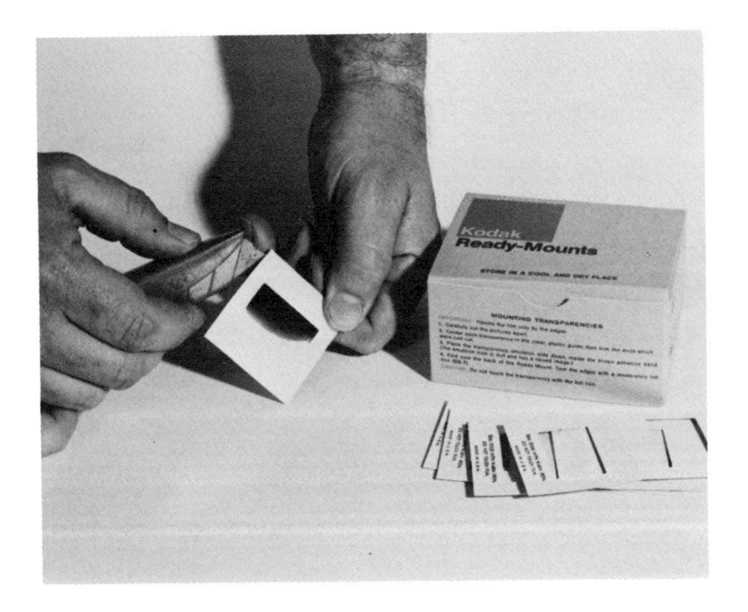

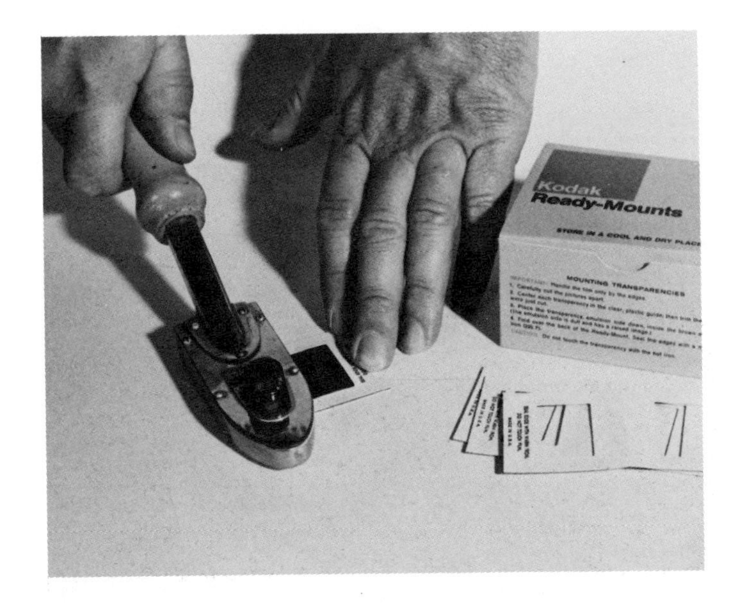

... and put it in a new heat-sealing mount. While any warm iron may be used, a tacking iron gives excellent control. Put mount on a hard surface and use considerable pressure at full tacking iron heat.

DISC RECORDINGS

Put about two good squeezes of Joy or other liquid detergent in about 16 oz. of warm water, in a tray. Using a soft cloth ...

... wetted thoroughly and squeezed out, wash the disc with short curved strokes that follow the grooves. Go around the disc at least three times, being careful to keep liquid off the label.

Without rinsing, stand the discs against a wall or cabinet and allow to air-dry several hours or overnight.

CASSETTE TAPES

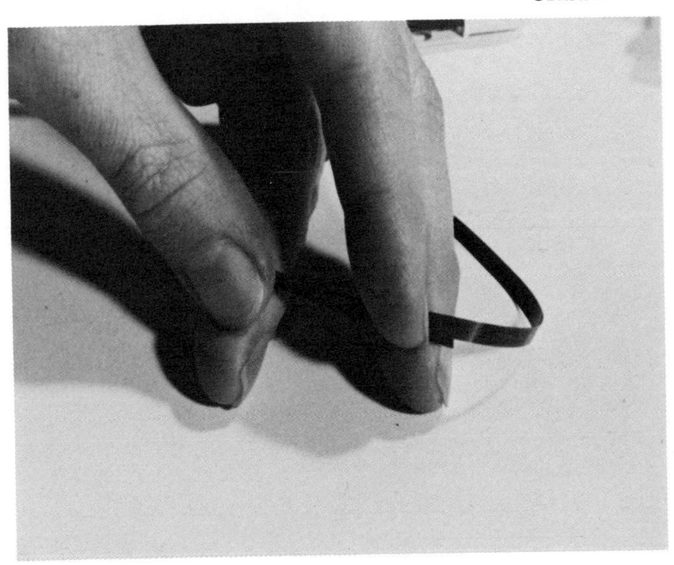

Lap two ends of tape together and hold as shown.

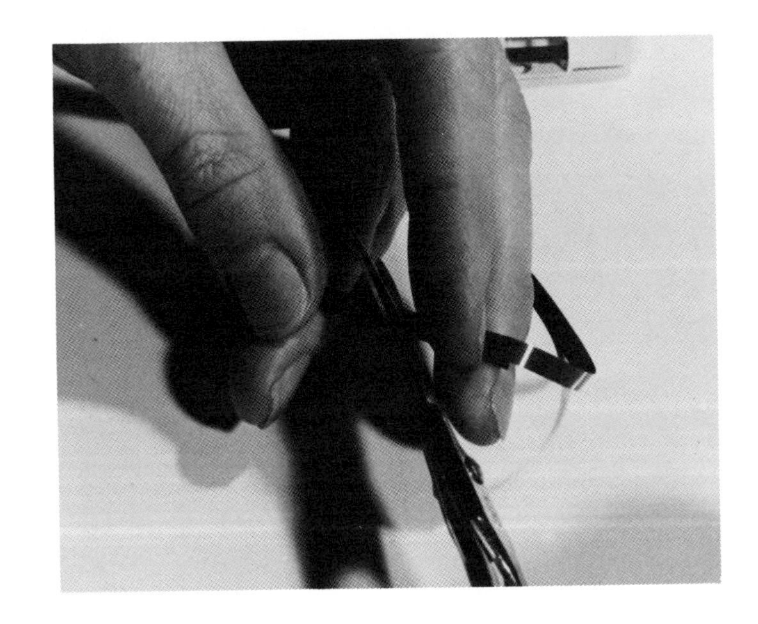

Cut tape diagonally, assuring both ends the same cut angle.

Put the two ends down on a smooth, dry surface and try to butt them together. It may be easier to overlap them and pull the fingers apart. Keep the tape straight.

Put a piece of special tape-splicing tape across only the non-recorded side of the tape.

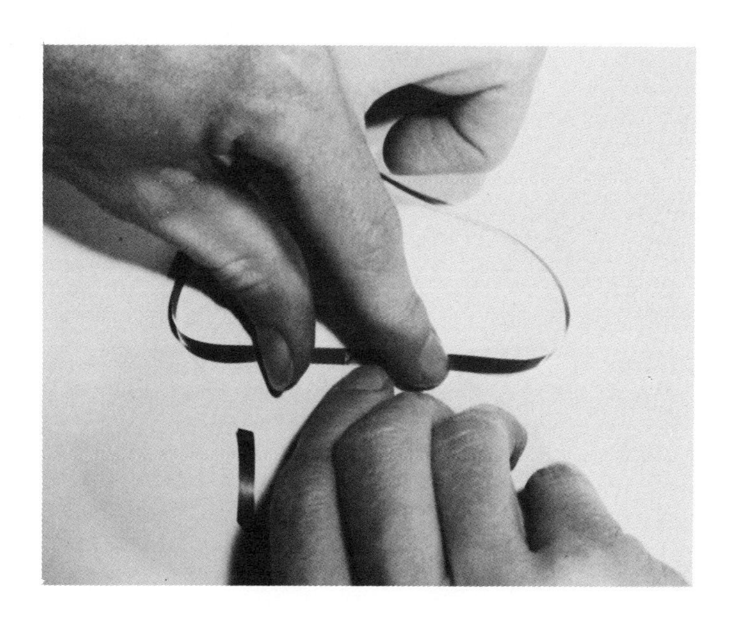

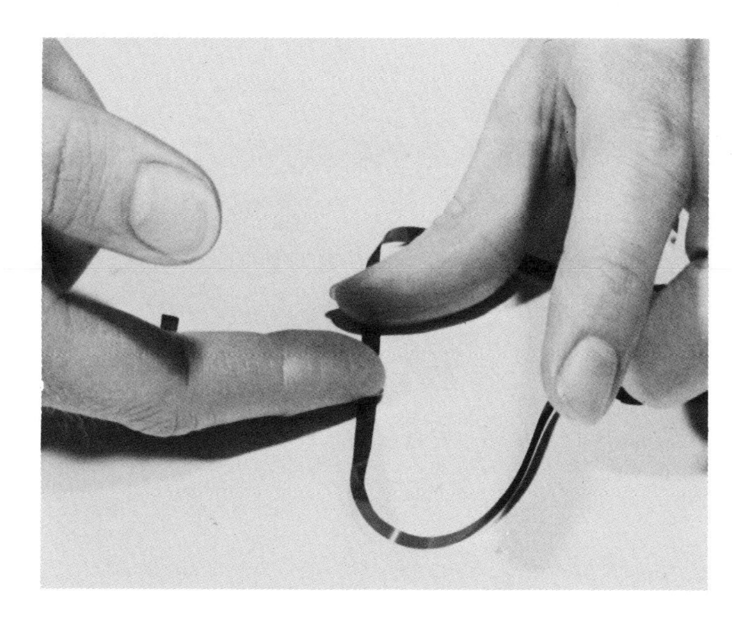

Burnish the splicing tape down ...

... and cut off excess tape, cutting very slightly into the tape. This technique works best with C-30; C-45; and C-60 cassettes. C-90 and C-120 are almost too thin to handle and tend to curl at the moment of splicing.

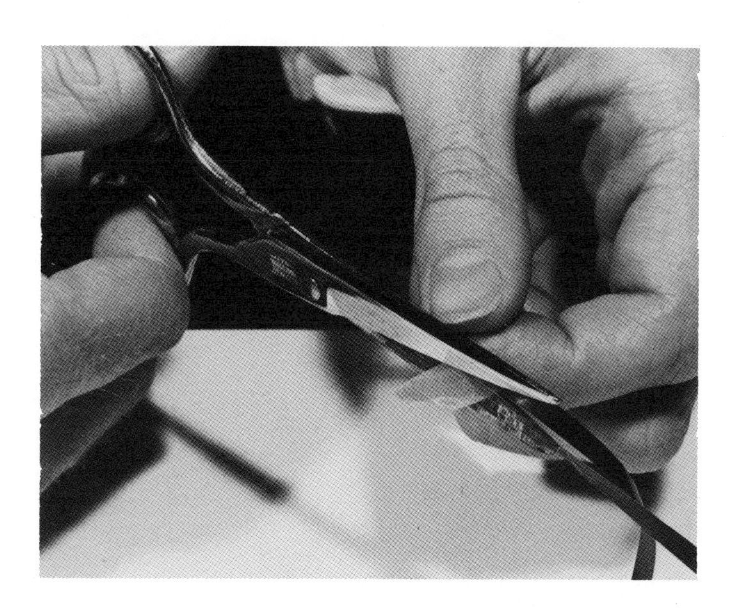

PART IV

APPENDICES

Appendix A

TOOLS

The photograph below shows what would constitute a basic set of tools needed to perform most of the repair procedures described in this book. This set also fits nicely in a small tool box, making it handy for on-the-spot repairs. One of the authors keeps such a kit in his car to eliminate the need to return to the shop for some minor problem that occurs in a school.

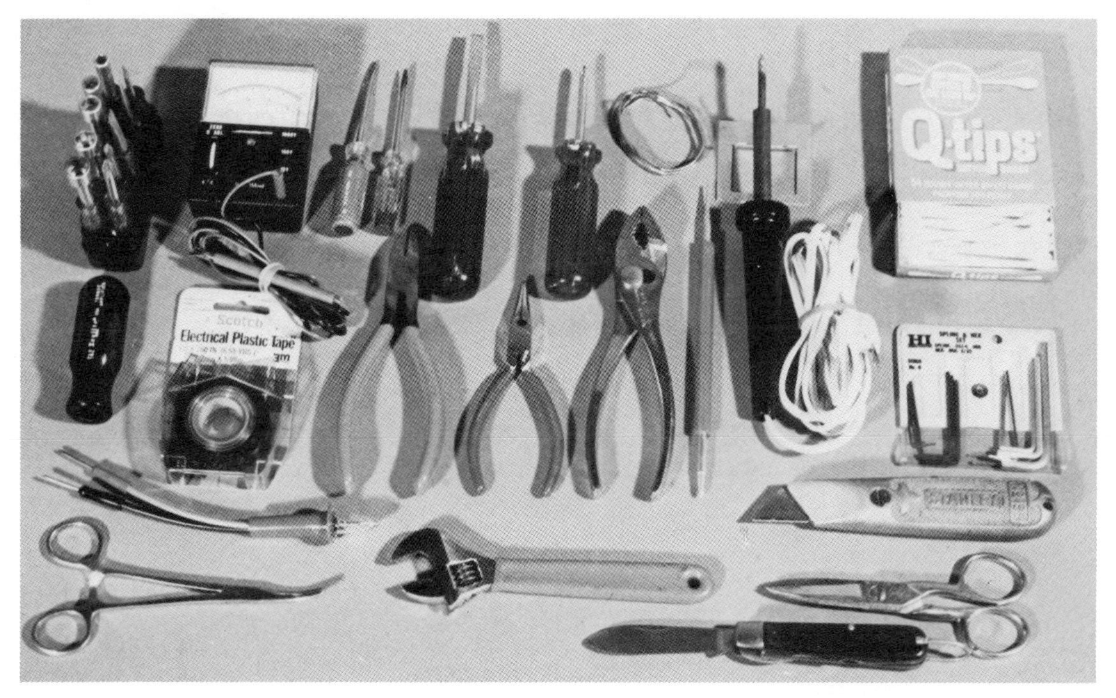

Briefly described, starting at the left of the top row and working across row by row:

A set of small socket wrenches and screwdrivers, grouped in a convenient plastic case with a common handle (shown just below the set).

A very simple volt-ohm-milliammeter, costing less than $10 (1978). The resistance ranges are the quickest way to check for a short between conductors of a cable, or a broken (or open) wire from one end of the cable to the other. The DC volts ranges will give you an idea of battery condition and supply voltage to transistor devices. AC volts can be used to check the line voltage, although this is relative and an average must be determined through repeated readings over days.

Two or more small screwdrivers with blades filed to meet the varied requirements of your equipment. A couple of larger screwdrivers (these have reversible blades, offering slot or Phillips-head capability).

A coil or spool of rosin-core electrical solder, a small soldering iron (25 to 40 watts), and a soldering aid, preferably one with a pointed tip (rather than a brush). The tip of the soldering iron should be small enough to get into the connector pin clusters.

A box of Q-tips or other stick swabs, used in conjunction with solvents and cleaning fluids.

(Second row): A roll of plastic electrical insulating tape. Many brands and widths are available, but Scotch #33 in a 1/2"-width is especially recommended for its combination of excellent insulation and good long-term sticking quality.

A 6" pair of diagonal cutting pliers. Indispensable for cutting wires, and even stripping them if you can develop the skill of cutting through the insulation only and pulling it off.

Some kind of long-nose pliers for reaching into tight places to get hold of things, retrieving dropped nuts and screws, and holding wires while soldering.

A pair of common pliers. Useful for loosening knobs, shafts, and nuts for which there is no right-size socket wrench. Also good for holding nuts while screws and bolts are tightened.

A set of small spline and hex wrenches. Expect to buy more often ... they get lost, twisted, and smoothed off. Used primarily to remove recessed set screws in knobs and pulleys, or to tighten them.

(Bottom row): A neon tester. Great for quick checks for voltage at an outlet, and, by holding one wire in your fingers or hand while inserting the other, determining which is the "hot" line wire (see opening section on Electrical Safety).

A pair of forceps. Ideal retriever of parts from down in equipment, and as a holder during soldering.

A small crescent wrench. Applies a force to stuck nuts that can not be achieved with pliers or small socket wrenches.

Utility knife. The tool for opening packages containing new equipment. Also, used with a light touch, fine for removing insulation without cutting the braids, shields, or conductors (see Cables and Connectors appendix).

Pair of electricians or other short, stout scissors. Good for cutting insulating tape and general shop cutting. Also handy for cutting the fiber filler strands in some cable.

An electrician's knife. Usually kept a little duller than the utility knife, this knife can be used in place of the utility knife when you need to be especially careful not to cut conductor strands when removing insulation.

The quality and care of tools deserves some attention. Hand tools are the extension of the hands of a skilled craftsman. It is fairly safe to say that the person who is sloppy about the storage and condition of tools will be equally messy about the work done with them. Given the state of irresponsibility in American society today, tools should not be loaned. If they come back at all, they usually come back in bad condition.

Be careful of very low-cost imported tools. This is not an idle, wave-the-flag, buy-American statement, but is based on the generally better American tool metallurgy. Cheap crescent wrenches will not hold adjustment; cheap screwdrivers twist in the blade; cheap cutting pliers will not hold a cutting edge.

You should be able to acquire a starting set of tools for less than $50 (1978), but you should expect to spend about that much. You can also expect to add to the collection as specific needs arise, depending upon how much repair work you want to do.

Appendix B

CLEANERS AND SOLVENTS

Throughout this book, especially in the preventive maintenance sections, reference is repeatedly made to keeping things clean. The sheer human handling of audiovisual equipment gets it dirty. Chalk dust frequently showers down, particularly onto and into classroom record players.

Joy or other liquid detergent is recommended when detergent action is wanted without the danger of undissolved particles of a powder soap or detergent. When added to water to make a rather rich solution, it is good for cleaning classroom records.

Case and surface cleaners

Fantastik, 409, and similar cleaners of this type are good for wiping off case exteriors and base-plates of record players, tape recorders, etc. Do not saturate leatherette covers with these cleaners ... you may soak the fabric loose.

Pledge or other wax/cleaner provides a good finishing touch. The wax protects the surface and the lemon odor helps convince your client that you really cleaned things up. Sometimes this seems more important than anything you actually did.

Lava soap has an abrasive action that can be very helpful in removing some kinds of dirt, particularly that heavy accumulation of discoloration where hands frequently touch a piece of equipment. It is usually best to moisten both the bar of soap and the cloth, wring out the cloth, rub it on the bar, and then use the paste of soap that has transferred to the cloth to do the cleaning. Do not use this soap on optical surfaces, or on any plastics that must stay clear.

For cleaning actual mechanisms, there are a number of specialized agents available.

WD-40 is probably the most commonly distributed cleaner/lubricant for mechanisms. LPS-1 is probably similar, but its claim of being "greaseless" would recommend it if electrical contacts are involved. (A greasy film is the enemy of good electrical connection.) Wissh is a general cleaner especially recommended for electrical contacts.

There has been some discussion in the trade magazines about the safety of solvents in areas where plastic is used. Many of the electronic assemblies are encased in and supported by plastic elements. Lighter Fluid, while rather flammable, is a good widely available petroleum-based solvent. It should not affect plastics and its rapid evaporation reduces the time anything is likely to be exposed to it.

Tape Head Cleaner is very good for its intended purpose, and some other cleaning as well. It would be expensive as a general mechanical cleaning solvent. Only the kind expressly sold as a video head cleaner should be used on video heads.

A good contrast between two types of cleaners is provided by the belt cleaner and the lighter fluid. The belt cleaner will leave clean plastics slightly fogged. The petroleum-based lighter fluid does not.

Solvents for cleaning mechanisms

Be sensitive to solvent bases

The question of which solvents to use is a difficult one. For general cleaning, it is usually best to start with something water based first, and if that doesn't do it, move up to a petroleum-based solvent. If that fails, it might be worth asking yourself if the cleaning is all that important, before moving on to those that are abrasive, or are known to cut plastics. Pure Acetone will cut almost anything, but is so potent that we have not even mentioned it as a viable choice. (Now that we have mentioned it, Acetone will remove most magic-marker graffiti. If you use it, apply it to a cloth and immediately rub very lightly the area to be cleaned with the moist area of the cloth. Acetone evaporates so rapidly that the wetting action must be repeated, but always just a little at a time. Watch carefully what you are doing to the surface and finish. Several applications of Pledge will usually restore some uniformity to the surface after an Acetone cleaning treatment.)

Appendix C

LUBRICANTS AND ADHESIVES

Most of the time we are concerned with getting audiovisual mechanisms to work more easily, and we do this by cleaning with solvents and lubricating with oil, silicone, or graphite. Today's mechanisms are designed for a very wide assortment of lubricants, and they are not interchangeable. You can not take that can of oil labeled Singer, intended for use in sewing machines, and use it anywhere in a Singer projector. Singer recommends about a half-a-dozen specific lubricants for use in different parts of the projector. Always be particularly wary of indiscriminate lubrication of any of the clutch areas, which are associated with the spooling or winding function of film or tape.

Oil comes in a variety of viscosities, with additional detergent and heat withstanding qualities. Light 3-in-1 has been sold widely for years. The oil is good but the can is rather gross for limited oiling. This can be controlled by applying the oil first to a toothpick, letting it run down to the end, and applying the drop that forms to the thing to be oiled. There are also a number of oilers marketed, full of thin oil, that permit needle-type control of the oil flow (center of picture).

Widely available lubricants

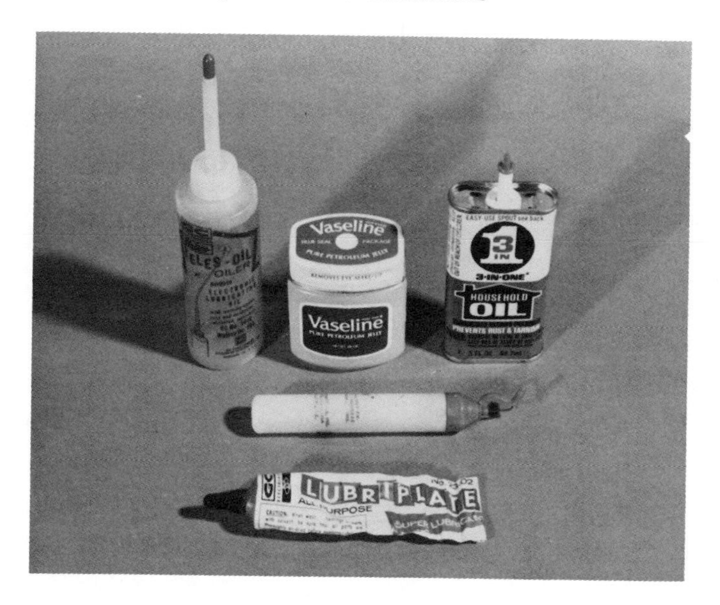

Having a slightly heavier oil available is also helpful. This could be a light-weight motor oil or an oil sold in a plastic oiler for electronic/mechanical equipment.

If you want to use a light grease, for example on plates where parts of mechanisms slide back and forth (speed change in some record players, linkages in cassette recorders), either use Vaseline or a special light grease like Lubriplate or a synthetic gun grease.

Do not assume that all lubricants will mix well together. When oiling fast running parts such as motor shafts, which also get pretty hot, it is a good idea to flood the shaft and bearing rather liberally with a petroleum solvent such as lighter fluid. Spin the shaft by hand or with a few-seconds burst of power. Do this several times, in an effort to flush out the old and gummy oil. Dry the area with a tissue, then apply the new oil, again working it in by hand operation or short bursts of power. Always wipe off any excess oil to reduce the tendency of lint and dirt to cling to the surface oil.

In one way of thinking, the adhesives are opposites of lubricants. Unfortunately, we can not use them to predictably slow things down. But if lubricants keep things from sticking together, an assortment of modern adhesives is indispensable for putting broken things back together and keeping them whole units.

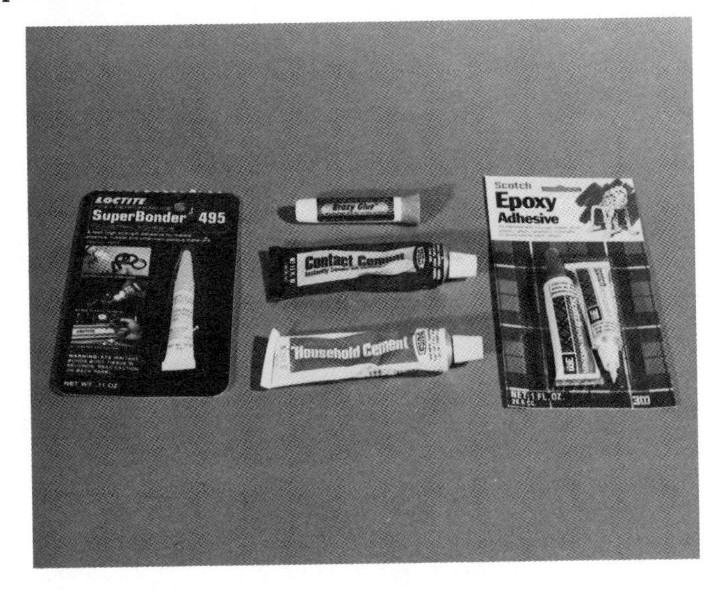

Stock a variety of adhesives

The first rule of any adhesive is that the surfaces must be clean--chemically clean. This is one case where a cleaner that bites into the surface is welcome. Getting parts clean enough for good adhesion is especially difficult in areas where oil or other lubricant has been on the surface of the broken part.

For plastics and quick, light repair of coverings, one of the clear household-type cements works well. Not all plastics respond, and if you don't succeed, try one of the new super cements.

These new cements include Eastman 910 Adhesive, Superbonder 495, Krazy Glue, etc. All of these require perfectly mated surfaces, typical of fractured plastic. Do not expect them to do well on porous materials, or on granular metal surfaces such as broken pot-metal. Also, heed the warning on the labels about sticking yourself together. For this they are truly superior.

In areas where flexibility is required, a Contact Cement is very good. It also works well where it is possible to coat both surfaces to be joined, let the cement set up for about 10 minutes, and then put them in contact for a permanent bond. Contact cement is good for repair of peeling cover material, or you can use one of the casein glues, like Elmers.

Epoxy cements are characterized by the need to mix two parts just before use. Epoxy cement is really nice where it is necessary to fill a small space, as where a chip is missing. It does have a creeping viscosity until it sets, and you may have to work with it to prevent its running out onto the surface.

Appendix D

SOLDERING

Most circuit connections in electronic equipment are made by soldering. Wires today are more and more frequently joined by various "quick-disconnect" couplings, wire nuts, and solderless crimp connectors. While power plugs are usually attached with terminal screws, and one type of 1/4" phone plug uses tiny screws (that are about as well removed and the connections soldered), all the other connectors are attached to the wires by solder.

Soldering is not difficult, if a few simple rules and techniques are followed. Like all skills, it should improve with practice, and some pure practice is recommended before attempting soldering "for real."

We might also say a word about the converse of soldering--unsoldering. Service work requires quite a lot of unsoldering, either to remove parts, to clear a hole in lugs and connectors, or to get rid of wire fragments. It is as important to become skillful at unsoldering to get things apart as it is to be good at soldering to get them together.

Good soldering requires all of the following:

1. Clean metal, usually scraped that way with a knife.
2. A good grade of rosin-core solder, either 40/60 or 50/50 (lead and tin). A good grade is not the cheapest you can buy, and it should never be acid-core for any electronics work.
3. A clean soldering iron tip, hot enough to melt the solder instantly when it is touched to the tip.

Before going into the soldering and unsoldering procedures, let's consider some terms and problems. One soldering term is "tinning." We tin the tip of most soldering irons to retard oxidation, which forms a barrier to efficient heat transfer. We also tin wires and terminals, sometimes to hold the strands of wire together and make them easier to manage, sometimes because a pre-tinned wire being soldered to a pre-tinned lug or connector terminal will solder instantly upon application of heat.

"Flux" is another term related to soldering. Rosin is the flux used for electronics soldering and it is manufactured into the center of the solder; hence the expression "rosin-core." There is also an "acid-core" solder, and there are liquid and paste fluxes. These should be left to plumbers, tinners and sheet metal workers. Heat speeds oxidation and oxidized metal does not accept solder. The acid flows over the hot metal, keeping the air off and lightly etching the surface, making a very clean area for bonding.

Acid can also continue to combine with moisture in the air, working over years to eat through thin wires. Acid and lead are basic battery ingredients, and we do not need strange voltages being developed within the circuits. Acid corrosion often approaches a crystalline growth, which if it is conductive due to the moisture it attracts, can cause unstable circuit values.

There will be times when soldering just doesn't seem to go right, and you may be sorely tempted to apply some soldering paste found in a shop or relative's tool box. Don't. Only rosin-core solder provides an acceptable flux for electronics work.

The greatest problem in soldering today is the extensive use of plastics, both as cable insulation and as the separating insulator in connectors and components. There is also a problem with overheating solid-state transistors and integrated circuits, but since those repairs are beyond the scope of this book, except for the possible discovery of a faulty connection on a circuit board (as in cassette recorders), we can disregard this problem.

The key to minimum damage to plastic components is the use of a clean soldering iron tip, hot enough to melt solder instantly upon contact. The most commonly observed bad technique is that of using an iron too cool to melt solder, but plenty hot enough to melt plastics, and leaving it in contact long enough to destroy everything while waiting for enough heat to melt the solder.

Still another problem arises from trying to solder metals that can not be soldered. Only brass, copper, silver and gold plating can be easily soldered. Ferrous metals (those that will cling to a magnet) can not be soldered. Aluminum is not easy to solder, and requires special fluxes and solders to get it to solder at all.

Generally, electronic solder will not make a mechanically sound joint. For instance, you could not expect to solder a motor shaft or a broken projector arm back together, even if they were made of solderable metals. "Silver soldering" with a torch might achieve this, but that is very hard solder and the heat required would destroy electronic components. You might, however, make some kind of bolted sleeve which you could fill with solder to obtain rigidity. In this case the sleeve and bolts would be carrying the mechanical stress, the solder serving only as a molded "shim."

Finally, you can not expect to solder anything very large with a small soldering iron intended for electronics work. Large metal areas or objects function as a "heat sink," which is a metal device used to dissipate heat from transistors or resistors that would otherwise be destroyed by the heat at which they operate. Likewise, the large metal object conducts the heat away from the area of contact with the soldering iron. It does this so rapidly that the small iron can not get the metal hot enough to melt solder, making a satisfactory soldered joint impossible.

Soldering

If you are using a heat element-type soldering iron, plug it in as you begin to get ready to work. And don't forget to unplug it when you are finished. Current practice is to keep a rather moist (but not outright wet) viscose sponge on the work bench to wipe off the tip. A damp cloth works equally well.

If the soldering gun-type iron is used, it is imperative to squeeze the trigger and wait until the tip is hot enough to melt solder before applying the tip to wires or parts. It is a distressing sight to an old hand to watch an inexperienced person put the tip on the connection area, then trigger the gun. All the plastic begins to recede and soften, and still the wires are not hot enough to melt solder.

Cut wires to length, remove whatever insulation is necessary, and lightly scrape the wires, trying to get bright metal all the way around (but don't make a fetish of it ... just sort of turn the wire as you are scraping) without nicking the wire or cutting any strands.

At this point a "third hand" can be very helpful. Either use one hand attached to a helper, or use a small vise, clamp, or clip-type of third hand. They are easy to make, as shown.

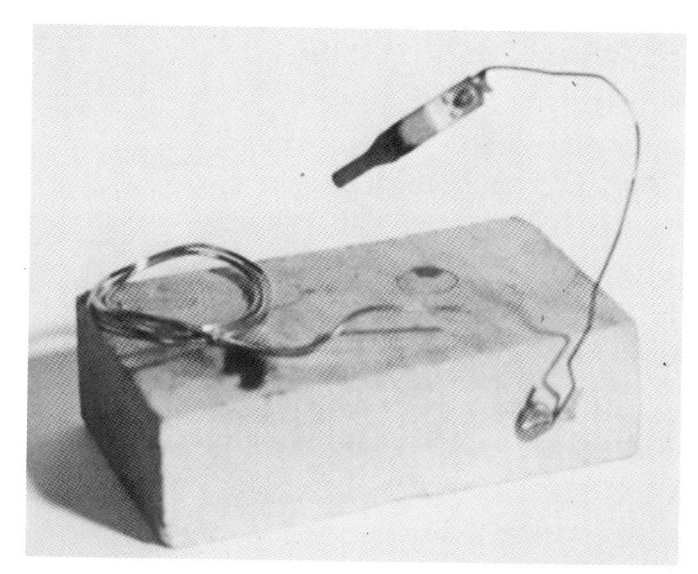

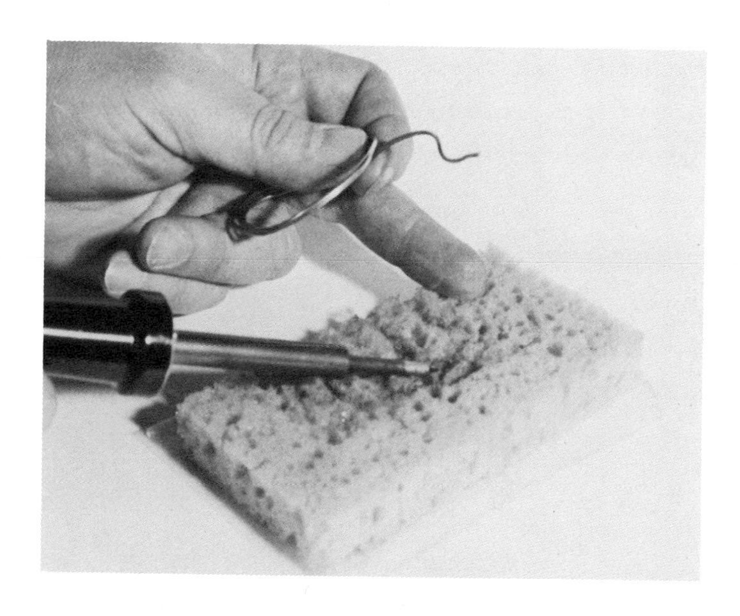

Having gotten the wire or connector to stay in place, take the solder in one hand and the iron in the other. Wipe off the tip and touch the solder to it. It should melt instantly. This little bit of solder re-tins the tip and serves as an excellent heat conduit to the joint.

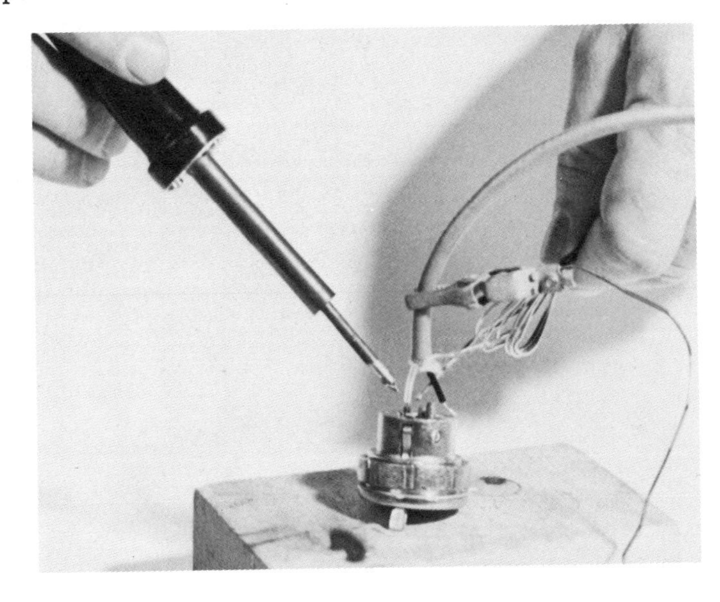

Make solder joint quickly

Now bring the tip, the solder, and the wire, lug, or connector together simultaneously. Remember that heat rises and if you can position the tip a little on the underside of the work, bringing the solder in from the side or above, a very quick, clean solder-joint is possible. The rule is that the metal to be soldered must be hot enough to melt the solder, or a cold joint will result. But it is possible to get the metal that hot simultaneously with the melting of the solder on the tip, and you will have to get good at this or you will melt all the plastic insulation. Let the tip of the soldering iron linger just a moment longer after you remove the solder, then pull the tip away and let the joint cool, or blow on it if you feel a need to cool things more quickly. Do not attempt to position wires, parts, or test joints until you are sure the solder has set. Movement while the solder is cooling crystallizes the solder, making the surface appear dull and the joint less than secure.

How thoroughly you wrap wires around lugs is a matter of personal preference. Those who always build things with new parts and rarely get involved in repair tend to be thorough wrappers prior to soldering. Those who have to get this kind of work undone for repair are less likely to make it that tough for the next guy. Certainly twisting wires together or using hook splices prior to soldering is desirable. Wires should also be hooked through lugs or around other adjacent wires. But more than just hooking makes disconnection very difficult when it has to be done while the solder is in a molten state. All of which brings us to ...

Unsoldering

To rewire or change a connector, to make some tests, and to replace components, you must be able to unsolder. Often it is best just to cut a wire, rather than subject the plastic to all the heat required to unsolder, then again to as much as is needed to resolder the connection.

Don't overlook constructive destruction. It is usually easier to cut a cable and cut each wire at the connector pin, melt the solder and rap the connector sharply on the bench top to dislodge the fragment of wire left in the pin, than it is to try to unsolder and remove the wires one at a time when they are part of the whole cable.

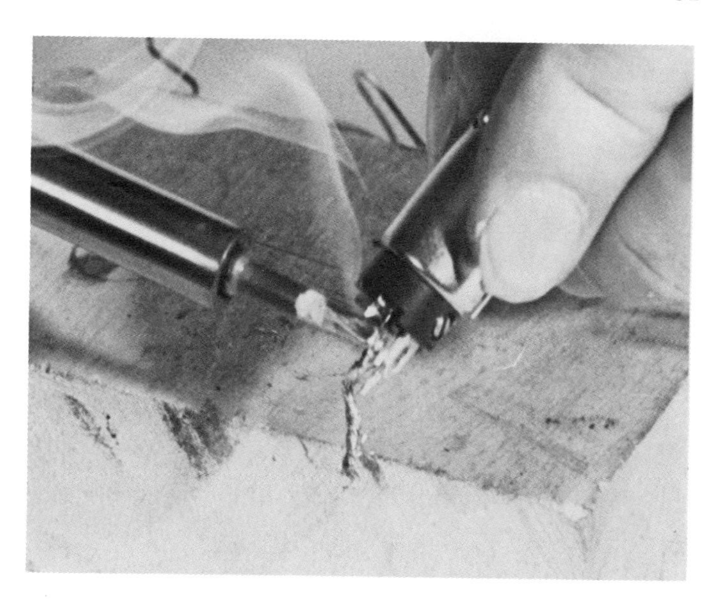

When doing this rapping procedure, it is best to hold the connector by some part other than the pin in which you are trying to melt the solder, if possible. Any tool used to hold the connector is also a great "heat sink," and will remove the soldering heat about as fast as you are trying to add it with the soldering iron.

Wires that have been twisted through lugs during manufacture can often be clipped at the top of the loop, greatly simplifying untwisting and removal while the solder is in a molten state.

There is also a device known as a solder sucker. These are particularly effective on circuit boards, where their sudden vacuum will even clear the small hole in a board while the solder is melted. This book is really not involved with repairs on circuit boards, and a solder sucker, while a convenience, is hardly necessary for the level of repair covered by this book.

Finally, a precaution on unsoldering. During the rapping technique of removing solder, the hot ball of molten solder tends to fly downward. If it spatters on a tile or concrete floor, it is easily loosened and scraped up. But it really gets exciting when it gets into denim fabric, especially in one's lap. It's also hard to get out of the pile of carpet. Try to aim your rapping in a direction that will keep solder splatters on the bench top or other covered work surface.

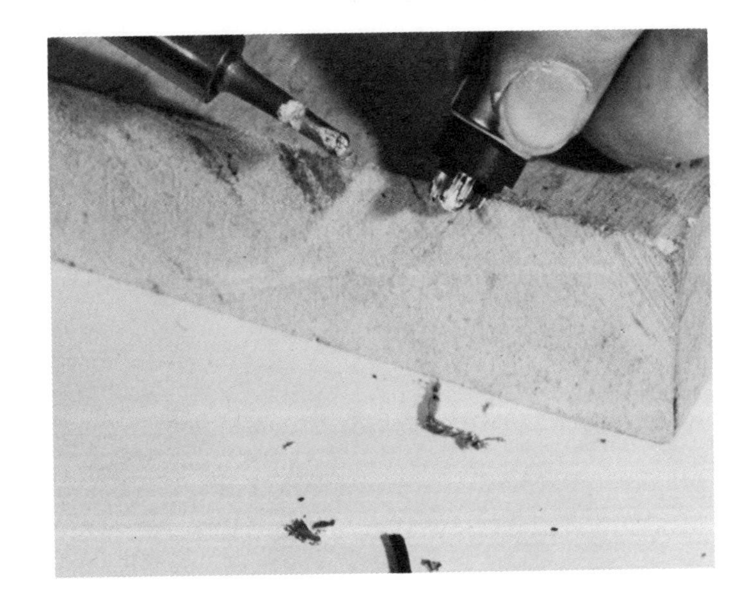

Appendix E

BASIC ELECTRICITY

You don't need to know a lot about basic electricity to get through most of the day-to-day problems related to audiovisual equipment. We are going to try to tie each theoretical idea to some practical application, hoping that you don't bog down in a lot of seemingly irrelevant scientific principles.

A VOLT is a unit of electrical pressure. The typical wall outlet measures about 117 volts. Anything from about 110 to 120 is fine for most audiovisual equipment. You do have trouble with lamp burn-out as you get to the high end of this range. This is often especially noticeable in a new building. If you suspect your voltage is high, you can ask your utility company to put a recording meter on it for a few days. Tell them why you think the voltage is high. They rarely admit anything, but suddenly the lamps seem to last longer.

An AMPERE (referred to as an "amp") is the current or electron flow unit. Amps are usually encountered as a rating on circuit breakers and fuses, the two most common protection devices against circuit overload. You may also see an amp rating on some of the higher current devices, such as laminators, dry mount presses, and thermal transparency makers. This rating may also be expressed in watts.

The WATT is the unit of electrical power. (It used to be a fair indicator of the brightness of a projector lamp, but the new high-efficiency designs have made the watt unreliable for these comparisons.) The watt is related to the volt and the ampere by the equation: Watts = Volts x Amperes. That form of the equation doesn't do us a whole lot of good in audiovisual work. But solving for

$$\text{Amps} = \frac{\text{Watts}}{\text{Volts}}$$

can sure come in handy. Let's take an example.

To keep our example really simple, always round the volts off to 100. We can claim that extra 17% as a safety factor, and most of us can move a decimal point two places to the left.

You're going to have the staff in for coffee and an in-service session on dry mounting and thermal transparency making. You know from experience (having overloaded the circuits and tripped the breakers before) that there are two circuits providing power to the room, with two outlets for each circuit. A check of the power panel shows that each breaker has a 20 on the switch, meaning 20 amperes for each circuit.

The label on the drymount press says it's 800 watts. The thermal transparency maker is 1, 000 watts. The coffee maker is also 1, 000 watts. Now it's true that each of these devices has a thermostat and they may not be on all the time, or all at the same time. But while the coffee is brewing and the press is warming up, they will be on for sure. If we add up the two 1, 000-watt devices and divide by our rounded off 100 volts, we get 20 amperes. That's pretty close to the limit for one circuit. It would be better to plug the transparency maker and dry mount press into one outlet (1800 watts divided by 100 volts is about 18 amps) and the coffee maker into the other. And if you only have one circuit? It's either got to be hot coffee down the hall (on somebody else's circuit) or cooler coffee in your own room.

Let's take one more example--one that comes up every few years. You are going to get the media center of your dreams and are asked to help with the specifications. You have managed to get "wet" carrels, complete with fluorescent lights and outlets, and a work room with counter space for a few production machines such as a dry mount press and laminator. Suddenly the architect looks at you and asks, "How much power do you think all this equipment will take?" You give him the "Who knows?" look, but that won't bail you out this time. Ask how many amps he is planning per circuit. That will probably be around 20. Now remember that each circuit is money. They won't want to underwire, but if the project goes over estimate, something will get cut. It probably won't be the circuit, but it might be something you really wanted. The point is, this is no time to ask for the moon. So ask for time. A day or two, or a week.

Now you've got to do a power inventory. You can either do it arithmetically, or by actual count. Get the production room out of the way first. If we use the figures from the first example, you will need about 8 amps for the dry mount press and the laminator will need about 9 amps more. That's 17 amps, allowing only 3 amps margin on a 20 amp circuit. If there are additional outlets, you could have problems if other equipment is added later. Ask the architect whether this can be handled by a single 20 amp circuit. (This is also a good time to ask the architect to provide outlet strips along work counters to make equipment use more convenient.)

Then try to figure out your carrel circuits. A cassette recorder or a small filmstrip viewer draws so little current that an overload is almost inconceivable. Those fluorescent lights won't add much either. But some of the projection devices for carrel use could run to 200 or 300 watts. One regular 500-watt filmstrip projector used in a carrel would use how much? By now you should have said about 5 amps.

$$\frac{500 \text{ Watts}}{100 \text{ Volts}} = 5 \text{ Amps}$$

Only you know your use patterns and what kind of equipment you have, or hope to have. Working with your architect, you should be able to work out a power circuit scheme that will make your dreams come true.

There are two more terms we need to mention to round out the discussion of basic electricity. They are resistance and impedance. They're somewhat related ideas, as their roots "resist" and "impede" would suggest.

RESISTANCE is the easier one, because it is always the same. Well, almost always. A projection lamp is a good example, because the lamp filament has pure resistance. A 500-watt lamp operating at 117 volts has about 27 ohms resistance. The OHM is the unit of electrical resistance. The "resistance ohm" doesn't have much application in audiovisual repair work. We do check cables to be sure they have not developed resistance or shorts because of broken wires. And there is a resistance problem that causes lamps to burn out when they are cold. How many times have you had a lamp burn out while you were reading? Isn't it usually a bright flash just as you turn the lamp on?

In the example of the last paragraph, we said the lamp had 27 ohms resistance when lit, using 500 watts of power. Those 27 ohms are calculated by Ohm's Law:

$$\text{Amperes} = \frac{\text{500 Watts}}{\text{117 Volts}} = 4.27 \qquad \text{Ohms} = \frac{\text{117 Volts}}{\text{4.27 Amps}} = 27.4$$

Now let's assume the projector was left in a car overnight and the temperature dropped to 20° F. Suppose this causes the resistance to drop to 20 ohms. (Most components having resistance maintain a fairly constant value regardless of temperature, but lamp filaments drop in value when they are cold.) Solving our equations in reverse, we now have:

$$\text{Amperes} = \frac{\text{117 Volts}}{\text{20 Ohms}} = 5.85 \qquad \text{Watts} = \text{117 Volts X 5.85 Amps} = \text{684.4 Watts}$$

This means that at the moment we turn the lamp on, before it has a chance to get hot, it will use 684 watts, about a 38% overload. While it only lasts a moment, this overload may burn the lamp out.

It would have been better to keep the projector in the building overnight and transport it in the warm part of the car, or pre-warm it by running the fan for at least ten minutes before turning the lamp on. There is always an excessive current drawn when a lamp is turned on, but the warmer it is, the lower the excess, and the less likely it is to burn the lamp out.

And then there's IMPEDANCE. It's measured in ohms too. It relates to AC circuits. There is usually some sort of magnetic device involved. And it's not constant ... it varies with frequency even though the parts all look and act essentially the same. Obviously, impedance is way beyond the scope of this book. But it keeps coming up in audiovisual work, particularly when we talk about microphones and speakers, or when we interconnect a record player and tape recorder (or two or more tape recorders) to dub recordings from one form to another or to make duplicates, or when we get involved with television cables for antennas, cameras, recorders and monitors.

Our primary concern is that impedances "match." The best match results in the most efficient transfer of energy, resulting in full, undistorted sound, or in clear, contrasty pictures. The match is rarely mathematically exact, but there are limits to the degree of mismatch that is permissible, and these limits can vary from one device to another. When impedances do not match, the reduction in energy transfer is similar to introducing resistance into the circuit, and to that extent the concepts of resistance and impedance are related.

Specific discussions of impedance-matching occur in the next appendix (How We Use Magnetism) under microphones and speakers, and in the appendix on Cables and Connectors (as related to television).

Appendix F

HOW WE USE MAGNETISM

If we disregard the actual amplifier circuits (which are considered beyond the scope of this book), most of the audiovisual electronics with which we are concerned involve a magnetic property, its corollary, and a second related property. If you have ever taken a general science of physics course, at least two of these principles should have been demonstrated.

1. The first property, illustrated at right, is that an electric current is generated in a coil of wire when that coil is passed through a magnetic field. At this time (1978), this is the source of almost all utility power used to operate our audiovisual devices. It is also the principle of most microphones, and with a slight variant, of high-quality phono cartridges.

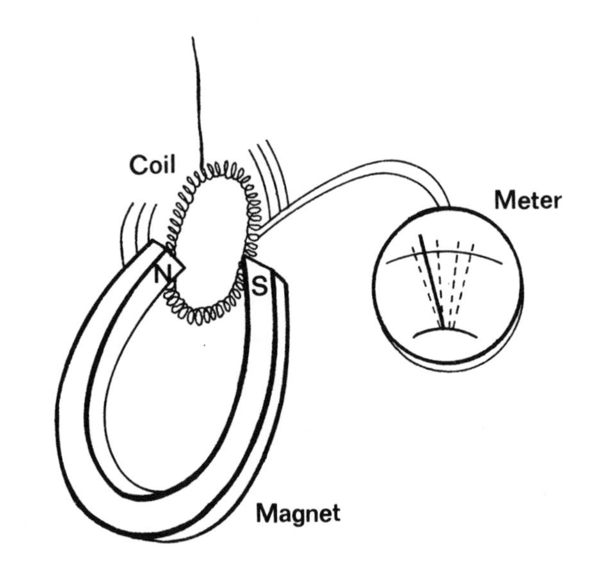

2. The corollary to the first property is that a current passing through a coil of wire freely suspended in a magnetic field will produce a polarized (North & South) field in the coil, causing the coil to move in the field of the magnet. This principle is basic to all speakers, most modern headphones, and, with considerable oversimplification, to the motors that drive record players and tape recorders, and the cooling fans and mechanism of motion picture and other projectors.

   The first half of this property, that "a current passing through a coil of wire ... will produce a polarized field

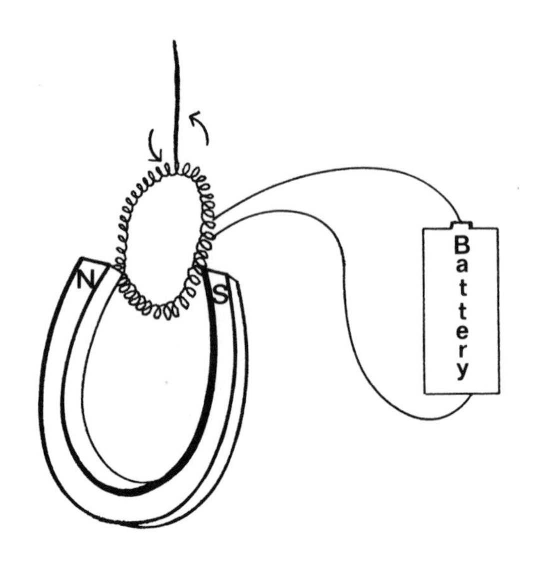

in the coil," is the basis of how we get the varying magnetic field used for magnetic tape recording. (And we vary the first principle, moving the magnetized tape over the coil to produce a feeble current, when we play the tape.)

3. The third property is known as induction. When an alternating current passes through a coil that shares a common iron core with a second coil, a current is "induced" in the second coil. Once again, it is a constantly expanding and contracting magnetic field in the core that actually permits induction. It's really like the first principle, except that physical motion is replaced by the motion of electrons and the magnetic field. Unfortunately, this field can also extend beyond the iron core, and is capable of inducing the hum of its oscillations into near-by microphones, phono and tape heads. More about these later.

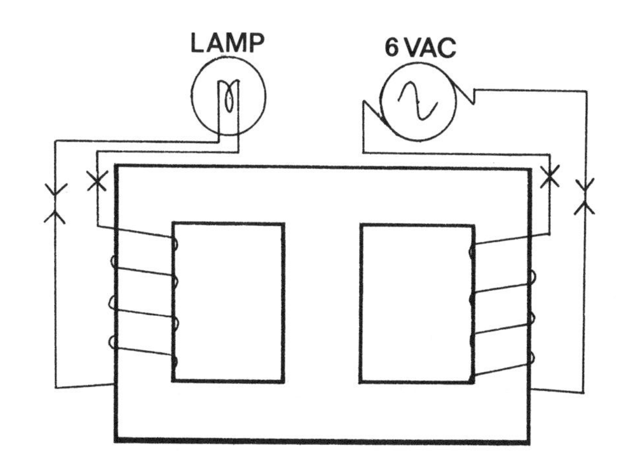

The component consisting of the coils and core is called a transformer. Transformers are used for isolation to reduce the shock hazard from audiovisual equipment. We use them to change the 117-volt power line to the lower voltages required by transistors (5 to 20 volts, usually, and around 20 volts for some of the newer, more efficient projection lamp designs). We also use transformers for something called "impedance matching." This will be discussed in the paragraphs on microphones and speakers that follow.

MAGNETIC PRINCIPLE DEVICES
(And a Few Others)

MICROPHONES convert the physical pressure variations of the sound wave into electrical impulses to permit amplification and recording or transmission. The sound wave impinging upon the microphone diaphragm causes a coil to move in a magnetic field, generating a

Actual microphone element

very tiny current. This is the principle of the Dynamic Microphone, the type most often encountered in audiovisual work.

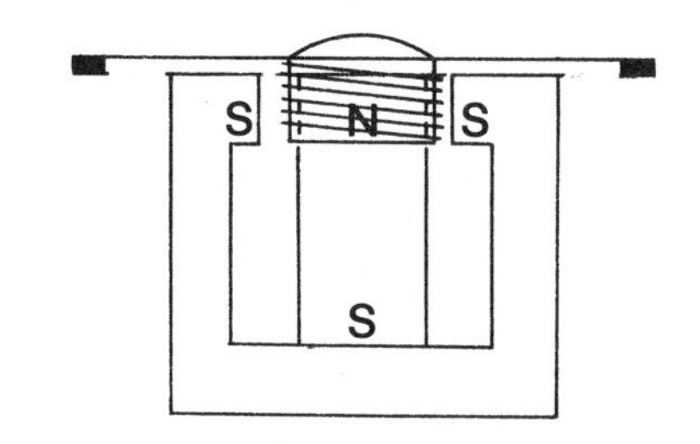

Without wanting to labor the point, it must be said that microphones are delicate instruments and require careful handling if they are to give reliable service, good sensitivity, and stay free of distortion. The lightness of many tape recorder microphones seems to reduce the shock when they are dropped, and they are amazingly durable, compared with the product of ten or 20 years ago. But careless handling will inevitably shorten useful life.

There are many horrible examples of microphone handling: blowing into the microphone to test it, twirling it by the cord in rock and club entertainment, throwing the mic. to someone off camera on network TV. And then there's the security problem. Every kid seems to want to be a rock star and needs a microphone to practice. Most audiovisual microphones are grossly unsuited to this type of work, but by the time they find that out, we have lost another microphone.

Blowing into a microphone is just stupid. Blowing across it isn't much better. If the diaphragm is designed to respond to the light zephyr of a sound wave there is no way it can withstand the gale of that "test blow." Designers work for a practical compromise, either stiffening the diaphragm or inserting a "blast screen." Either expedient reduces microphone sensitivity, which we usually want about as high as possible. It's a losing battle, but one worth continuing to fight. Demonstrating the advantages of light tapping with a fingernail is more positive than dire threats when trying to discourage this microphone-destroying practice.

Microphone cables are rather complex and delicate. This matter is fully treated under audio cables (Cables and Connectors Appendix). A break at the plug end can be repaired by cutting and replacing the plug. A break at the mic. end of the small plastic cassette recorder mics. is usually not repairable. Use of small table and floor stands, whenever possible, reduces handling and prolongs life. And while we are talking about cables, let's bring up storage bins. It usually takes a master of packaging to get all those cords back in the bins provided in the equipment. Wedging all that in, or tightly wrapping the cord around the microphone, puts great bending strain on the cord. It would be much better to store the microphone and cord loosely in a larger box or in a desk or cabinet drawer.

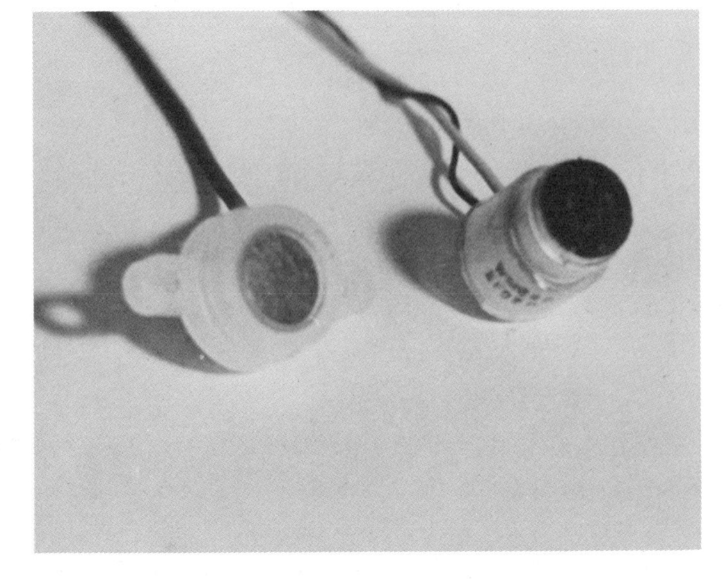

Electret condenser microphone

There is another type of microphone coming into wide use with audiovisual recording and public address equipment. It is called an ELECTRET CONDENSER MICROPHONE. This microphone is non-magnetic, using the principle of what might be called a static battery (the electret retains a high voltage charge under which the material was formed, but delivers virtually no current). In condenser microphones, the charged area changes with sound pressure on the diaphragm. This change is converted by a transistor that is usually part of the microphone. When the microphone is built-in, the voltage for the transistor is derived from the circuit. If the microphone is external, it requires a battery in the base. This battery should be changed once a year to assure reliable operation and prevent corrosion.

Condenser microphones, before the advent of the electret, were expensive and required bulky external power supplies. Their advantages of wide frequency response, rugged diaphragms, and great sensitivity made them the choice wherever the associated equipment could be accommodated. Spending $35-$50 (1978) for an inexpensive Electret Condenser Microphone would be the most inexpensive way to greatly improve recording quality and sensitivity with almost any tape recorder.

Two other aspects of microphones should be considered to cope with them in audiovisual equipment.

The first of these is what is known as "polar pattern." A typical pattern is shown at right. The concentric rings of the circle refer to pressure sensitivity levels. The microphone is assumed to be in the center. The heavy line of irregular shape traces the microphone's sensitivity from all directions. If the microphone's line is a circle, it is considered to be omnidirectional. This should be thought of as a sphere of sensitivity that surrounds the head of the microphone, responding equally to any sources located at the same distance around the microphone. If you are recording a conference with people all around the table, this is the kind of microphone you want, but be careful of any air-conditioning outlets located directly overhead, since that air rush is also within the sphere and will be recorded.

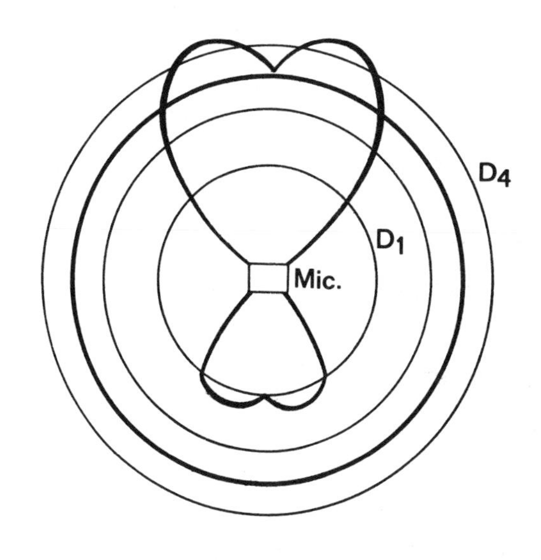

The opposite of the omnidirectional pattern is the unidirectional pattern. In this case all the sensitivity, or certainly the greatest part of it, is directly in front of the microphone screen. This is the kind of microphone we want for public address work, where we want to reject the sound from the PA speakers in order to minimize feedback (that whistling, howling noise heard all too often--see Part II, Public Address Systems and Sound Lecterns). Unidirectional microphones are also fine for recording a lecturer who is seated or at a rostrum, especially if the location is rather noisy.

Finally there is a bi-polar or "cardioid" pattern. Such a microphone has an area of greatest sensitivity in front, some degree of lesser sensitivity in back, and least sensitivity at the sides. This polar pattern can be worked to some advantage when recording music, where we might let the front favor the vocalist, with the louder accompanying instruments arranged at the back and sides to reduce their volume and keep them in balance with the singer.

These polar pattern options are only available in more expensive (about $50) microphones. But each model, regardless of price, has to have some kind of polar pattern. It's not all as obvious as it sounds (no pun intended), but if you know about the patterns, they can be used to advantage.

Microphone impedance must also be considered. This is an electrical characteristic. The impedance must "match" the associated equipment. Since the advent of transistor equipment almost all microphones have been "low-impedance," but some older tube equipment, particularly old public address installations, may still require "high-impedance" microphones.

A high impedance is usually around 20,000 ohms. Cables for these microphones are very vulnerable to hum pick-up from nearby power lines ... not an unusual situation on stages and church altars, where lighting power seems to be concentrated. Usually a high-impedance microphone has about 20 feet of cord attached, and under favorable conditions this can be lengthened by a 20- or 30-foot extension, but that's about all. There is no difference in the performance of high- and low-impedance microphones, but they can not be used interchangeably.

For years broadcast and professional applications specified low-impedance microphones. Low impedance ranges from 50 to 500 ohms, but even in this confined range, the microphones may not work interchangeably. Neither is the size of the plug any assurance that just because you can plug it in, the microphone will match. This is especially true of small cassette recorder mics.

The table of specifications in the owners manual will give a microphone's input impedance. Some of the plastic microphones have an impedance value molded into the case where the cord comes out. If you are trying to buy a replacement microphone, the safest way is to take the equipment along and have the salesperson try it for good sensitivity and lack of distortion. If it meets these two criteria, it's an OK match.

It is characteristic of low-impedance microphone cables to be much freer of hum pick-up than high-impedance cable. The twist of the wires within the cable tends to cancel hum currents induced into the wire from nearby power wiring. The low impedance is also less vulnerable to hum because it is based on current transfer, rather than voltage. The cable for most low-impedance devices could be extended up to 100 feet under good circumstances (not too much power wiring adjacent to the cable), but there would be some loss of sensitivity because of the resistance of the long cable. (This would be slight enough to permit compensation by advancing the volume control in most equipment.)

There can be a problem of hum pick-up from transformers in audiovisual equipment, especially if the microphone is used right next to the device. If you find that a given recorder makes a recording with hum along with the sound, move the microphone several feet from the recorder and the problem should disappear. This would not be a problem with built-in or separate electret microphones because they do not operate on a magnetic principle.

Microphone technique can make a lot of difference in the results you get. In electronics the term "signal-to-noise ratio" is frequently used. Signal is the sound you want. Everything else is noise. A high signal-to-noise ratio means the information is very clear and almost everything else drops away. The best technique for speech seems to be talking across (rather than into) the microphone, with the grille or screen two to three inches away from the mouth. A pleasant voice level should be maintained and turning the head away from the microphone should be avoided. Scripts should be held beyond the microphone, not between the mouth and the microphone.

Built-in microphones present some special problems. Since they are so close to the mechanism, they will have a tendency to record its sound as noise. This means that the signal must be greater than the noise, and that is achieved by keeping your head just above the microphone in the device while you are recording. These built-in microphones rarely do a good job of recording conferences because no one is as close to the microphone as the recorder mechanism is.

No microphone, however sensitive, can make something of the sound pressure that isn't there in the first place. This doesn't mean that people have to shout, but it does mean that they have to give the microphone some sound to work with. Children are particularly difficult in this regard because of their light voice quality. But if they can be heard from one end of the playground to the other, there is no reason why they can't be taught to speak up on the stage or when recording in the classroom. We are frequently asked to "live-mic." a whole stage for public address. This is generally just not possible. The potential for feedback becomes enormous when many microphones are all operating right at the "ringing point." (Ringing is that odd, echo-like sound that occurs just before the whole system begins to howl.) Getting the actors to speak up and project their voices will do more than anything we can hope to do with electronics. Not every seemingly technical problem has a technical solution.

SPEAKERS use the second basic magnetic principle (that a current passing through a coil in a permanent magnetic field will produce motion) to convert electrical energy into a pressure wave in the air that we call sound. The cut-away drawing at right shows the voice coil attached to a paper diaphragm known as the speaker cone. The coil operates in a very narrow circular gap that brings all the magnetic force into an intense field around the coil.

Comparison of the diagram at right with that of the dynamic microphone (page 97) shows the construction to be almost identical. When small speakers are used in headsets, even the size is comparable, but generally speakers run from 3 to 12 inches in diameter in audio-visual equipment (microphone diaphragms are usually from 1/4 to 1 inch in diameter).

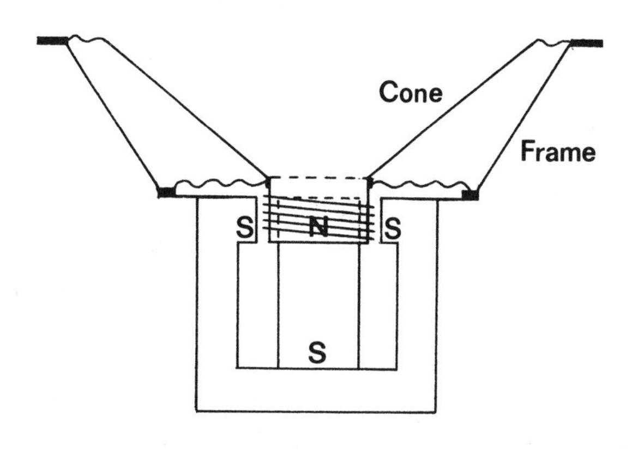

As a general rule, the heavier the magnet, the more efficient the speaker. That rule has an interesting application. Suppose a small cassette recorder is rated at 1.5 watts output and has a self-contained 4"-speaker with about a 5 oz. -magnet. If you plug a 6"-speaker with a 12 oz. -magnet into the external speaker jack, you will realize considerably louder sound. This is primarily due to the heavier magnet and greater efficiency, rather than to the larger diameter speaker cone. The watt output rating of the amplifier has not changed, but is more efficiently converted to sound energy.

Speaker baffles (the boards they are mounted on) and enclosures have a marked effect upon speaker sound and performance. In the past, a need for powerful, extended bass range required use of an enclosure of considerable size (2' x 2' x 3' minimum). The introduction of powerful transistor amplifiers made practical the use of much smaller enclosures with special speaker designs. Efficiency was sacrificed for size. Most audiovisual equipment does not have a high (in excess of 25 watts) output rating. This should be considered if an application suggests use of small high fidelity "bookshelf" speakers in combination with standard audiovisual record players or tape recorders. Because institutional rooms are often quite large, you may end up with sound of excellent quality, but never enough volume to really carry the content of the recording.

Speakers are usually rated for their watt rating and their impedance value. This is often stamped on the back of the magnet structure, sometimes with the weight of the magnet as well. When replacement speakers are selected, they should have a watt rating at least equal to that of the amplifier in the equipment. Failure to do this results in burn-out of the voice coil if the device is played at full volume.

Impedance matching of speakers is another consideration. If a replacement is being selected, it should have the same impedance as the original speaker. You can get by with 3. 2 ohms on a 4-ohm output (that would be considered a "match" by most technicians). An 8-ohm speaker could be connected to either a 4-ohm or a 16-ohm output, as well as its perfect match, an 8-ohm output. But a 3. 2-ohm speaker on a 16-ohm output would be a moderately severe mismatch. It will work, but the volume should be kept no higher than half, to prevent overloading the amplifier. An old rule of thumb holds that lower impedance outputs can be used to feed higher impedance loads, but never the other way around. It doesn't always work out that way, but it's pretty good advice.

When more than one speaker is to be connected to one amplifier, things get pretty involved. If both speakers are to operate in the same room, speaker "phasing" must be considered. Speakers are said to be "in-phase" when both cones move forward together, rather than one pushing and one pulling at the air in the room. The easiest way to get two speakers in phase is to operate the equipment with one speaker connected, touching the wires to the other speaker and listening intently to the volume level. Reverse these wires and listen again. Try this several times. The wires should be attached in the combination that produces the loudest volume. If you must do this while you are very near one speaker, get someone else to stand out in the room where it is easier to judge the volume level.

There are also different ways to connect the speakers, whether used in the same room or in different locations. The two basic wiring configurations are:

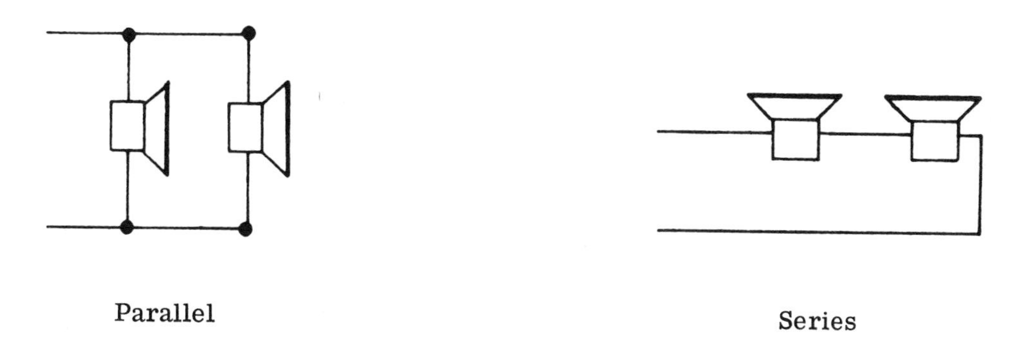

Parallel

Series

Combinations of these are also possible.

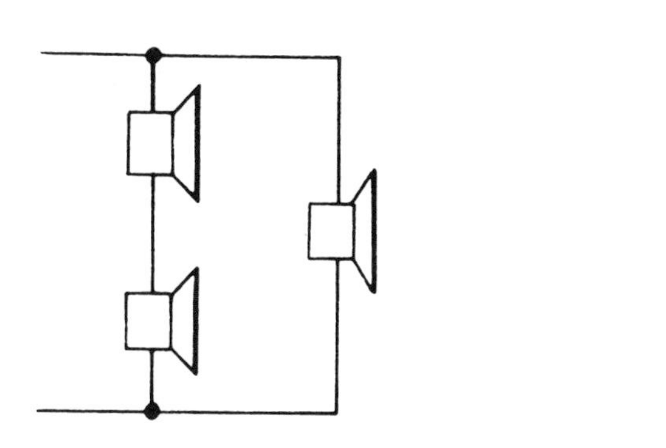

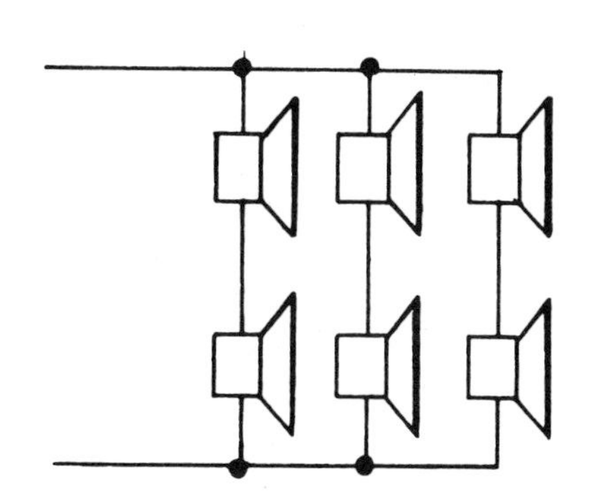

The most important thing to remember is that the TOTAL LOAD IMPEDANCE OF THE SPEAKERS MUST NOT BE LOWER THAN THE OUTPUT IMPEDANCE OF THE AMPLIFIER. Overloading is the most common cause of burned out amplifiers. It takes equipment out of service and requires a service technician to repair the damage.

Handling the mathematics of multiple speaker connections is a little difficult, but there are some short-cuts. The easiest calculation is for speakers in series, because in this case the total impedance is equal to the sum of all the individual speakers. All you have to do is add them up. But speakers are rarely wired in series.

Speakers in parallel have a total impedance equal to the reciprocal of the sum of the reciprocals of all the speakers. Mathematically the equation is: $\frac{1}{Rt} = \frac{1}{R_1} + \frac{1}{R_2} + \frac{1}{R_n}$

Let's try an example. Assume you have a tape recorder with a 3.2-ohm speaker in it. Since that rating is stamped on the speaker, it is safe to assume that it is also the output impedance of the amplifier in the tape recorder. Now you want to add two more speakers to play background music in three separate offices. You are able to buy two more 3.2-ohm speakers, or you can take some out of discarded equipment. First, let's see what the impedance is going to look like if all three speakers are wired in parallel.

$$\frac{1}{Rt} = \frac{1}{3.2} + \frac{1}{3.2} + \frac{1}{3.2} \quad \frac{1}{Rt} = .31 + .31 + 3.1 \quad \frac{1}{Rt} = .93 \quad Rt = 1.07$$

This gives us an opportunity to show the first short-cut. WHEN ALL SPEAKERS HAVE THE SAME IMPEDANCE, THE TOTAL IMPEDANCE OF THE SPEAKERS WIRED IN PARALLEL IS EQUAL TO THE IMPEDANCE OF ONE SPEAKER, DIVIDED BY THE TOTAL NUMBER OF SPEAKERS. $\frac{3.2}{3} = 1.0666.$ That certainly does simplify things.

Now, from the discussion preceeding this example, we know it would be bad practice to try to load the amplifier's 3.2-ohm output with a 1.07-ohm speaker load. On the other hand, if all speakers are wired in series, we will have 9.6 ohms. From a loading standpoint, that would be much safer, and all the speakers would play at the same volume, but the mismatch is pretty bad, and will possibly decrease the power available and introduce slight distortion. How can we come closer to the 3.2-ohm output impedance and still use all three speakers?

A series/parallel arrangement will do this, and we have two options in this particular example.

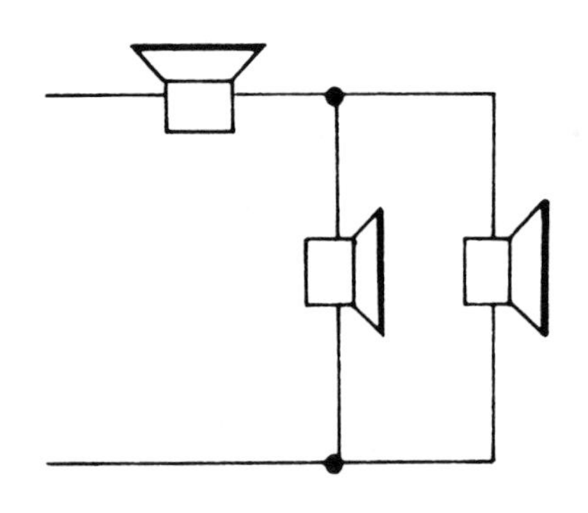

Option 1

Option 1 wires two speakers in parallel, then adds the third speaker in series with the parallel pair. The total impedance is 4.8 ohms.

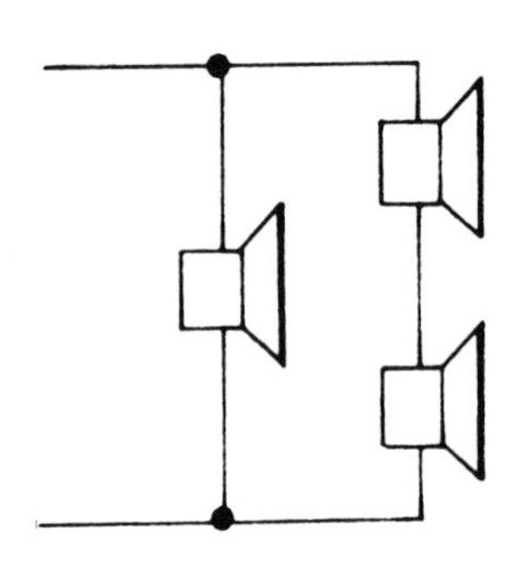

Option 2

Option 2 wires two speakers in series, then adds the third speaker in parallel with the series pair. The total impedance is 2.14 ohms.

Option 1 would be a safer load for a 3.2-ohm output. Option 2 should be easier to achieve in practice if you were hoping to use the output jack on the recorder (because the internal speaker would already be wired in parallel with that jack) and should present no problem as a load if the volume is kept around half-way setting. Full volume should absolutely be avoided with this load. Below are the details of how these output jacks work circuit-wise, and how you might file a plug tip to permit use of the internal speaker at the same time the external ones are playing. Just

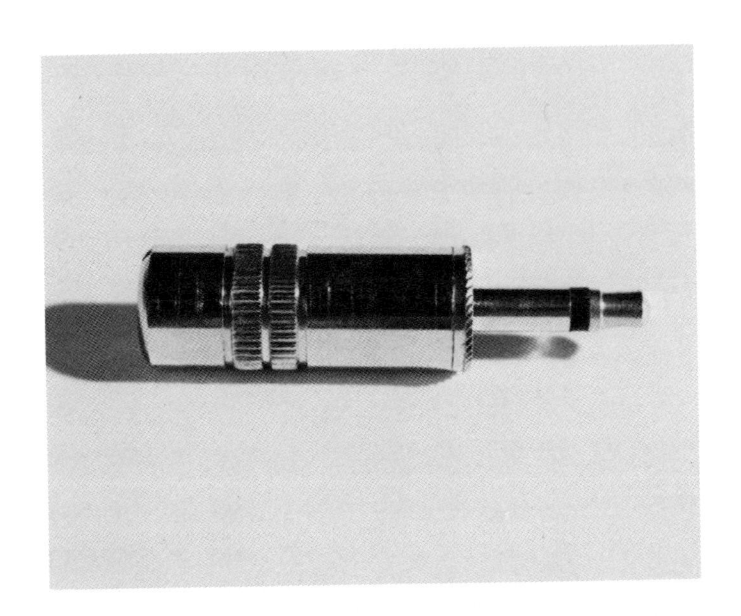

Plug before filing

Plug opens circuit and cuts off internal speaker

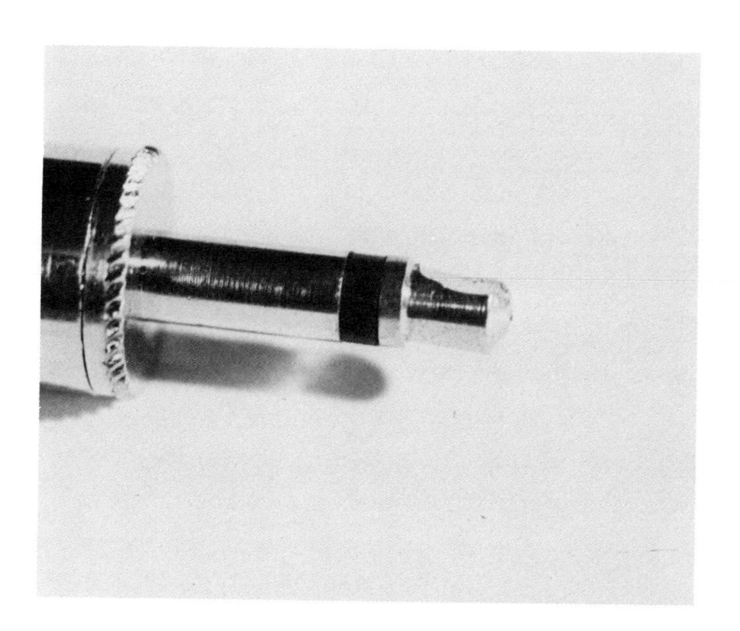

Plug after filing down

Flat spot on plug prevents jack from disconnecting internal speaker

how much filing is required depends upon the device. It's a question of file, try, file, try, until you get the connection without turning off the internal speaker.

If you will look back over the examples above, you will see the other general short-cut. WHEN SPEAKERS ARE CONNECTED IN PARALLEL, THE TOTAL IMPEDANCE WILL BE LESS THAN THAT OF THE SPEAKER WITH THE LOWEST IMPEDANCE. This is useful if we are doing something simple like adding just one speaker, and it is rated at 8 ohms. We know this is going to be something lower than 3.2 because that's the value we have established for the internal speaker. Let's solve it and see just how far off we would be if we just added the 8-ohm speaker in parallel:

$$\frac{1}{Rt} = \frac{1}{3.2} + \frac{1}{8} = \quad \frac{1}{Rt} = .32 + .125 \quad \frac{1}{Rt} = .435 \quad Rt = 2.29$$

That's certainly lower than 3.2, but again we could get by with it if we can keep the volume somewhat less than full. It would surely beat going through all the re-wiring, and even then the best match we could achieve would be a series 11.2, which is a fairly bad match.

To really get a match like this right, it is also possible to use "matching transformers." Usually found only in very large sound systems, these transformers use basic principle 3, transferring energy between two coils on a common core. The coil windings are "tapped" to offer a variety of impedances, both to the amplifier and to the load, essentially matching them. Schools, offices and industrial plants often have paging and background music systems. If you think you have a problem needing transformer matching, you should get in touch with the installers or maintainers of these systems, both for advice and as a source of the transformers you might need.

In all of our examples of speaker connection, another very evident thing would be happening. Not all the speakers would play at the same volume. That might or might not be a problem. In our office example, it might be desirable to have individual volume controls on each speaker. Fortunately, many people have multi-speaker installations in cars these days. Among the accessories available for such installations is the speaker level control. Known in electronics as an "L Pad," this control will vary the volume on one speaker without changing the load and varying all the rest. As the L Pad adds resistance to make the speaker play softer, it compensates by putting proportionally less resistance across the line, essentially keeping the impedance constant for that speaker.

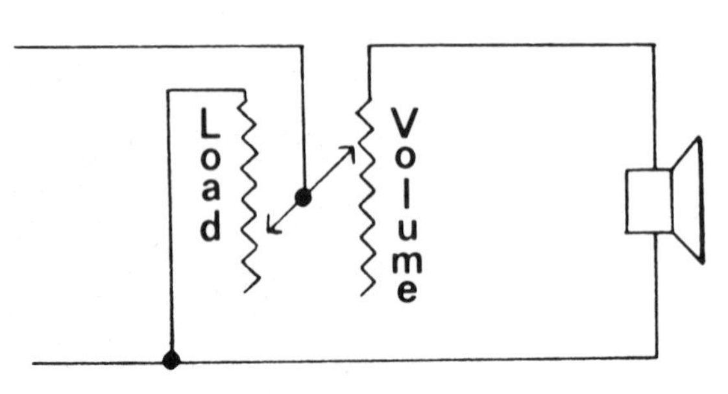

Circuit of L Pad

If the varying levels of the speakers in a given series/parallel circuit is a problem, add L Pads to the individual speakers as needed. Sometimes it is possible to make this difference in volume work for us, particularly in public address systems.

There is also another system of impedance-matching known as "Constant Voltage Line." This system is widely used in very large multi-speaker systems and requires transformers which are not commonly available except through the installers of these large systems. These systems usually require experienced technical service. The reason for introducing constant voltage line here is that you might find some strange figures like 70.7 volts or some other voltage rating on the output strip of a power amplifier. Unless you know what you are doing, these connections should be avoided and speakers should be matched by impedance to the connections marked 4, 8, 16 on the same terminal strip. When working with these amplifiers, it is important to watch the power rating of the speakers too, since it is very easy to burn out a 10-watt speaker with a 25-watt amplifier. If this combination is all you have, go ahead and use it, but keep the volume setting no more than half. (The volume setting is not proportional to the watts of output. Power increase is much greater in the upper half of the control's rotation.)

HEADSETS used with audiovisual equipment fall into three categories. They are shown below:

Diaphragm magnetic

Cone magnetic

Acoustical with Distributor

Diaphragm magnetic headsets date back to crystal sets. They usually have an impedance in the order of 2,000 ohms and should not be mixed with systems using lower-impedance cone magnetic headsets, even if the plugs do match. (It is not uncommon to see 2,000-ohm headsets plugged into 4- or 8-ohm output jacks. We get by with this mismatch, probably because of the very low power transfer required ... the diaphragm is almost in our ears!) The cords will not stand rough institutional use and repair of them is hardly worth the effort. Replacement plastic-jacketed cords are available, if they can be found.

Cone magnetic headsets are really miniature speakers. They are usually around 8 ohms impedance and therefore readily match the headset jacks of most record players, tape recorders, sound filmstrip and slide viewers, etc. They have been designed for institutional use and feature more durable cords and washable plastic headbands and ear cushions. (They won't stand being dunked, but they should be wiped off more often than they usually are.)

Acoustical with distributor headsets consist really of a plastic tube which forms a conduit for the sound wave produced by a regular speaker inside the distributor, carrying the sound wave into a hollow plastic molded headset. These headsets eliminate most of the cord problem, there being only the cord from the device to the distributor. Kinks in the tubes do not seem to cut off sound transmission, and replacement tubing is available from the manufacturers and is easily installed. The valves in the outlet ports of the distributor should be kept clean and checked occasionally for proper closure when no headset is plugged in. This can be done by operating the distributor at low volume and rotating the small outlet holes past one ear. Any increase in volume would indicate a leaking port valve. These valves maintain the pressure to the headsets in use and reduce sound of the distributor in the room. Headsets not actually in use should be unplugged to allow the valves to close.

PHONO PICK-UPS are either magnetic "reluctance" types in higher quality equipment, or ceramic cartridge/needle combinations in the average quality equipment.

Magnetic

Ceramic

Magnetic cartridges tend to cost more, have replaceable needles, require more amplification, and, in the case of stereo, have better separation and lower distortion. They are also much more delicate and for that reason can sometimes not be used where many persons have access to the equipment. Like other magnetic/coil devices, they can be vulnerable to hum pick-up from adjacent power devices. Hum can usually be corrected by moving the record player away from any nearby powered device.

Ceramic cartridges are durable, can take relatively rough handling, require more pressure on the record, need less amplification because of their higher voltage output, and are replaced in their entirety (needle and element) each time replacement is necessary. This last idea is sound when normal needle wear is the reason for replacement, but rather costly when rough handling that breaks off the needle point is the most common reason for replacement. In-service training is recommended to reduce rough handling. A further step might be some sort of account charge for replacement cartridges.

Because of the range of groove widths still encountered in audiovisual work, a brief discussion of point size and its ramifications is in order.

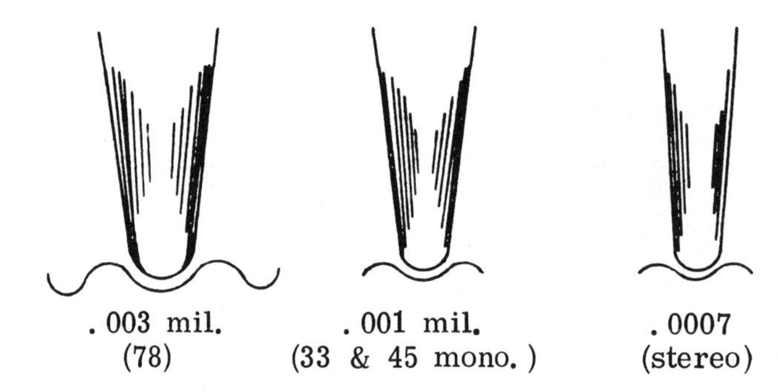

.003 mil. (78) .001 mil. (33 & 45 mono.) .0007 (stereo)

The program content of the record is reproduced by the needle point being moved back and forth by "wiggles" in the walls of the groove. When the master record was cut, the cutting stylus converted electrical energy to mechanical energy, producing variations in the groove walls proportional to the frequency, volume, and timbre of the original sound. In playing the record, mechanical energy from the rotating disc and wiggling groove is converted back into proportional electrical energy. When amplified and used to drive a speaker, the original sound is reproduced. To get the best reproduction, the needle must ride only on the groove walls. The needle point is polished to the proper diameter to do this.

There are two ways to look at matching the needle to the groove. If the .001-mil needle is used to play a standard groove 78 rpm. record, the needle is free to slop around in the oversize groove, thus producing distortion. The small needle can also get to the bottom of the groove, where it can "play" any dirt or irregularities that may be there. None of this helps to bring about a very good reproduction of the original, so try to use the right needle for the record you are playing. The other groove-matching problem is that of the oversize needle. If the needle is too large, it may not even be able to track the groove at all, and will go skidding across the record, leaving a nasty scratch along the way. If it does track, it can turn a stereo disc into a monaural one, as the oversize "chisel" can not track the separate information on either side of the groove and proceeds to average it out, shaping the soft vinyl as it goes. Once again, there is no substitute for the right needle size.

There is a related term in common use in small monaural record players ... the term "stereo compatible." This means that the needle size will track a stereo disc, and that the "compliance" of the cartridge is also ok for stereo records, even though the record player is monaural. Compliance is a term that describes the freedom of the needle point support system to track something as delicate as a tiny groove with separate information on each side of the groove. Lack of compliance can be just as devastating to a stereo groove as wrong needle size. The wrong combination can spell disaster for the disc forever. When replacing needles or needle/cartridge combinations, make an effort to use replacements which have the same specifications as the original. All manufacturers have extensive interchangeability lists and your electronic parts or audiovisual dealer should be able to supply a proper replacement. Since the primary aim of the maintenance program is to provide minimum interruption of the instructional program, a small supply of spare needles and/or cartridges should be kept on hand. And don't forget to order more when you get down to two or three spares.

MAGNETIC TAPE RECORDING is achieved without changing electrical to mechanical energy, unless you insist on including the tape moving system (but we have the equivalent of that in a record player). The tape head is a very small and sophisticated electro-magnet. The tape coating contains iron oxide with millions of microscopic magnetic domains. As the tape passes over the erase head (almost the same as the record/play head) the domains are aligned by the magnetism produced by a high-frequency (30, 000 cycles or more) current passing through the coil of the erase head. A fraction of a second later, the tape passes over the gap of the record head. At this point a magnetic field is generated by the coil of the record head. The field consists of a small amount of the erase current, called bias, and the variations produced by the audio signal coming from the record amplifier. This composite field aligns the domains in the tape coating, producing a magnetic equivalent of the original program material. The realignment will last in the tape until it is subjected to another strong magnetic field, such as that of the erase head.

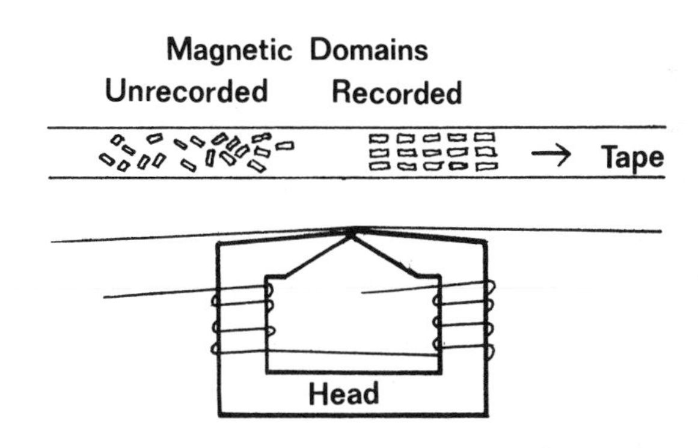

When the "magnetized" tape is passed over the play head (which is usually the record head, now connected to the input end of the amplifier), it induces a tiny current into the coils of the head. When this current is amplified and fed through a speaker, it becomes a reproduction of the original sound.

Because we use so many magnetic devices in audiovisual equipment, and a number of these have strong permanent magnet fields, we need to be careful in the storage and handling of tape to avoid accidental erasure (full or partial). In routine audiovisual work we are rarely concerned with the extreme measures used to maintain archival permanence. But some science kits contain magnets, and tapes should be stored separately, if they are used with the kit. It is also not good practice to casually leave cassettes on top of the cassette recorder, especially over the speaker. Even this strong field does not seem to do immediate damage, indicating that the tape has considerable resistance to accidental erasure. On the other hand, bulk tape erasers are available and can be used to erase quickly and thoroughly the content of any magnetic tape.

Video tape works the same way as audio tape does in recording principle. The mechanism is much more involved because a very high recording speed must be attained to record the full gray scale of the picture, from black to white, or the full color spectrum. Because of the critical nature of the picture and the more abrasive recording head contact (due to the speed), video tape can not be re-used as often as audio tape. Momentary white or black streaks in the picture are called drop-out. When they become obvious, the tape should be discarded.

MOTORS are among the most trouble-free components in audiovisual equipment. The type most commonly found is called an "induction" motor. It is so called because the magnetic field produced by the line power in the stationary part of the motor induces current and a magnetic field in the rotating part of the motor. By design and construction the rotor (or armature) field is just slightly offset from the field of the stationary magnet. As it tries to align through attraction and repulsion of the magnetic poles, the armature turns. This rotation supplies the power for cooling fans and the drive mechanism of all the projectors, many of the tape recorders (line-operated), and most phono turntables. There is nothing to wear out in these motors, so a little cleaning and lubrication is all the attention they ever require (although the dust collected by the cooling fan can make annual cleaning and oiling desirable in some locations).

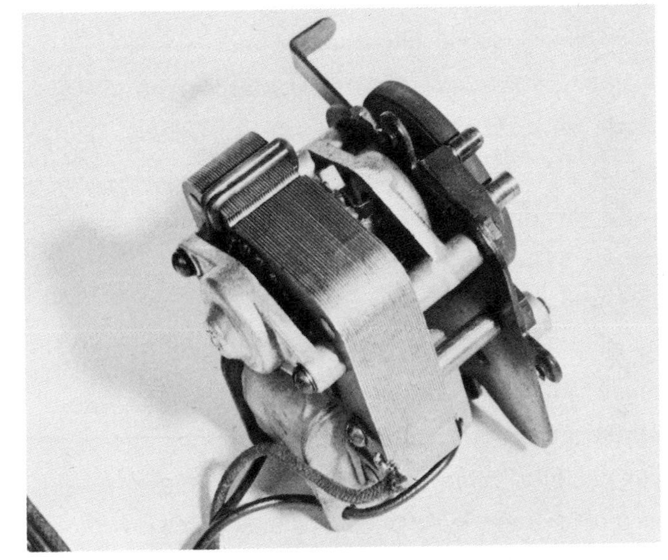

Small induction motor

There are two other types of motors found in some tape recorders. Very good tape recorders may have "synchronous" drive motors. These are a special type of induction motors that run with the same speed accuracy as an electric clock. Speed accuracy is particularly important in tapes for broadcast because program length must be constant in order to assure tight scheduling.

Small cassette recorders designed to operate from batteries or the power line have small direct-current (the kind that comes from batteries) motors. They are not very powerful, but do an adequate job in the cassette application.

If you have a mechanical drive problem (doesn't run at all, or doesn't run at constant speed, or doesn't seem to have enough power), the motor is usually the last thing to suspect. There are frequently special switches designed to stop the motor; e.g., when the tape runs out. The switch on the microphone of small cassette recorders will start and stop the drive motor. Weak batteries will prevent good power delivery by the motor. So will gummy bearings and slipping belts along the drive chain of pulleys, idler wheels, etc.

Some of the most recent quality tape recorders, and also the better small cassette recorders, use an electronic circuit to maintain constant motor speed. A component failure in these circuits may cause the motor to vary in speed, or not to run at all.

Most motors will turn rather freely when the shaft is twisted with the fingers and there is no mechanical load (belts and idler wheels removed from contact with the motor shaft). A drop of oil applied to the motor shaft by first oiling a toothpick, and then touching the drop on the toothpick to the shaft where it enters the bearing, will loosen up most sluggish motor armatures. After the oil is applied, the motor should be run for a few seconds to work the oil into the bearing. Then take a Q-Tip or piece of tissue and wipe off all excess oil on the shaft before reassembling the piece of equipment.

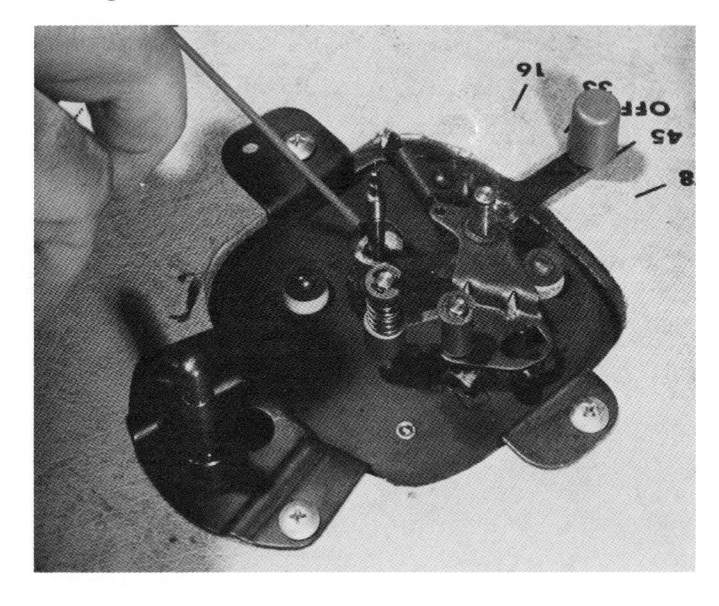

Shaft should turn freely

In some cases, especially old record players, the lubricant on the shaft turns to "varnish" because of age and heat from the motor. When this happens, the motor must be removed from the equipment and carefully disassembled (paying particular attention to where any little spacer washers are located in the assembly). It helps to lay out all the parts in some approximation of where they came from. When the armature has been removed from the bearings, the brown varnish is plainly visible where the shaft went through the bearings. Wash out the bearings with some petroleum solvent like lighter fluid or kerosene, using a Q-Tip or pipe-cleaner. Wipe off the shaft with a rag or tissue wetted with the solvent. The varnish is best removed by twisting the shaft in a loop of crocus cloth held between the fingers. Crocus cloth is an industrial fabric coated with an extremely fine polishing abrasive. It should be available from any good hardware store or a machine shop may be willing to sell a single piece. Torn into 1"-strips as needed, it will last for years.

Remove motor from the rest of the mechanical assembly.

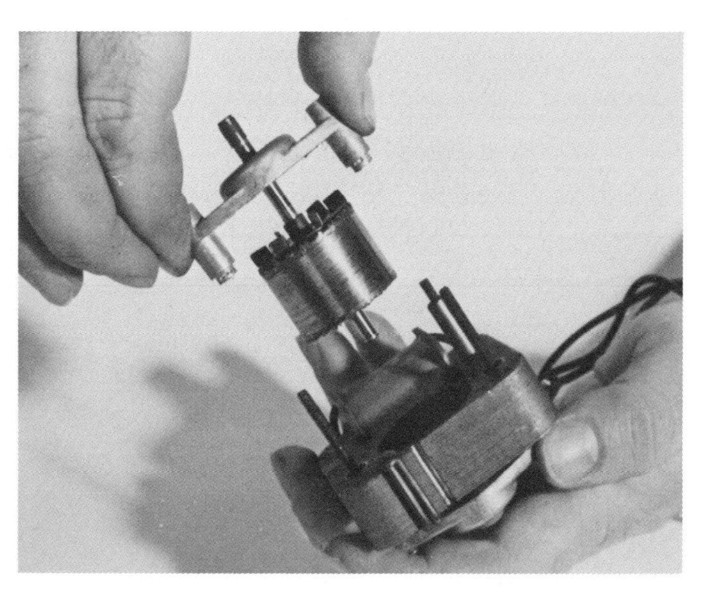

Take the motor apart as far as possible. Bearings may not come off both ends of armature shaft.

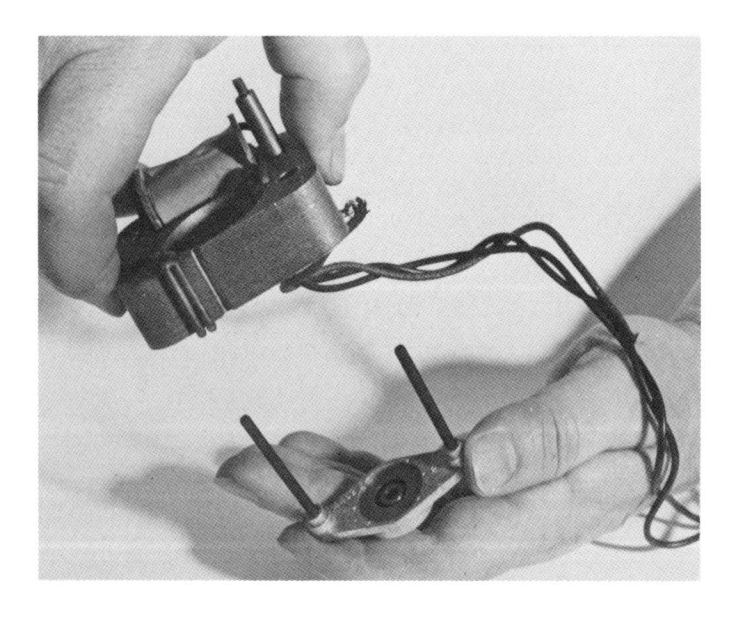

Be careful to remember where any spacers may have been along assembly bolts.

Wash off both ends of shaft with a Q-tip ...

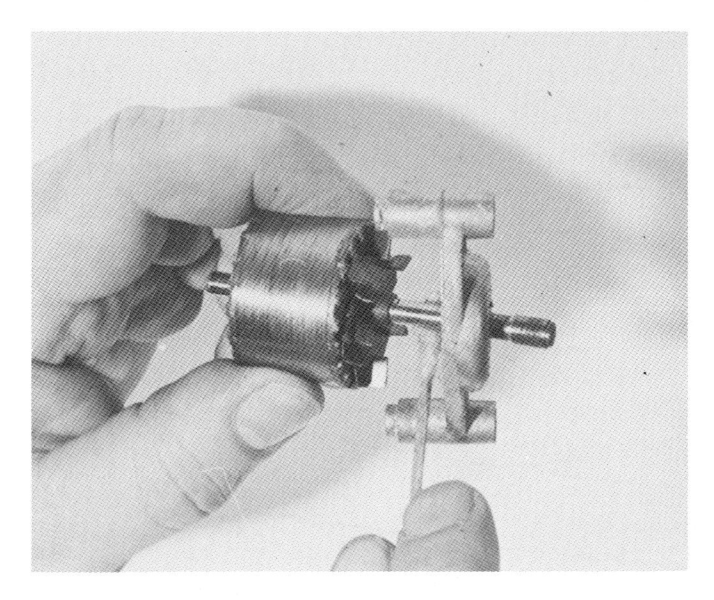

... saturated with a solvent or cleaning/lubricating fluid like WD-40.

Similarly, clean out any bearing that will clear the motor shaft.

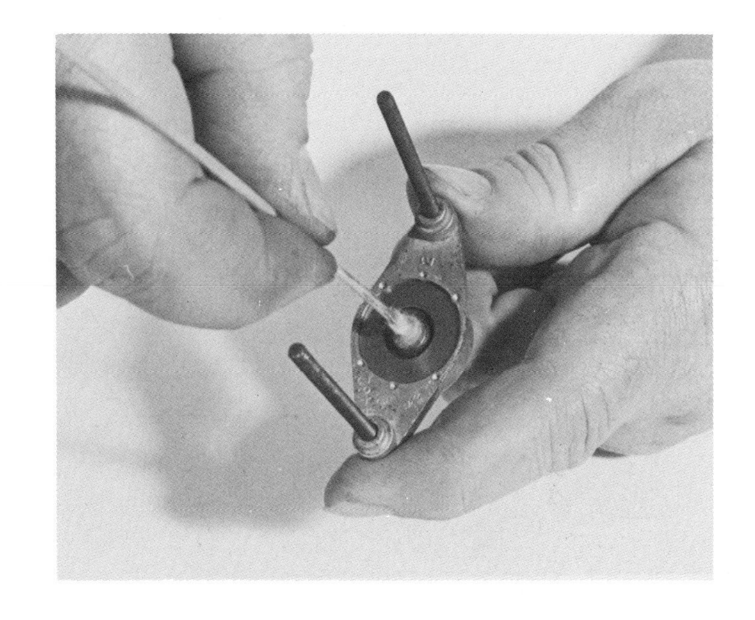

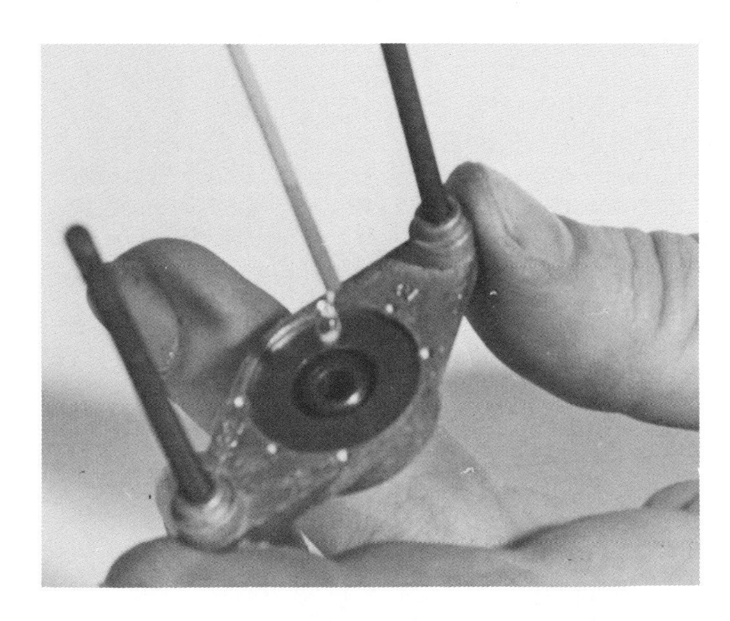

Put a drop of oil in the bearing before reassembly.

Put another drop of oil on the shaft at the other bearing.

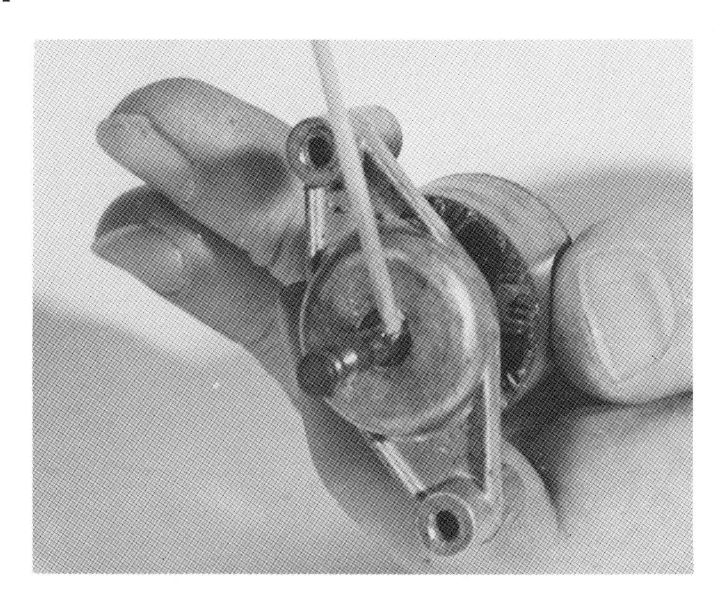

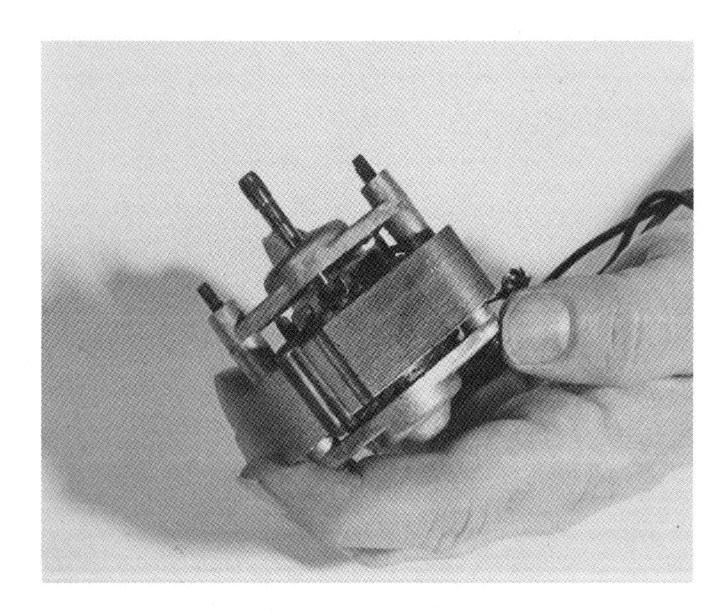

Carefully reassemble the motor, being sure that any spacers and shaft washers are back in place.

Partially tighten the nuts that hold the motor assembly together. If necessary, tighten them all the way and back them off about a turn.

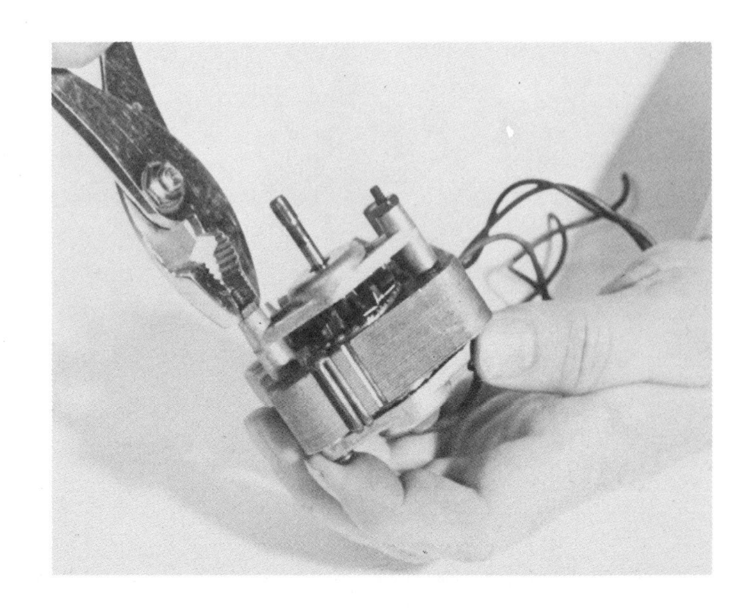

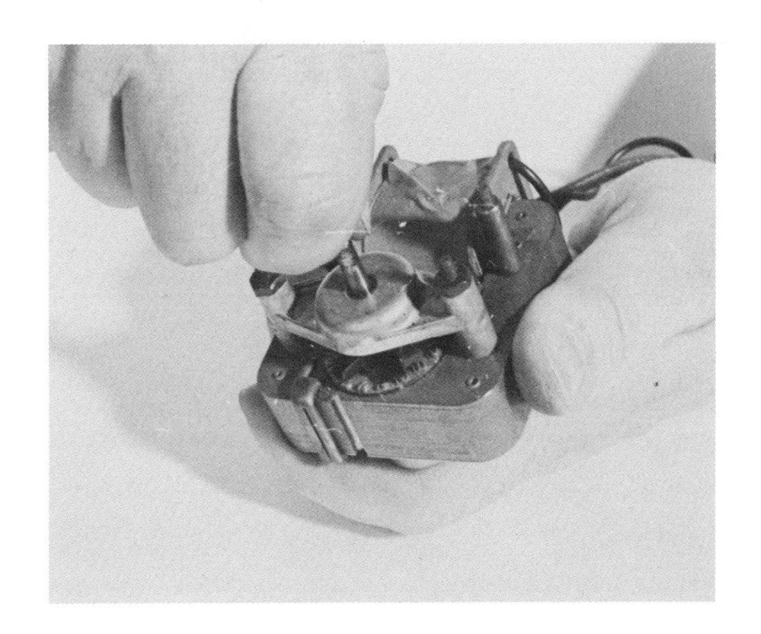

Grasp the shaft tightly and move it back and forth (to align the bearings), trying to spin it with the fingers. When it is free turning, tighten the assembly nuts.

When the shaft and bearings have been cleaned they should be lightly oiled and the motor carefully reassembled. These motors have "self-aligning bearings" that tend to get out of alignment when the motor is taken apart. Some of the designs also allow some adjustment of the centering of the armature in the stator magnet. Before fully tightening the two screws that hold the bearing assemblies on either side of the stator, the centering should be checked visually and the armature shaft rotated between the fingers to be sure it is turning freely. If the armature needs centering, the bearing housings can be tapped lightly in the required direction, using a screwdriver and light hammer. If the centering is good but the shaft does not turn freely, grip the shaft tightly with the fingers. Do not rotate the shaft, but try to move it in a circular direction. It will not actually move, but the pressure exerted on the bearings by this attempted movement will align the bearings and free the shaft considerably. When everything is centered and rotating freely, tighten the two bearing screws. Apply power to the motor and let it "run-in" for a few minutes. Turn the motor off and check the shaft again for free rotation. It will usually spin quite freely now. This completes the repair of the motor and it can be returned to the piece of equipment.

If you feel that this rather involved, though essentially simple, procedure takes more time or skill than you have, you can always send the piece of equipment out for service by a technician. But if you do get involved in anything this complex, you would be well advised to pick a time when you can be sure you will be able to complete the job. The memory of just which screws and washers go where can be very short indeed, and there is a real risk of never completing the repair if you let the work "grow cold."

TRANSFORMERS are the most trouble-free of all components. They also do their inductive energy transfer with great efficiency. Circuit design usually allows them to run warm, but not hot. Only experience can tell you what is alarmingly hot for a transformer. There is also a characteristic odor associated with transformer failure. It's like the odor you may have smelled when a fluorescent lamp ballast burns out. Transformer replacement should be left to a qualified service technician because there are often a number of wires involved, replacements must match electrically, and it is often difficult to buy replacements. Because of all this, it is also one of the more time-consuming repairs, often requiring correspondence with the manufacturer to get the right replacement.

Appendix G

HOW WE CONTROL LIGHT

Light is, of course, essential to the visual aspect of any audiovisual storage and retrieval system. Through the use of a camera or by contact printing on film as in the diazo process, we use light to store images on film. There is no point in discussing cameras in this book because they are usually not amenable to repair by any but highly skilled and often factory-trained technicians. We will, however, include a very basic diagram of the essential parts of a camera because it will be useful for comparison and a complete understanding of what the storing and re-creating optical systems do.

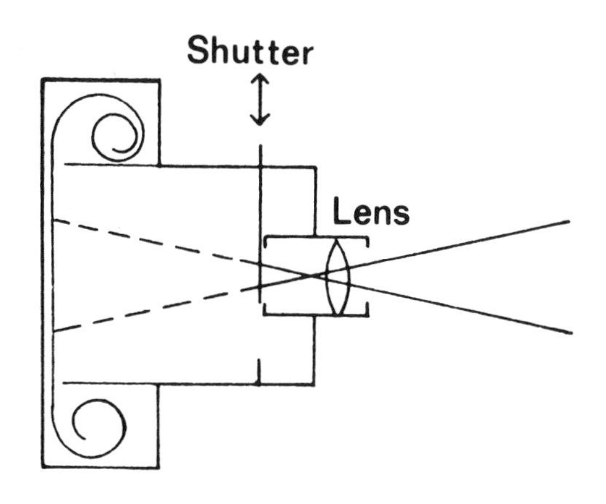

CAMERAS are really light-tight boxes whose function is to keep out stray light while admitting only light from the image we are trying to store. The box also provides the structure that maintains the required distance between lens and film for sharp focus, permits mounting of the shutter mechanism, and supports and contains whatever film advance or change mechanism is used. The function of the lens is to bring the external image into sharp focus at the size reduction the camera is designed for. The shutter controls the time duration of the film exposure. Most better lenses have an iris mechanism that controls the amount of light the lens admits in a unit of time. These opening sizes are calibrated in an odd sequence of "f" numbers, designed and calculated so that each smaller number admits twice the light of its successor. Shutters are usually calibrated in fractions of a second, with possible maximum times of several seconds.

Cameras also include some form of finder to permit the photographer to know what is included in the photograph. Focus and light meter functions are also incorporated in most modern camera designs.

So, for the production of an image on film, we usually employ an external light source (the sun, flood or flash lamps) to light the subject being photographed. The box of the camera keeps this light off the sensitive film, permitting only that image focused on the film by the lens to be exposed for the time the shutter is open. By some chemical process we develop the image on the film and desensitize it to any further change from exposure to light.

We should make some mention here of the fact that not all our film processes are dependent upon light. Several use heat or the infrared spectrum of light to expose the image on the film. Some of these processes yield an instantly available "dry" processed image, while at least one requires development in very hot water.

When we want to use the image in audio-visual work, we customarily make some conversion of it to a larger image. The simplest device for this is the magnifying filmstrip viewer. We provide some kind of light diffusing screen just behind the film image, illuminating it with existing daylight or artificial light, or we provide self-contained illumination. Between the film and the eye, we place a magnifying lens which makes the film image appear large enough to be useful. The lamp in most of these devices is a regular 7 1/2-watt Christmas tree or sewing machine lamp. Some means is usually provided for mechanically advancing the filmstrip. Viewers of this type are also available for slides, and for the Viewmaster stereo reels.

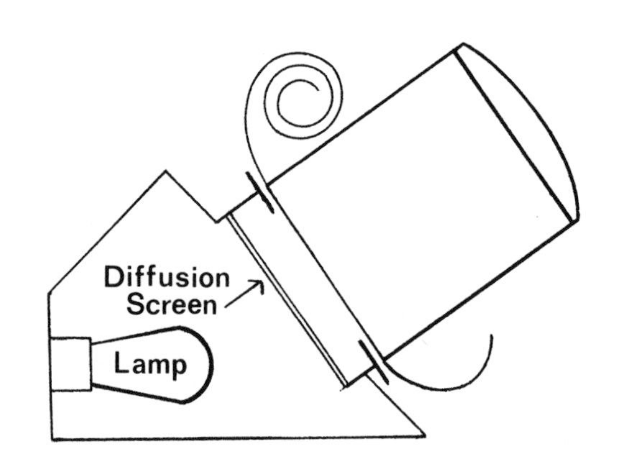

Once we get beyond the simple magnifier lens viewers we are into some form of image projection. We have deliberately retraced our camera drawing outline, but have modified it to make it a projector. Now we box the light to prevent its illuminating the room, remove the shutter (in those devices where image persistence is desired), and provide some focusing scheme for the lens. Unfortunately, that isn't the whole story because most projectors need several more elements to make them functionally efficient. Because of lamp developments over the past 15 years, we will offer several diagrams of projector optical systems.

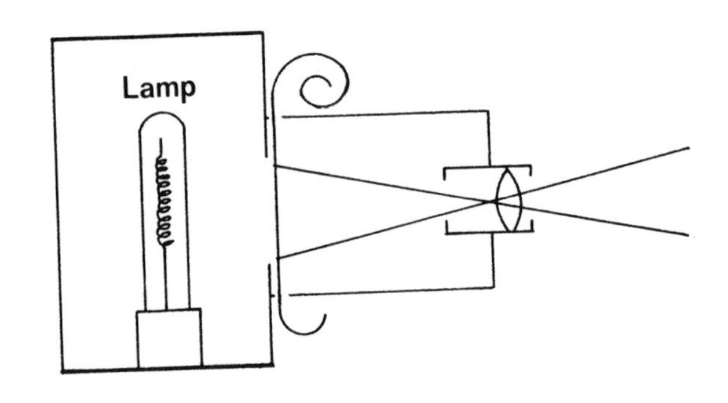

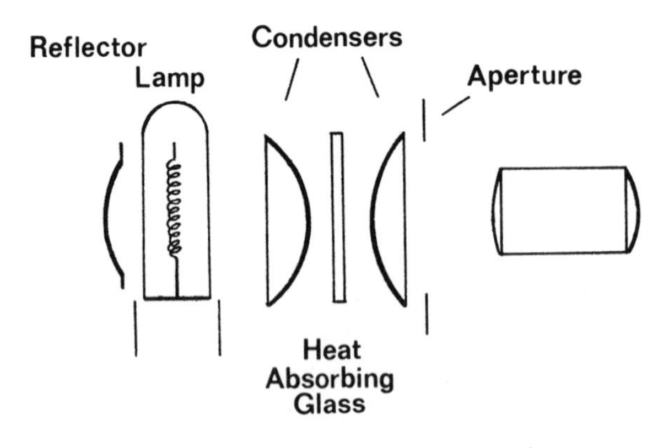

Older slide or filmstrip system

For around 50 years, almost all projectors contained these optical elements. The lamp provides a small, solid area of illumination by virtue of the way the filament coils are positioned in the support structure. A system of pins or flanges on the lamp base assures that the filament will be aligned parallel to the film "gate," guaranteeing full and even illumination of the film image.

Older projection lamp

The efficiency of the illumination was improved by placing a concave mirror behind the lamp, reflecting light back into the area of the filament. In older projectors these mirrors are often dirty or tarnished. Some effort can be expended on cleaning them, but an all-out effort may cause more damage to the reflecting surface. Glass mirrors may be cleaned by gently washing the surface with warm water and liquid detergent on a soft cloth or Q-Tip. Rinse the surface with clear water and blot dry with a soft cloth or let it air dry. Metal mirrors will often brighten with the use of a liquid metal polish, but this should always be applied with a soft cloth and care should be taken to avoid a polish that contains polishing abrasive. It is always wise to try soap and water first, since removal of the accumulated film will restore much of the brightness without risking damage to the reflecting surface.

Between the lamp and the film are usually between one and three pieces of glass. One or two of these are the condenser lenses. Their function is to gather the light rays from the lamp and concentrate them uniformly across the area of the film image. Depending upon the lamp used and the design of the projector, these lenses have precise optical specifications and should not be interchanged between makes and models of projectors just because they do, or can be made to, fit the holders. It is also common for these lenses to have different curvatures on the front and back surfaces. Sometimes this is barely perceptible, but reversal will degrade performance. Do not take the condenser lenses for granted. Kids love to take them out and use them for magnifying glasses. You may have to take them out for cleaning. Getting them back properly is best done by making a small sketch before removing them. Exaggerate the curvatures in your sketch to avoid accidental reversal. Where there are very slight differences in curvature, your finger tips will often sense differences that your eyes do not. Placing the lens on a piece of clean paper on a table and sighting across the table will also show the difference in curve as a difference between the distance separating the lens rim and the paper, first on one side, then on the other. Taking time to make such a sketch when a new projector is first removed from its carton can be a great help in subsequent servicing.

A piece of plain but slightly greenish glass among the condenser lenses is heat-absorbing glass. A projector will work without this glass ... and may even be a bit brighter. But condenser lens systems concentrate a lot of heat, as well as light, on the film. For maximum film life all the elements provided by the optical designer should be in place. Replacement condenser lenses and heat-absorbing glass can be ordered through dealers from whom the equipment was purchased. Cracked glass (from the high lamp heat) should be replaced, but it will work well enough until replacements can be obtained.

While not a part of the illumination or optical system in the sense of helping to reproduce the film image, the cooling fan or blower merits some discussion. While one manufacturer offered a projector with a 300-watt lamp and no cooling blower, others have fan-cooled lamps of 150 watts and lower. If a projector burns out lamps rapidly, or brings complaints about "smelling hot," the cooling system should be checked. Sometimes the fan blade is blocked because it has slipped on the motor shaft, or something may have been dropped into the projector from the top of the lamp house. The most common problem is gummy motor bearings resulting from the dust drawn in by the fan combining with the oil at the bearings. Blowing the motor area and fan blade clean with compressed air, cleaning the shaft with a little solvent, and relubricating with a drop of light oil on each end of the motor shaft will usually clear the problem. With careful technique you may even be able to do this without removing the motor. A complete cleaning and repair technique is described under Motors in the How We Use Magnetism Appendix.

Returning to the light-path of the projector, the light passes through the condensers and is evenly distributed over the aperture in the film gate. The area of the film gate merits some attention in any routine cleaning and repair. The gate includes some system for keeping the film flat, usually with slight spring pressure. Some gates use small pieces of beveled glass, others are glassless. Any glass in this area should be cleaned carefully whenever the projector is being checked. Blow or brush away any dirt or film particles, then clean the glass with lens cleaner and tissue. Because this area is in the focal plane of the projection lens, any scratches will show, clearly or blurred, on the screen.

The gate also contains whatever film advance or slide change mechanism is used. These range from relatively simple, in filmstrip projectors, to the synchronized claw of motion picture projectors. See specific projector headings for details on these mechanisms.

After passing through the film image, the light reaches the projection lens. The projection lens takes the image on the film, inverts it, and focuses it on the screen. A very simple convex lens will do this job, but not very efficiently. (Efficiency in this case means a bright image.) The projection lenses usually consist of two or more glass elements in a metal or plastic "barrel." The barrel moves back and forth for focusing. Some are threaded, others use a rack and pinion gear to permit focusing by means of a "Focus" knob.

The projection lens needs care in cleaning since the clarity of the projected image is affected by it. The following procedure is recommended for cleaning all lenses. Do not worry about small bubbles in the lens glass or small scratches. There is really nothing you can do about them once they are there, and they won't degrade the image or brightness much. But you should make every effort to avoid adding any scratches.

First try to remove any solid particles of dirt by blowing the surface with Omit, Dust-Off, or similar product. (Your mouth is not a source of dry com-

Some helps for lens cleaning

pressed air.) A very soft lens brush is also good. Next, moisten a piece of lens cleaning tissue with a little lens cleaning fluid and very gently blot the surface of the lens. Throw away the first tissue, moisten a second one, and this time crumple the tissue slightly and, using short strokes, wipe the surface gently. Discard the second tissue and use a third one to polish the surface lightly, attempting to remove any marks left by the cleaning fluid. Remember, the tissues are much cheaper than a replacement lens. Use them gently with careless abandon.

The above discussion took us through what was the most commonly encountered optical system in audiovisual projectors. Now let's look at some variations, primarily brought about by recent lamp developments.

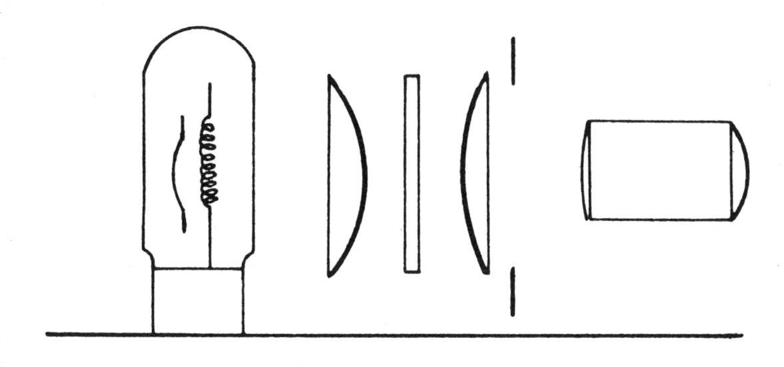

New slide or filmstrip system

The most evident change is inclusion of the mirror within the glass lamp envelope.

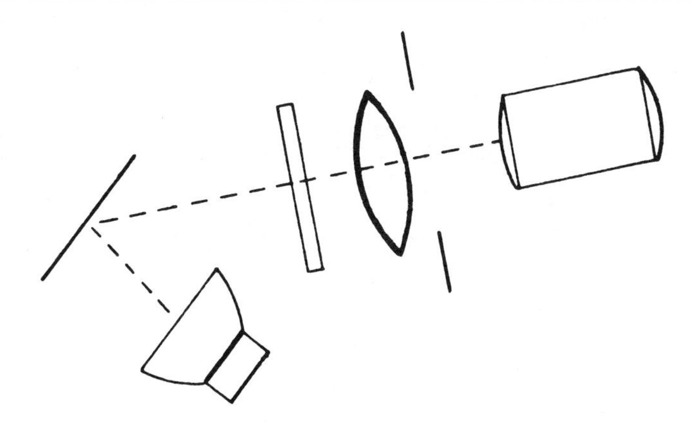

H-Series Carousel slide projectors

These use a very tiny quartz lamp in a larger reflector which is part of the lamp base. Lamps of this type are extremely efficient, equalling the older 500-watt system in brightness (and whiteness of the light) while consuming only 300 watts of power. This also made it possible to reduce projector noise because a lower volume of air is required to cool the lower-wattage light system. Condenser lenses are still used to distribute the light evenly across the slide.

Note the similarity between the diagram that follows and that of the "older slide or filmstrip system." The only addition to the optical path is that of the shutter. A shutter is used to darken the screen while the next frame of the film is being pulled into place. Since we do this 24 times per second with 16mm. sound film, the result would be a pronounced flicker on the screen. To speed up the flicker rate, one or two more blades are designed on the shutter.

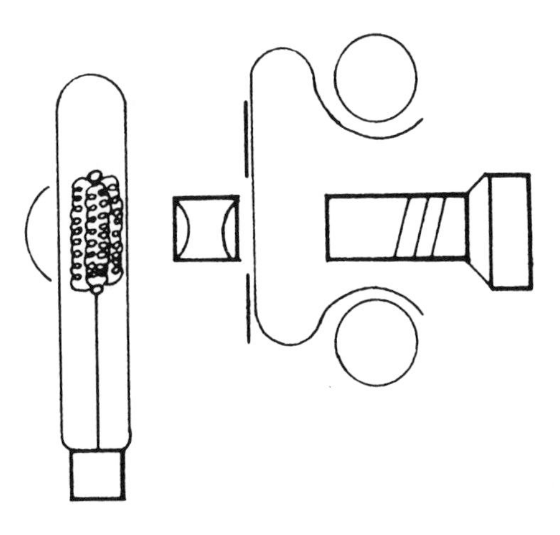

Earlier motion picture projector

This interrupts the light more frequently (and cuts down on image brightness) but the film is still advanced during one of the two or three interruptions. Keeping the film advance synchronized with the shutter requires a rather complex mechanism, but one that rarely gives any trouble. Blurry horizontal lines in the image, or a blur just above or below titles, are usually an indication of synchronization problems. The film has not stopped moving in the gate when the shutter is still open, and this movement of the film is seen as a blur.

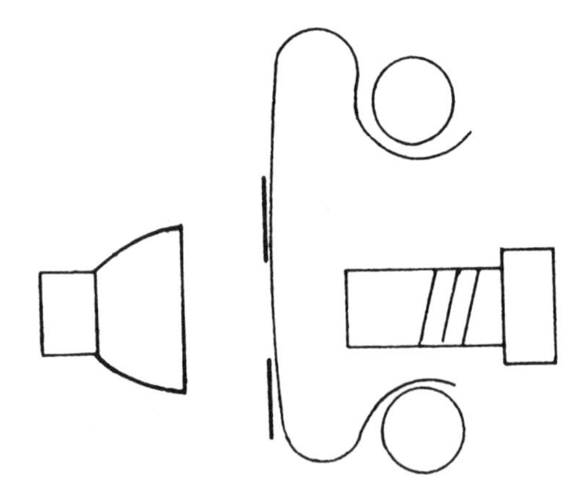

Recent motion picture projector

In recent years a great simplification in lamp structure, using lower voltage filaments and internal reflectors, has made it possible to eliminate the condenser lenses. At the same time, lamp efficiency has been tripled. Unfortunately this has not made the motion picture projector a first-magnitude brightness performer in the galaxy of audiovisual projectors. Concentrations of light still bring concentrations of heat, seemingly setting a limit to the light we can get through the small apertures of the 16mm. or Super 8mm. film frame. But it has reduced the power required to get a very good image on the screen.

The overhead projector introduces two elements in the optical system that we have not seen before. Very early overhead projectors used quite large and expensive condenser lenses to uniformly light the 10" x 10" film area. All designs now use a molded plastic "fresnel" lens for

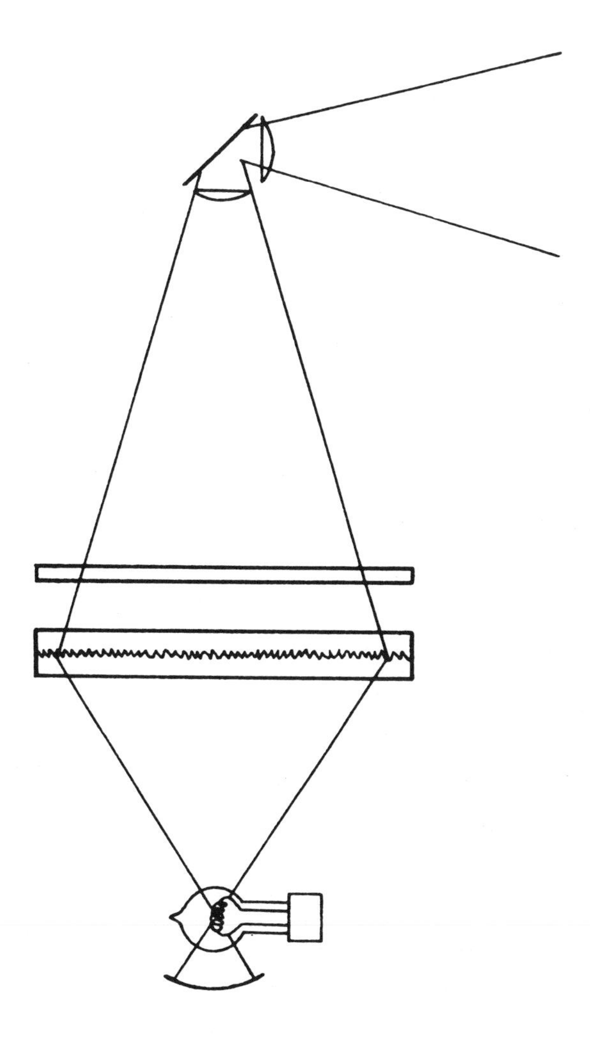

Overhead projector

this purpose. The concentric grooves of a fresnel lens are molded with a groove wall angle figured to refract light from a point source to come directly through at a right angle to the plane of the lens material. In practice, two such lenses are cemented face to face, making a unit about an inch below the stage glass of the overhead projector. Since these lenses are plastic and directly above the hot lamp, maintaining the flow of cooling air is especially important. Overheated fresnel lenses tend to sag in the center, or to get wavy. Either will destroy their optical properties and they will have to be replaced.

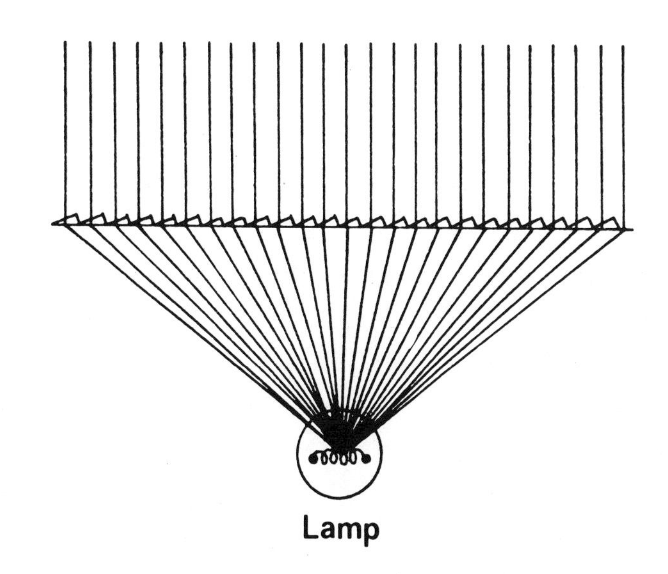

The other element unique to overhead projectors (and a few special lenses for rear-screen motion picture projection) is a mirror in the projection lens system. Early projectors and some high-quality or special-purpose overhead projectors use a very expensive barrel lens, with the mirror behind or above the lens. Most overhead projectors today use a sealed "lens head" with a lens horizontal to the stage, a 45° mirror inside the top of the head, and a second lens relatively vertical, facing the screen.

The stage glass and outside lens surfaces should be kept clean. Fresnel lens surfaces also accumulate a film, and this should be wiped off occasionally. Opening the heads for cleaning is not advisable. Any first-surface mirror (one on which the reflecting surface is applied to the front, rather than the back, of the mirror) requires incredible care in cleaning. Experience has shown that any improvement that might be realized by cleaning is outweighed by the dangers of scratching the mirror or failing to get the lens back into proper optical alignment.

Strange as it is, most of the things you can see when you look into an optical system (bubbles in the lens glass, flecks of black paint from the inside of the lens barrel, sometimes even cracks and chips in the lenses) are not noticeable on the screen image at all. It is best just to forget them.

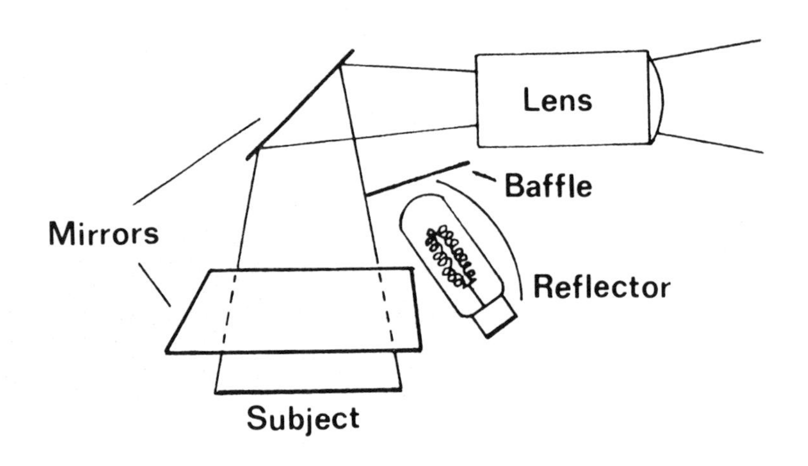

The opaque projector

The diagram above should quickly show why opaque projection is the dimmest of the lot: there is no direct optical path from the lamp to the screen. Opaque projectors use a lamp and a cluster of mirrors to put as much light as possible on the picture or object to be projected. A large first-surface mirror above the picture or object bends the light rays 90°, making it possible for a very large, long focal-length lens to focus the image on the screen. Considering that the only light available for projection is that reflected from an opaque picture or object, opaque projectors do quite well. The key to successful opaque projection is selection of relatively light (high reflectance) pictures and the tightest possible control of stray or ambient light in the room.

This discussion was originally intended to concern itself with how we control the light we want. But any practical discussion should also give some attention to controlling the light we don't want. We audiovisual types always seem to have to get in the dark before we can shed a little light on anything.

While theaters and industrial training rooms are usually built to preclude any need to control daylight, American schools have generally been exceeded only by greenhouses in the number of square feet of glass in the walls. This tradition probably dates back to non-existent artificial light in schools, with the brightness of the classroom subject to the vagaries of the weather. More recent arguments for expanses of glass run from some kind of "back to nature" concept to ease of breaking out in case of fire. Whatever the merits of any of these pro-window arguments, the projected image simply can not compete with any significant amount of uncontrollable ambient light. Color suffers dreadfully from ambient light, and more and more of the material in use is in color. Color television competes well, but relatively few schools at present (1978) have color origination equipment or cable systems with sufficient receivers for convenient color television distribution.

Daylight control systems range from dark window shades, sometimes with light-trap boxes at the sides, through heavy traverse drapery and the lighter special darkening drapes, to specially stippled or patterned blinds. Where designated rooms or auditoriums are to be used extensively for projection, the windows are sometimes painted--and this, if you have never seen it, looks about as bad as you imagine it would. But it's cheap and relatively permanent. Low-transmission glass helps, but is no real answer and is rarely used for replacement. Architectural designs using clerestory windows at sloped ceilings are almost impossible to darken.

Artificial light can also be a problem. Interior rooms with no ambient light when the lights are turned out provide no light for note-taking and can present student control problems. A simple solution to this problem is to install one or two low-wattage (20 watts) fluorescent lamps about two feet below the ceiling. Very stylish baffles can be made from wood-grained masonite and attached to the fixture to direct all light to the ceiling.

Easily built indirect light

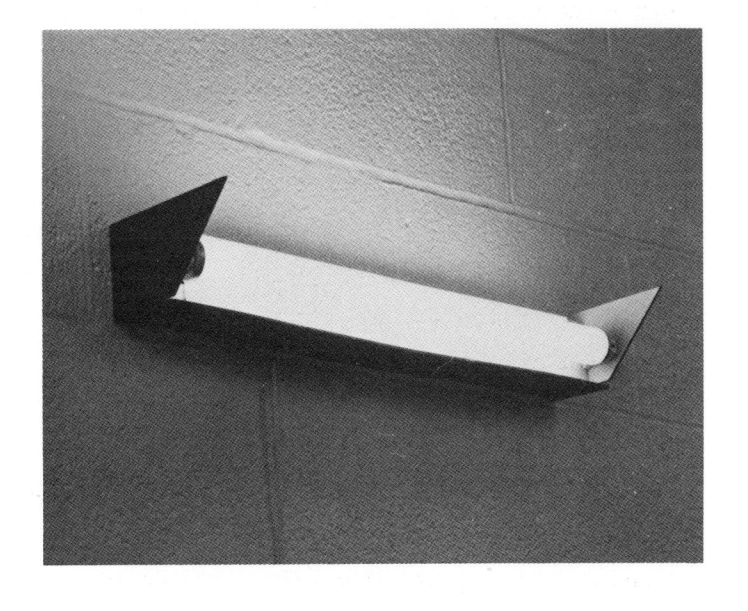

If recessed reflector lamps are used in a building, it is relatively inexpensive to replace switches with wall dimmer controls. Care should be taken to count the wattage of the circuit (add up the ratings of all the lamps) and to obtain a dimmer with sufficient capacity. Most are 600 watts, but 1,000-watt units are available. Whenever dimmable lamps are used, mark the proper dimming level on the control, set it, and leave it. It is amateurish and nauseating to vary the light level in a room constantly.

Light control is best resolved at the time a building is planned or remodeled. Modern teaching/learning modes use audiovisual equipment. There is no excuse for failing to build in light control that will facilitate the use of audiovisual materials. Generally, buildings that have easy light control are also more energy-efficient, an argument that should work where no amount of claims of audiovisual utilization gets a response from administrators and/or architects.

Appendix H

PROJECTION LAMPS

Excellent guides are published by Sylvania and General Electric, including dimensional outlines, all specifications, and even current models of projectors with the lamps they were designed to use. These guides may be obtained by writing:

GTE Sylvania
Photolamp Marketing Headquarters
100 Endicott St.
Danvers, MA 01923

General Electric Co.
Lamp Business Division
Nela Park
Cleveland, OH 44112

or upon request from your lamp supplier.

All projection lamps are now designated by the ANSI (American National Standards Institute) code: a three-letter group found on the top of the lamp. This code is universal for a given lamp configuration, regardless of manufacturer.

The life of a projection lamp as stated on the carton or top-stamp is an average life for that type of lamp, determined by the manufacturer for lamps operated at the specified voltage. Rough handling, thermal shock from turning on a super-chilled lamp (one left in a car overnight in the winter and not allowed to warm to room temperature before being turned on), operation at higher than rated voltage, use of a lamp other than that for which the projector was designed, or slow fans or blowers (resulting from gummy bearings, obstructions of blades or air intakes or outlets, or slipping drive belts) will all contribute to shorter than rated life.

In no case is rated life a guarantee of minimum time for a single lamp. If you have examined conditions of use and still feel that a lamp has burned out too quickly, try returning it to your dealer for credit. Manufacturers can usually determine by examination whether lamp failure was a result of manufacturing problems or conditions of use.

While reduced voltage will extend lamp life, the color temperature of a lamp must also be considered. Vivid blue skies can only result from white-hot lamp filaments. The nature of the light from incandescent filaments is that they are rich in the red-orange end of the spectrum, but weak in blue-violet light. It is difficult to reduce lamp voltage by a small specified amount anyway. Wall dimmers can not be used in series with the projector because of the induction motor used for the cooling fan. Carousel projectors incorporate a high-low lamp switch, using a high-wattage resistor cooled by the blower, to drop the voltage for the "low" position of the switch. Some motion picture and overhead projectors that use low voltage lamps offer switch-selected transformer taps to reduce the voltage for low light output.

You can demonstrate the effect of color temperature on color rendition of a slide by wiring a 600-watt wall dimmer to a Carousel projector as shown below.

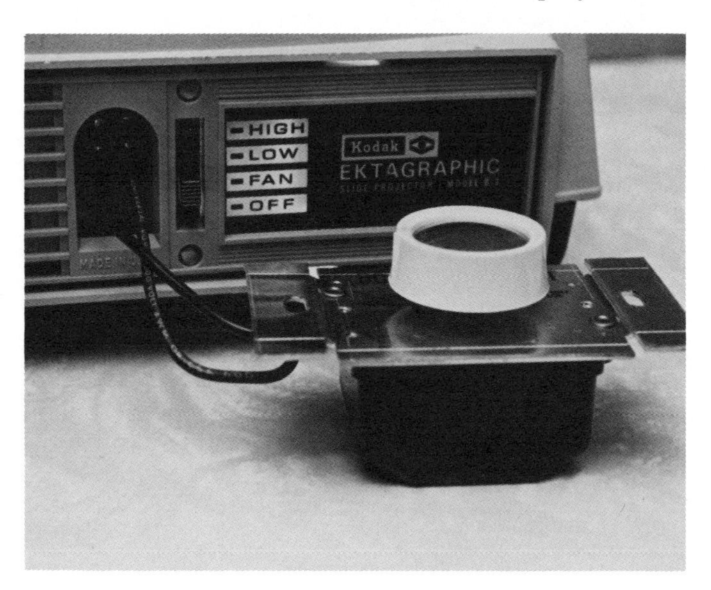

Insert a good quality color slide containing a fair percentage of blue sky in the gate, switch the projector to FAN, and advance the dimmer slowly. Watch the change in the blueness of the sky as you reach the higher end of the dimmer's rotation. Most of these controls will still not give full voltage to the lamp because of a slight voltage drop across the dimmer components.

NOTE: The above demonstration is possible because the Carousel projector provides access to the lamp circuit independent of the motor and slide change circuits. This access is normally used with dissolve control accessories. DO NOT try to wire a wall dimmer in series with the line cord of any projector that has a cooling or drive motor. These dimmers are designed to work with resistive loads only, and even if they would work, we would not want to lower the volume of air for cooling by slowing down the blower.

Some limited lamp substitution is possible, and tables of satisfactory substitutes are given in the lamp guides. If substitution is necessary, use only recommended alternate lamps. Just because you can get the base to fit the socket, and the lamp to light, is no guarantee of proper projection. Only the originally specified lamp or a recommended substitute will align optically, produce no more heat than the cooling system can handle, and operate for a reasonable life span.

While many projectors today include the recommended ANSI code on the model and serial number plate, it is a good idea to write the ANSI code letters of the original lamp on the projector housing with a marking pen when the projector is put in service. This can head off a lot of trouble later.

Appendix I

CABLES AND CONNECTORS

Cables and connectors cause more difficulty than anything, with the possible exception of burned-out lamps. And not without reason. Most household appliances get plugged in and left connected for weeks, months, or even years. It is not uncommon for audiovisual equipment, however, to be connected and disconnected daily, at least to and from power. Microphones and video equipment add even more cables and connectors, many of them requiring twisting to lock them in place, some having rather delicate pin and socket contacts. Because each cable and connector type is unique, we have divided this appendix into Power, Audio, and Television/Video cables and connectors.

Power Cables

As far as the wire used is concerned, power cables are the simplest structurally and the easiest to repair. Two-wire cables present no problems at all. Let's assume that you have determined that the cable is broken at the plug, and the plug is one that was molded onto the wire. First, cut the wire with a pair of diagonal cutting pliers about an inch back from the plug. The remaining cutting will be done with some kind of knife, and skill and delicacy is required to keep from cutting insulation where you shouldn't, or losing some of the wire strands, all of which are necessary if full power is to be delivered.

Further assuming that this is two-wire zip-cord, use the following procedure:

Carefully separate the wires by pulling them apart, after having cut through the joining insulation for about an inch.

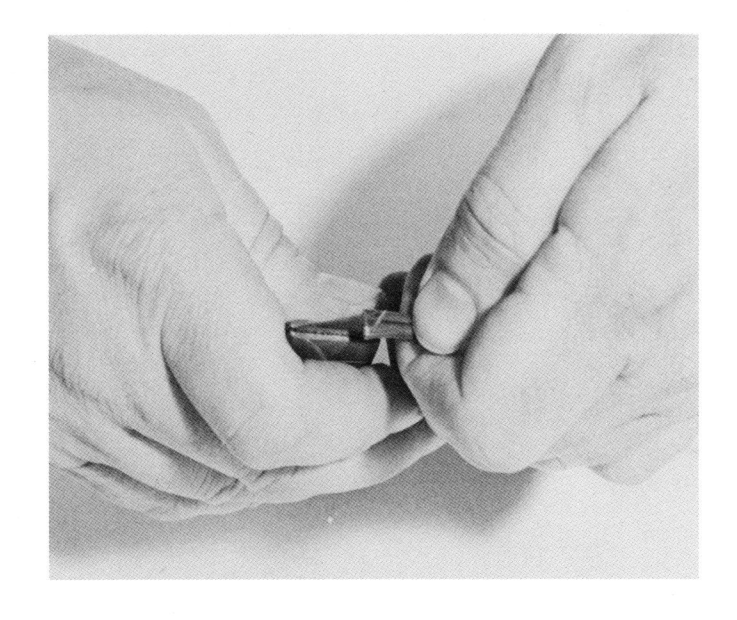

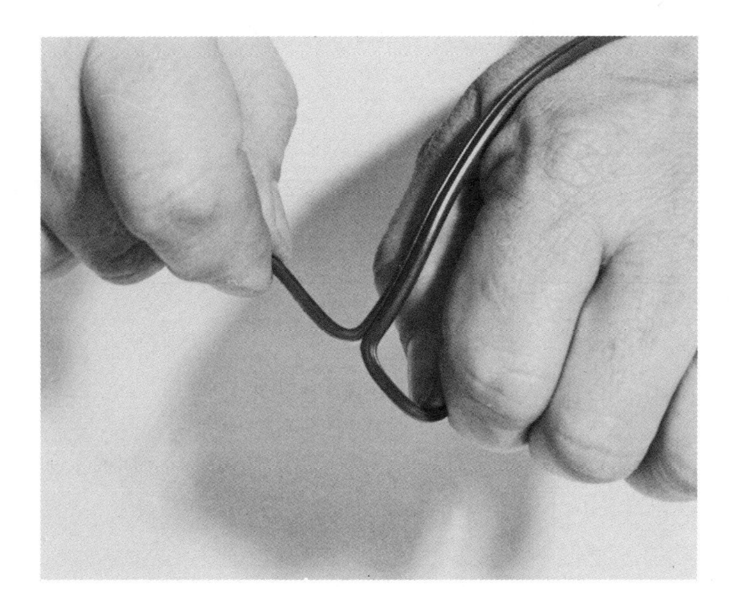

Pull until the wires are apart about an inch and a half from the end.

Using a knife that isn't too sharp, roll each wire under the blade, making a circumferential cut about 3/4" back from the end. This cut should be through the insulation, but if you end up pulling out more than three of the wire strands, you should cut back and start over.

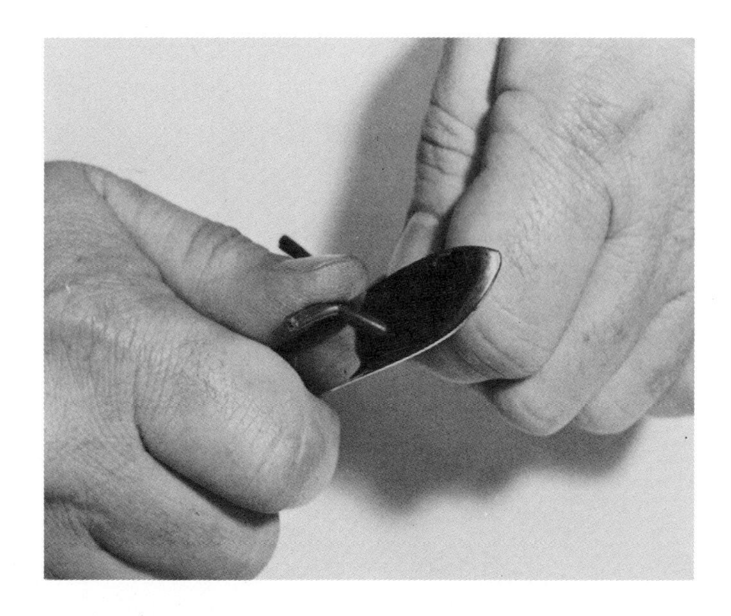

Hold the wire between the knife blade and your thumb and, working from the cut, pull the insulation off the wire. Repeat this procedure for the other wire too.

Now twist the strands of bare wire as tightly as you can between thumb and forefinger, in a clockwise direction (looking from the cut end of the wire). The direction is important to minimize unraveling of the strands when the terminal screw is tightened in the plug.

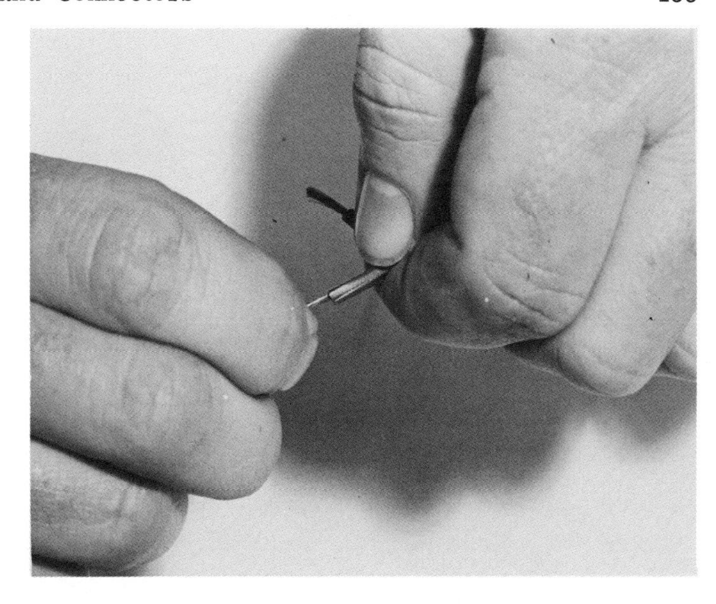

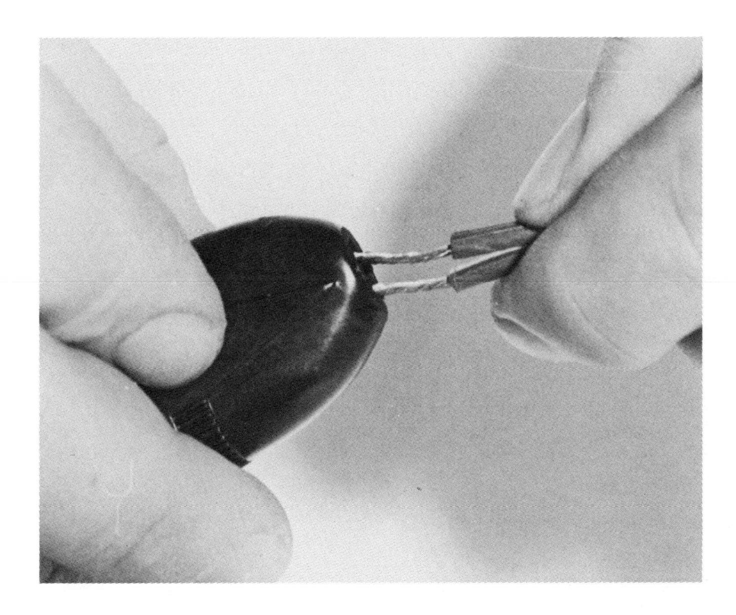

Push the wires through the plug shell, wrap each around a plug prong, bend the wire around the screw, again in a clockwise direction, and tighten the screw down. Carefully inspect the work for any single strands of wire that have not stayed under the screw head. One or two may be cut off, but if there

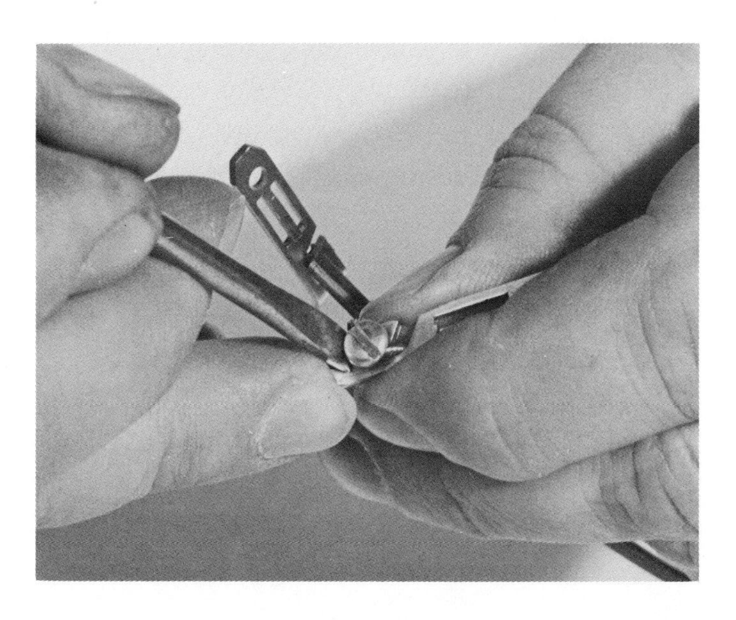

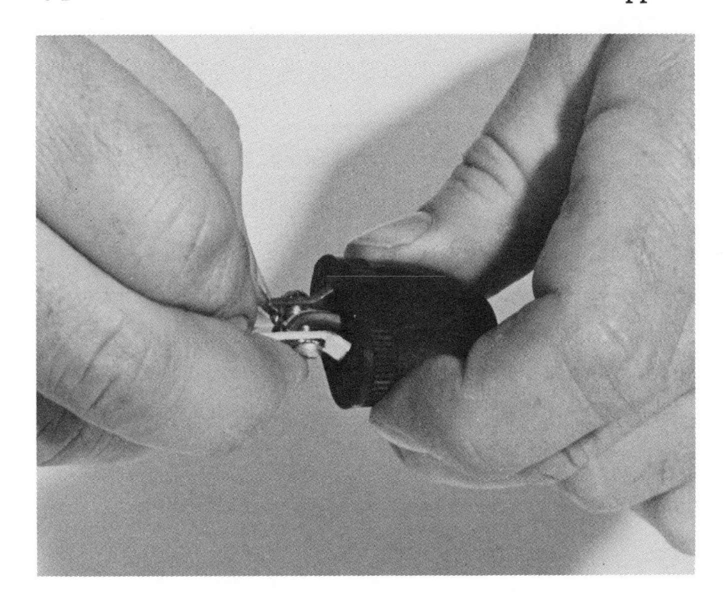

are more, back that screw off, re-twist the wires, and re-tighten the screw.

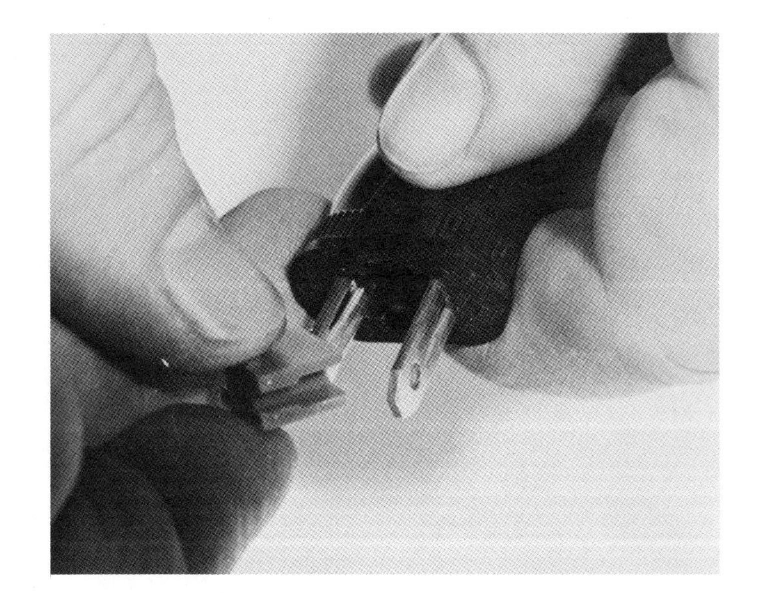

If the plug is the recommended type, re-assemble it. A plug that had a flat paper insulator over the prongs should now have this put back in place.

Assuming that you have a round power cord, there are a few variations in the procedure.

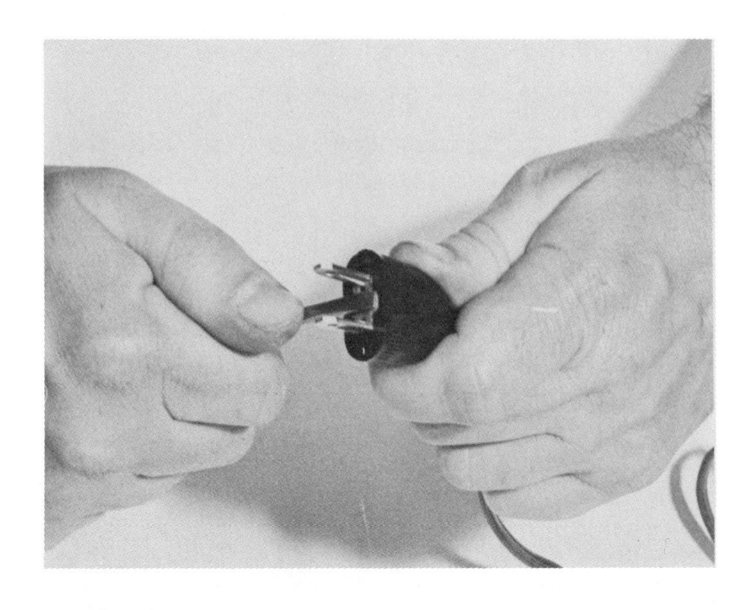

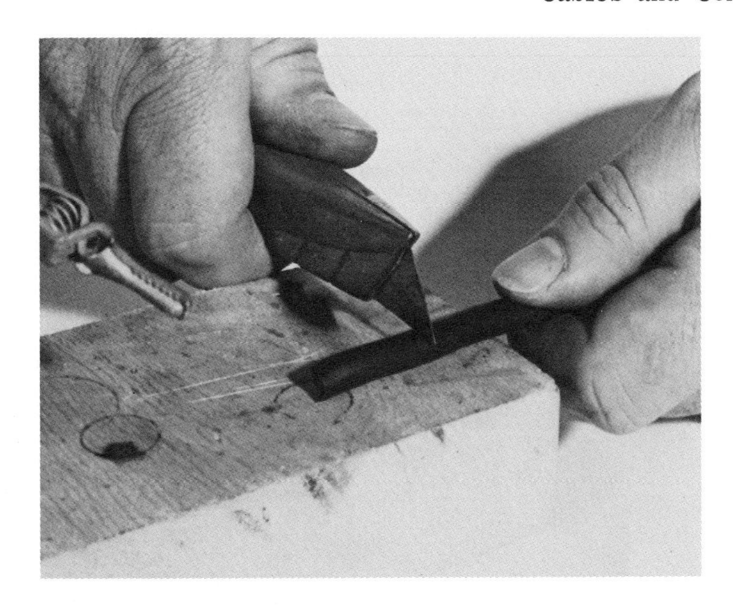

Having cut the wire an inch back from the old plug, roll the round insulation under a sharp knife (with very light pressure), about an inch and a half back from the end. Bend the wire at the cut to be sure the outer jacket is cut through, cutting lightly with the knife where it is not.

Now gently draw the blade along the jacket from the previous cut to the end. This should make it possible to peel the jacket off the wires and filler cord.

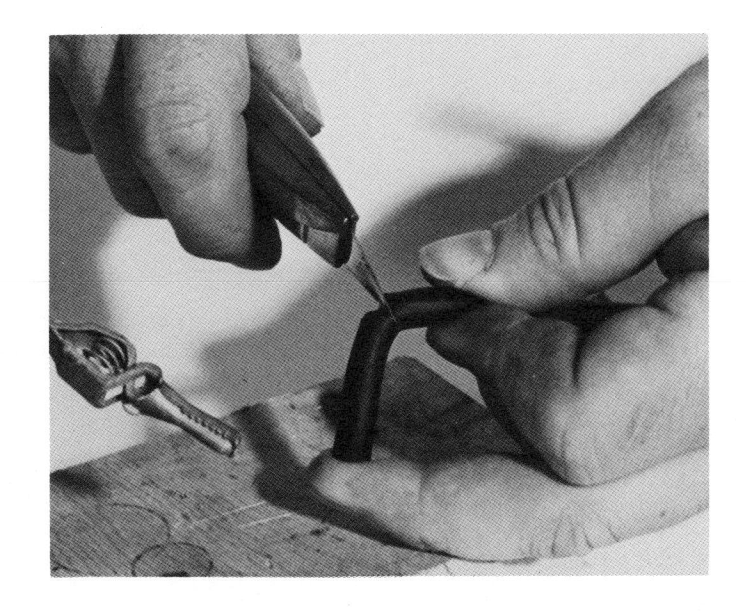

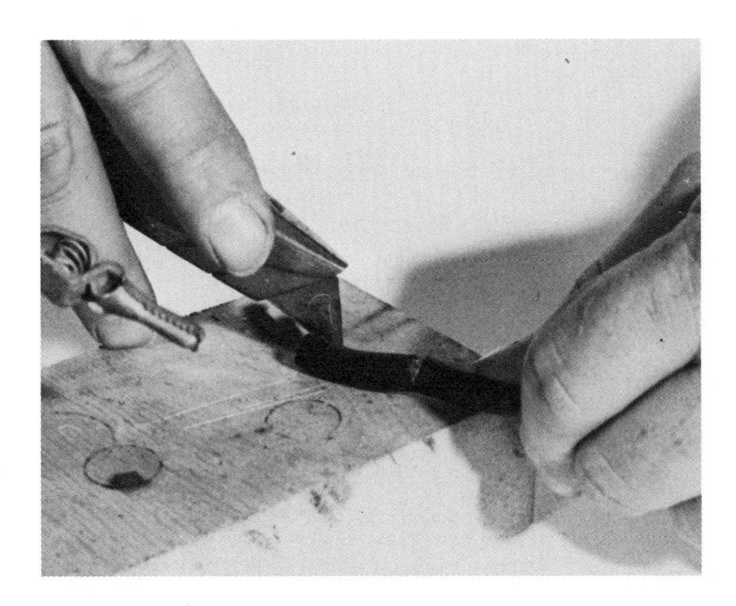

Fan out the wire and filler cord and cut off all the fillers, leaving only the two insulated wires.

Strip away the insulation from each wire as described under the zip-cord, above. Again, be careful not to cut any (or more than a very few) of the wire strands.

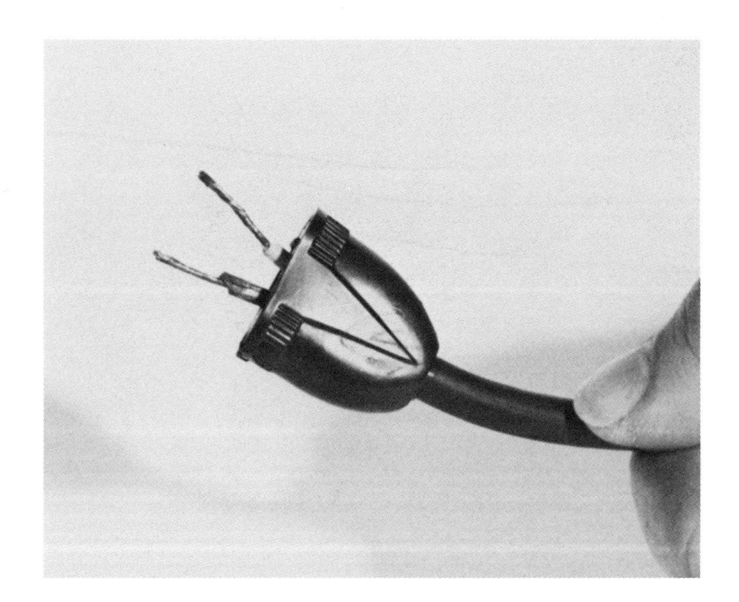

Push the full cable into the shell and install the wires in the plug as described under the zip-cord. A well replaced plug will have the full jacketed cable going right down into the shell.

What kinds of plugs should you get for these replacements? That is something of a problem. There is only

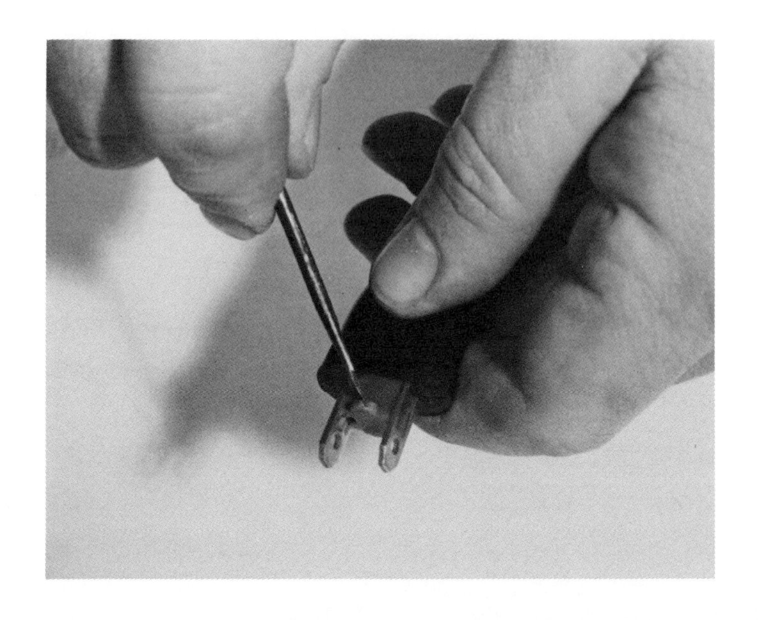

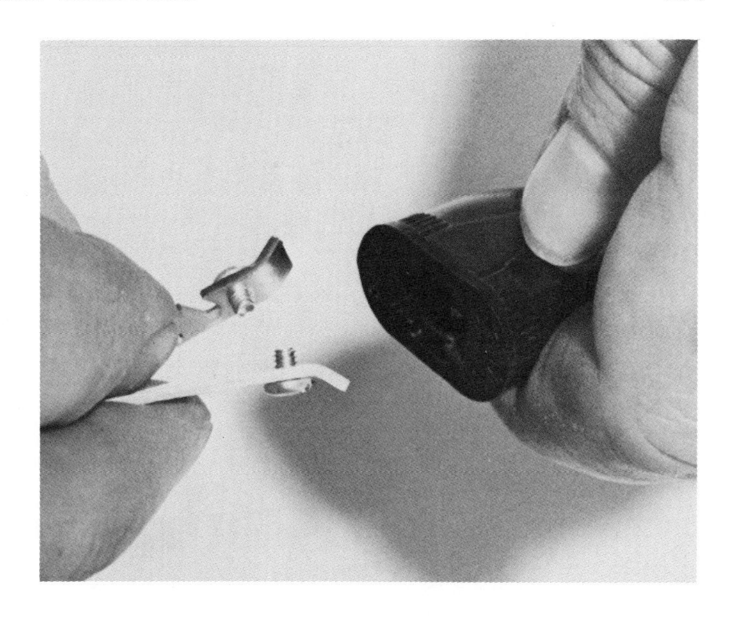

one that is unreservedly recommended. They aren't easy to find but they are available as Stock No. 41A300-5-010-9 at 10 for $2. 85 (1978) from Burstein-Applebee (see Bibliography for complete address).

Any substantial screw-attached plug will do. The problems are breakage with the plastic ones and bulkiness with the rubber ones.

The small, quick-attaching plugs made for zip-cord should not be used on institutional equipment, primarily because of the high current involved, particularly on projectors.

THREE-WIRE CORDS are made in both zip and round cords. The clue that you are dealing with this kind of cord is the 3-pin plug. The "ground" wire is always green-insulated and that wire always is attached to the large round ground prong of the plug. (See the opening section on Electrical Safety for a discussion of the role of this wire.)

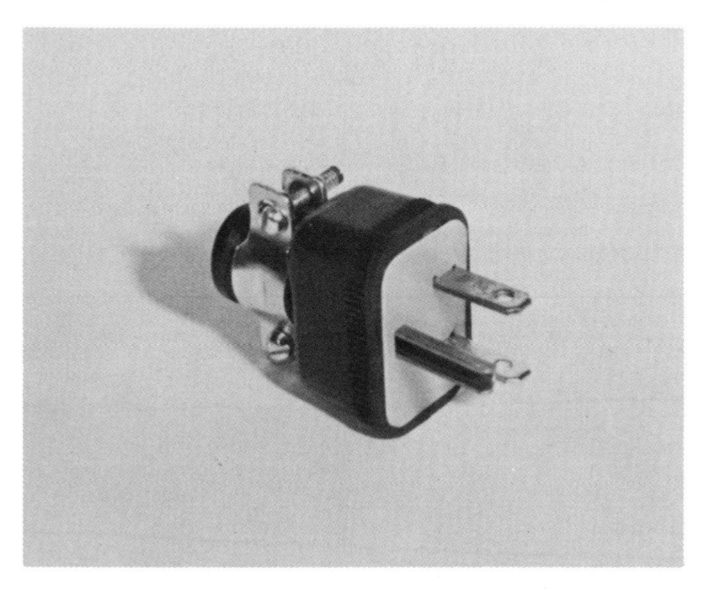

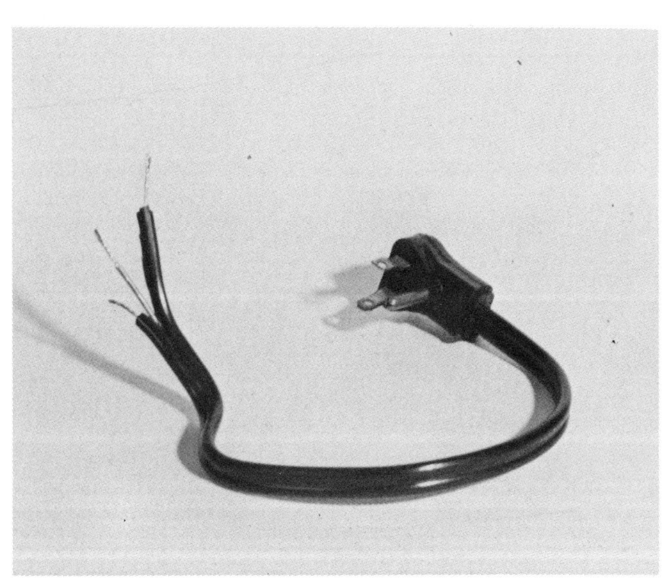

Only one relatively small 3-prong replacement plug has been identified--Eagle #126. A local hardware or electrical dealer may be able to order a box of them for you. If a small replacement plug can not be obtained, the best recommendation at this time seems to be to buy the shortest 3-wire replacement cable you can find, and either replace the whole cord, or cut the new cord about 6" back from the plug, cut the old cord about an inch above the plug, and splice and tape the wires together.

(A flat grey vinyl insulated, 6'-cord is Stock No. 41A445-8 at $1.85 each. An 8'-black rubber round cord is Stock No. 41A335-1 at $1.87. Both are available from Burstein-Applebee (see Bibliography for complete address).

The safest way to make a splice is to step cut the wires with 1 1/2" intervals. Do this to each end to be spliced.

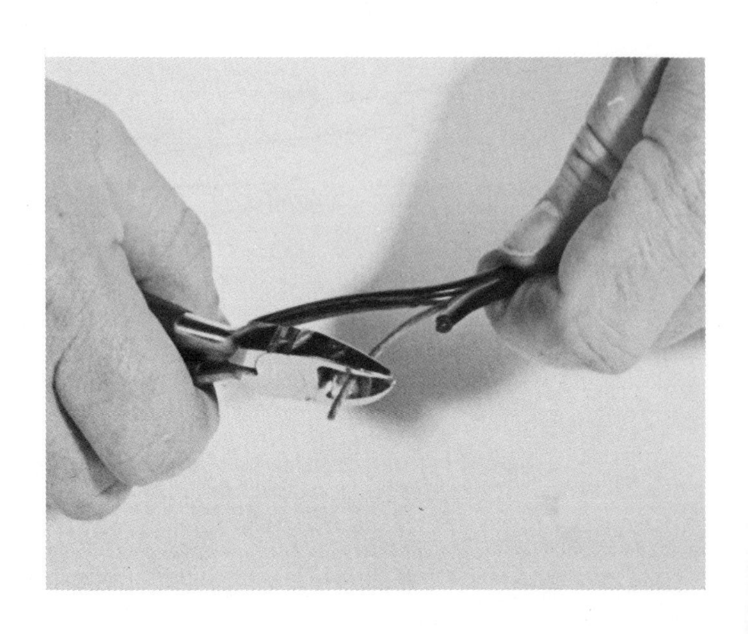

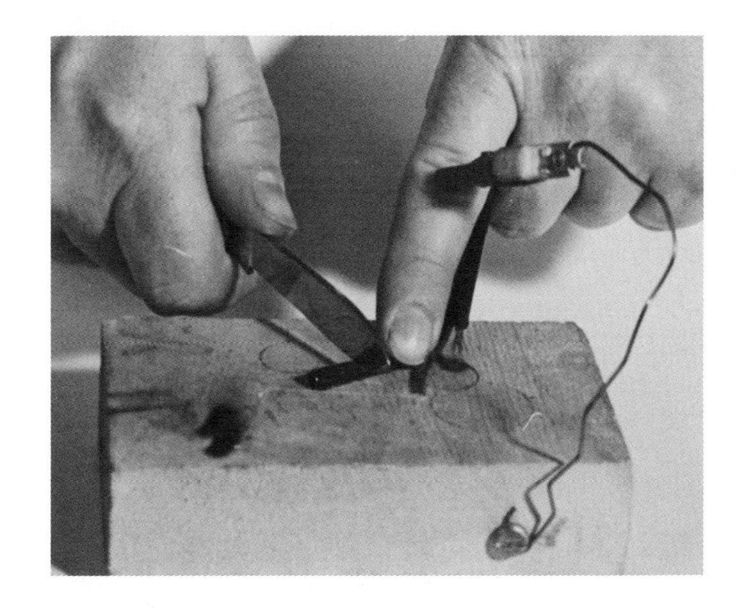

Next, strip the insulation from each separate wire, using the same procedure described under zip-cord, above.

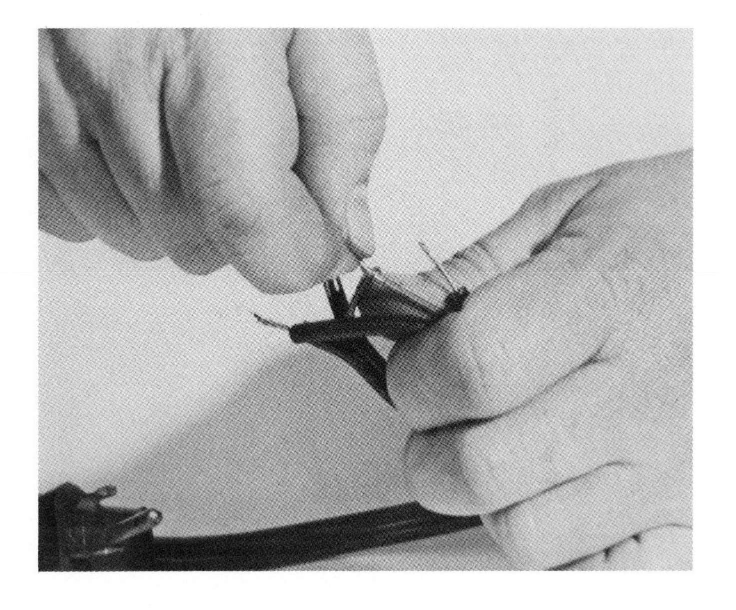

Cross each pair of wires as shown, and twist them together. For best power transfer and durability, each joint should be soldered. Fold each twisted splice, soldered or not, down along its wire and tape neatly with an overlap, each wrap about equal to half

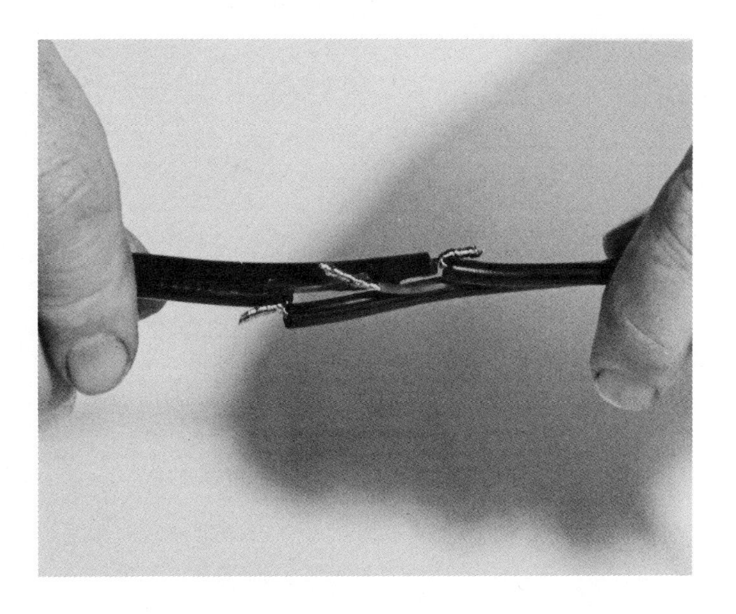

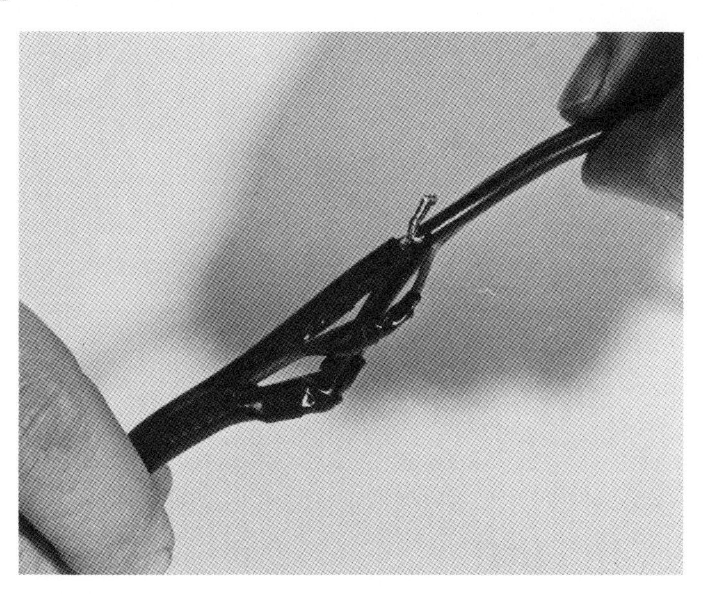

the width of the tape. Each wire should be taped separately, but not excessively. Finally, tape the whole set of wires into a neat bundle, starting about an inch back on the unseparated cable on one end and completing the taping an inch onto the other unseparated cable. While there are many good tapes on the market, Scotch No. 33 offers excellent insulation, great pliability, and consistent adhesion. NEVER use any tape other than a tape sold expressly for electrical insulation. Narrower tapes are usually easier to use and result in a neater job.

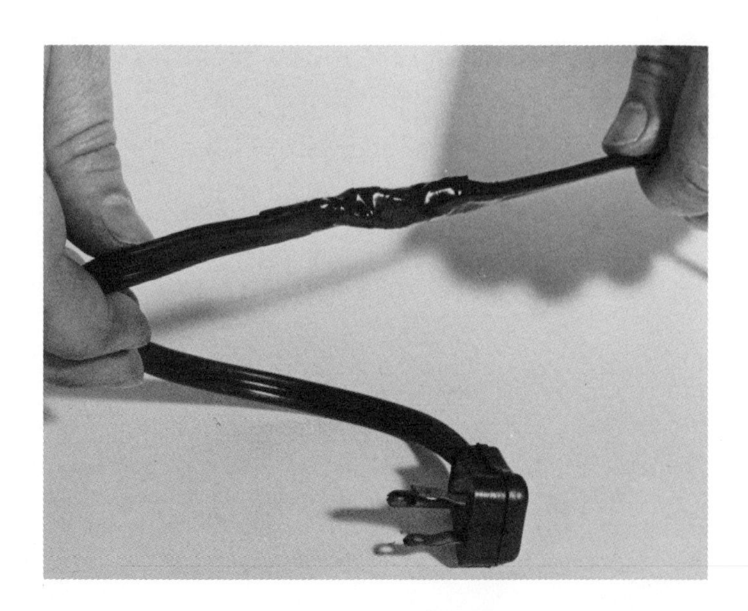

Audio Cables

The structure of an audio cable differs from the cable used for power. When the outer jacket is stripped away, a metal shield becomes visible. This shield may be a braid of interwoven wire, a flat spiral of about 20 strands of fine wire winding around the inner wires for the length of the cable, or it may be a metal foil with a bare wire that maintains conductivity along the foil. When the shield is pulled back, there will be one or two wires (even more for intercom and special applications) and some filler strands of some kind of fiber. If there are two wires, they are usually black and white and have a very gradual twist along the length of the cable.

The function of the shield is to keep nearby electrical fields from inducing hum into the circuit. It is generally effective, although in some stage and church altar areas, where power wiring is concentrated, it may be necessary to slowly re-position cable on the floor until a point of minimum hum is found.

The fiber filler adds strength, helps shape the cable, and promotes good flexibility.

Wires in the cable are rather small, since little current will be carried by the cable. The color-coding of the insulation is important because some wiring schemes will short-circuit if the wires are interchanged, especially with respect to the connection of the shield. The twist of the inner wires is another effort to reduce hum pick-up, this time by reversing small induced currents with each twist, causing them to cancel. And the insulation is especially chosen to minimize electrical capacitance, which would reduce the high frequency response of the microphone.

Single wire and shield cables are associated with high-impedance equipment, most often the older tube-type PA amplifiers and older reel-to-reel tape recorders. This cable can not be extended for more than about 20 feet without picking up hum, in most cases.

Dual wire and shield cables are used with low-impedance systems. This includes all better quality PA amplifiers of any period, and all newer transistor equipment. Low-impedance cables can stand 50 feet of extension without noticeable deterioration of the sound. Very long cable runs require a preamplifier near the microphone, boosting the feeble signal and reducing the vulnerability to line noise pick-up, which is itself a very small signal.

One of the surest ways to guarantee reliability of a PA system is to cut all lines back an inch from connectors each year and re-attach the connectors. When doing this, or when making any connector replacement, it is important to match the wires color for color. Sometimes both wires are broken and no insulation remains to determine which color went to which pin of the plug. In such cases it is best to attach the shield and just lightly tack-solder the wires. Do not assemble the connector

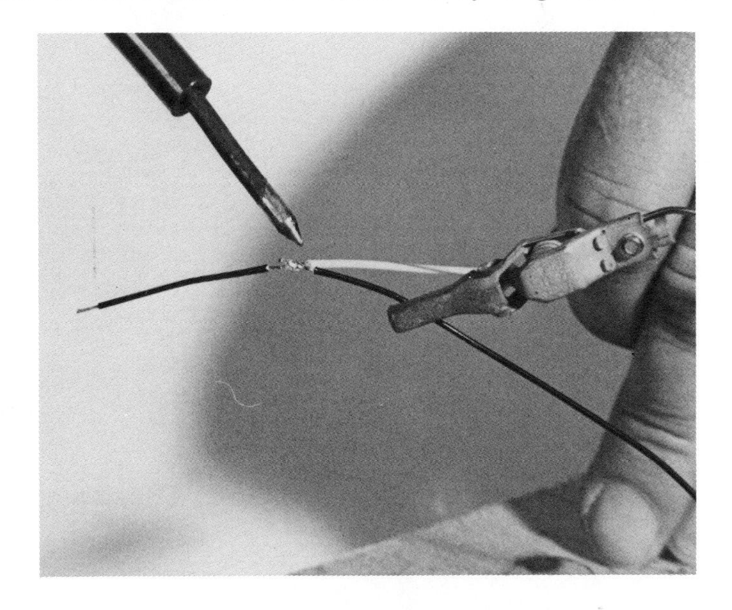

An example of "tack soldering" (above and top of next page). One wire is attached to the other by momentary melting of the solder, without forming a hook or wrapping a splice.

shell until the cable has been tested (you can expect some hum when the shell is off the connector, especially if you touch the wires). Connect the microphone to the amplifier with the cable you are repairing and try to talk through the system. If it works, success! Un-tack the wires and make a good, permanent connection. If it doesn't work, untack both wires and switch them in relation to the pins of the connector. This will normally make the system work. If it still does not, try combinations that attach one wire to the shield and the other wire to one or the other of the pins. Sometimes a system is wired this way in the amplifier, and rather than revise the whole system, it is expedient to just play along, making repairs that keep the system in operation without rebuilding it. The one time it is very desirable to maintain connection uniformity is where a large institution has a number of amplifiers, recorders, etc. and a limited number of good microphones. In such cases either the plant operations technicians or a maintenance contractor should spend the time it takes to get all the systems compatibly wired.

Shielded audio cable is prepared in the following manner:

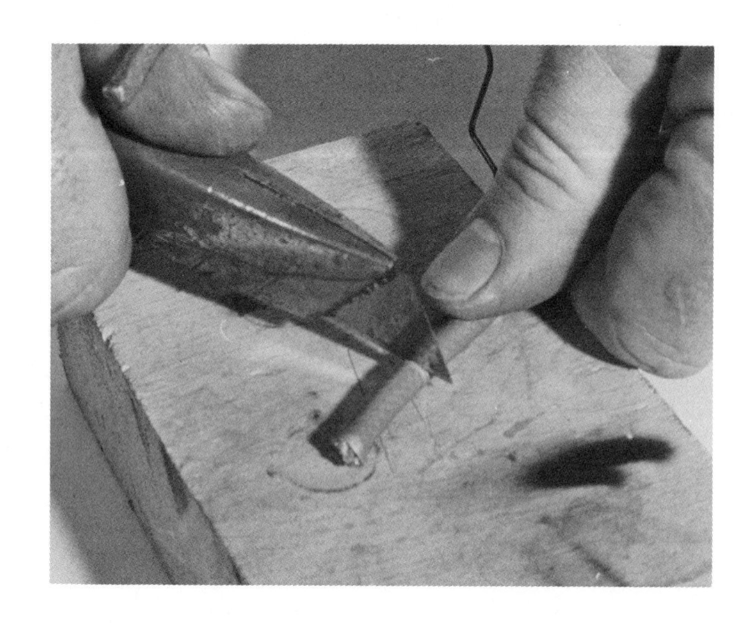

Roll the outer jacket under a knife blade about an inch from the end of the cable. The jacket can usually be pulled off after cutting by placing the wire between the thumb and the knife blade and pulling. If this does not work, slit the jacket from the cut to the end and peel the jacket away. Be careful not to cut much of the shield wire or braid.

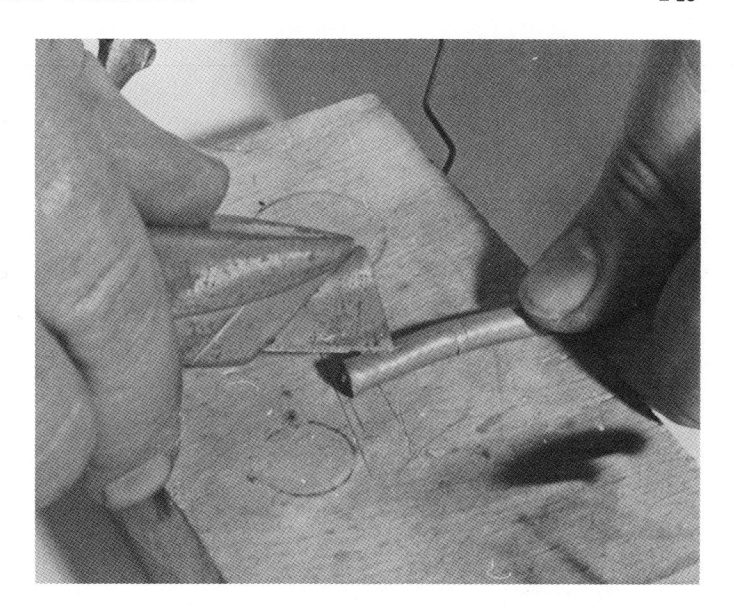

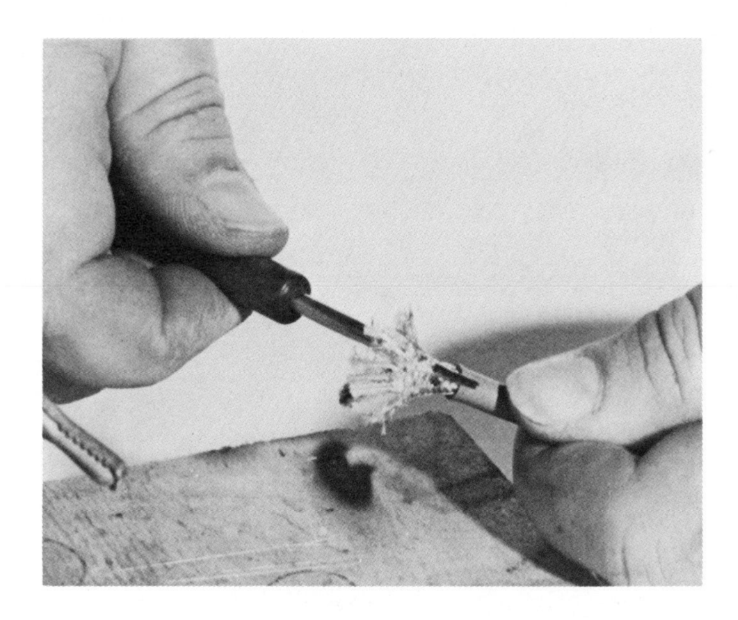

Now unbraid the shield with a pointed, but not sharp, tool. A "soldering aid" is ideal (see Tools appendix). When you have reduced the braid or wrap to a cluster of strands, twist as many together as it takes to make a diameter about that of the other wires. Cut the rest of the strands away.

Also cut and remove any fiber filler strands.

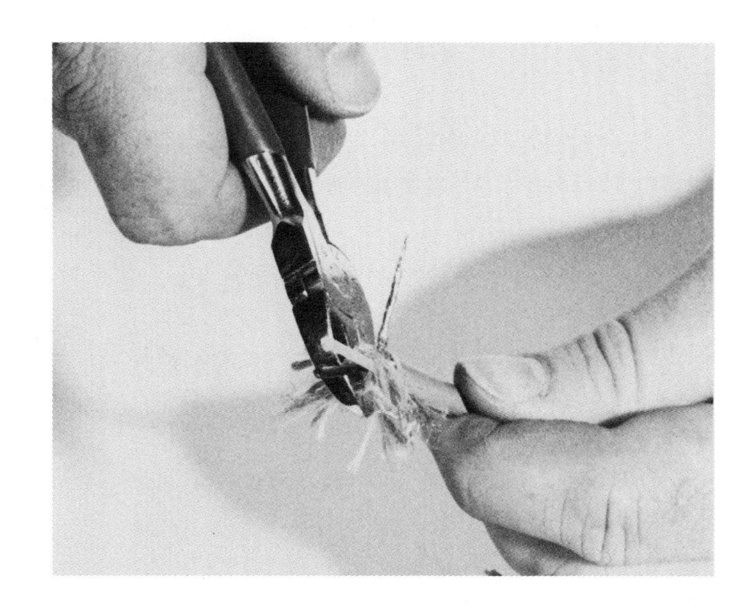

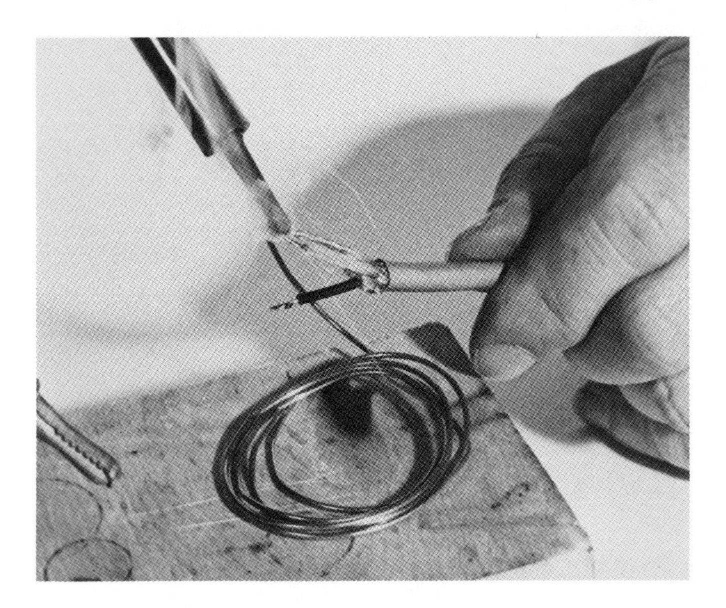

Carefully cut around the insulation of each wire, only 1/8" back from the end, and remove the insulation. Using as little heat as possible, "tin" (see Soldering appendix) the bare ends of the wire(s) and the twisted shield wires.

Cut the shield wires to the length of the other wire(s) and solder, usually to pin 1 of the connector.

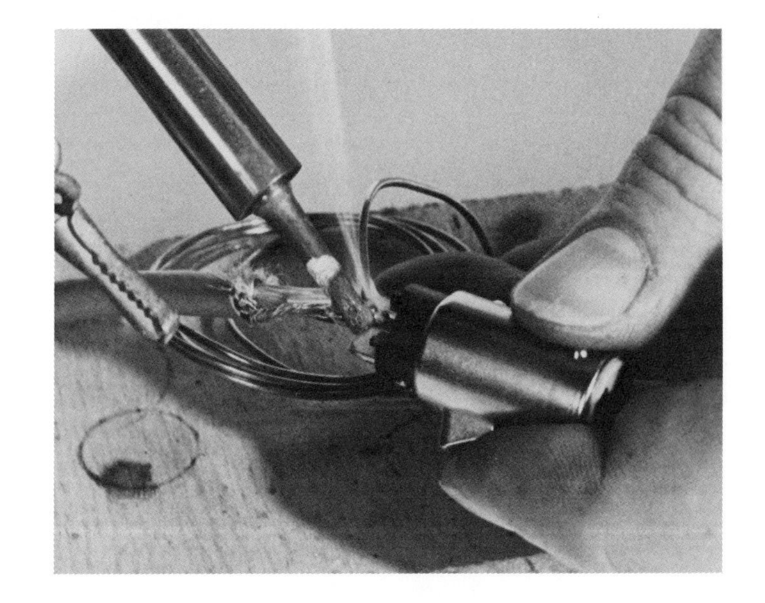

(If you have a microphone that hums when it or the stand is touched, there is some error in the shield connection. A properly wired shield connects the metal case of the microphone to the electronic "ground" of the amplifier, essentially "shielding" the whole system from hum-inducing fields.)

The procedure above has demonstrated connection to the most popular type of audio connector used in professional audio systems. These connectors are very durable, costing more but giving reliable service.

Some other types and the method of connection are shown below.

1/4" & 1/8" Plug

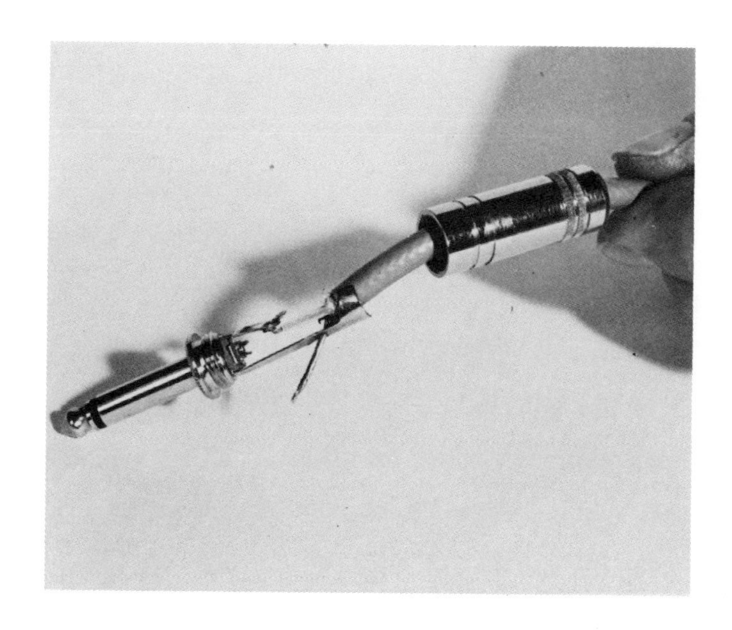

Strip and twist wires. If cable has two wires and shield, twist one wire with shield strands. Form hook and attach center wire ...

... push shield strands through hole in outer connector, bend back, solder and cut off excess. If shell does not have paper insert, put very little tape around center wire and connector and wire.

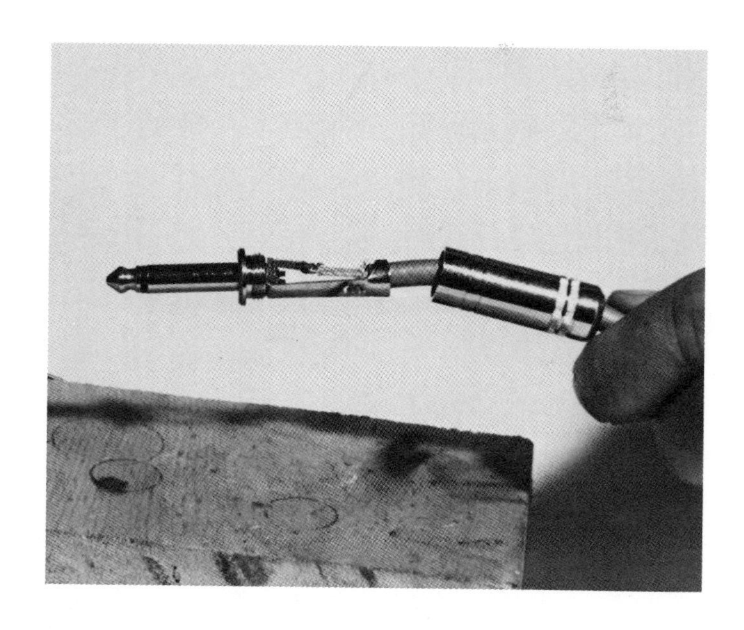

1/4" Cable Female

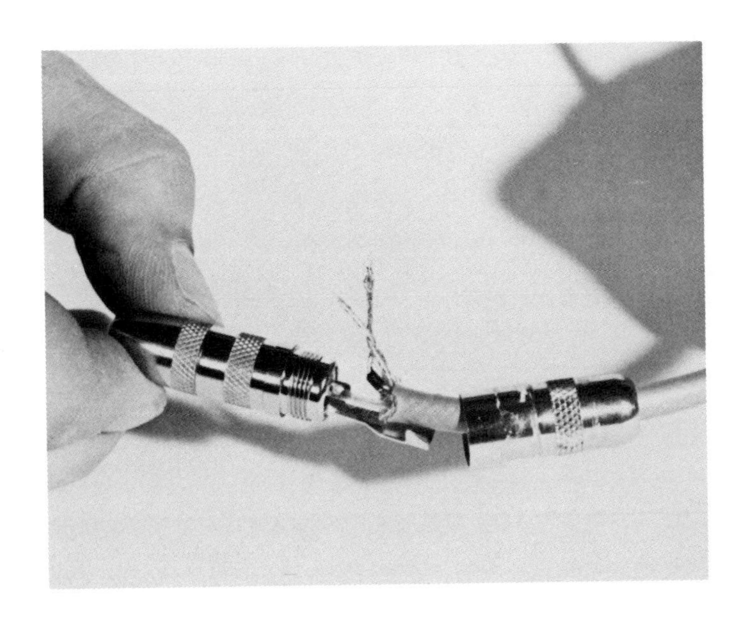

Prepare wire by cutting to length and stripping insulation. Form hook and attach wire to center lug, soldering to hold it in place.

If cable has two wires, twist one with shield strands. Hook these wires around outer connection point and solder. Bend the cable clamp around the jacket and tighten the shell to the cable jack.

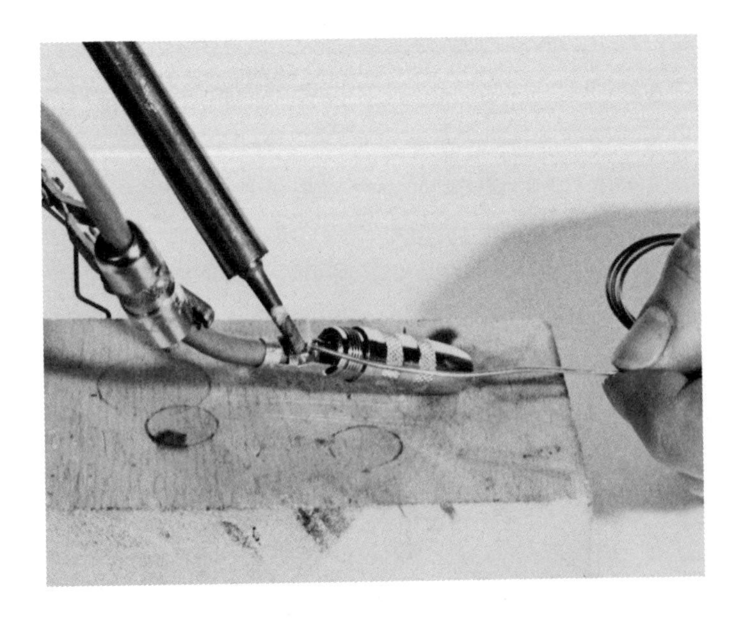

RCA Pin Plug

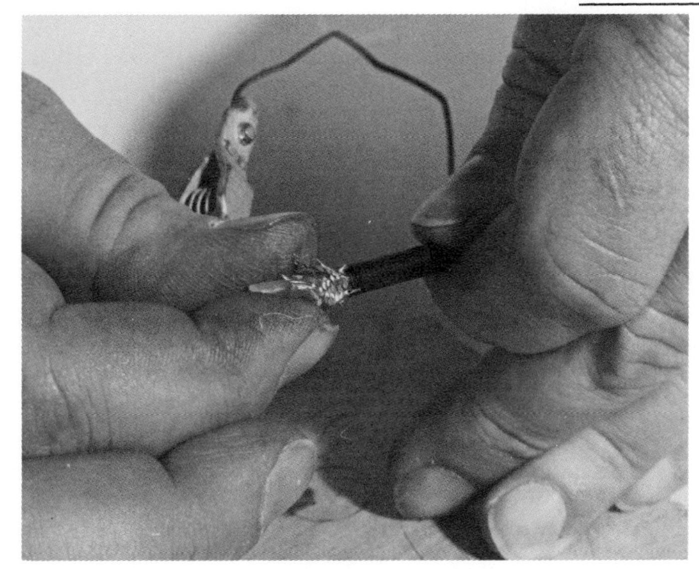

Just push braid back without cutting it.

Strip center insulation, insert wire into plug pin, and solder.

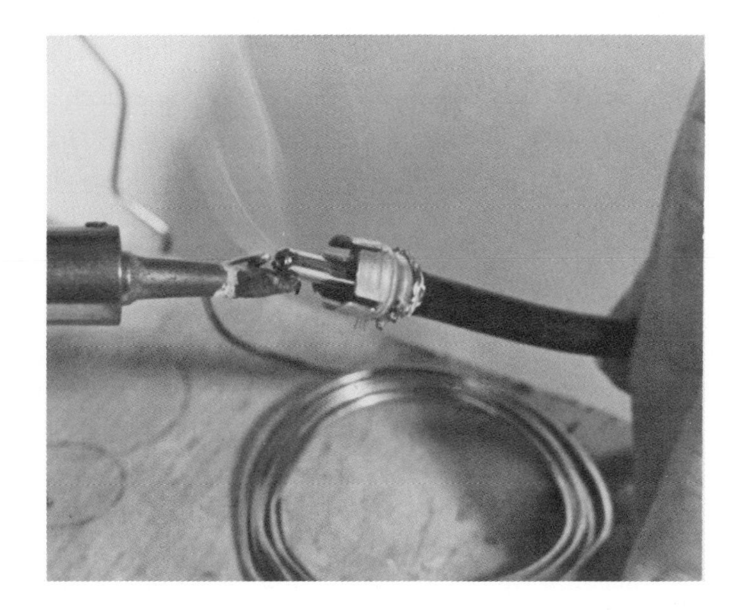

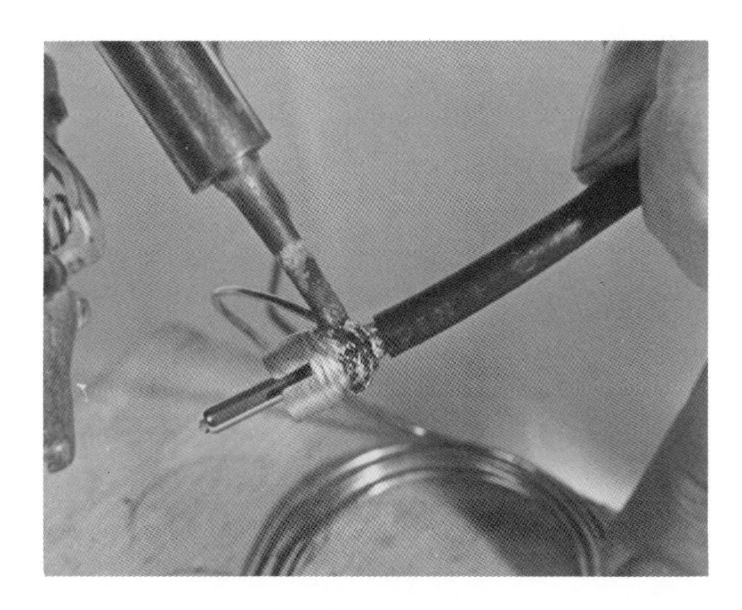

Push shield back down into contact with connector and solder, at least in two places, if not all around.

Television Cables

Most institutional television cable is "co-axial." The flat 300-ohm "twin-lead" is rarely seen, except to attach a pair of "rabbit ears" antenna to a receiver.

Co-axial cable is so-called because there is a center conductor, surrounded by a very uniform plastic insulating material with known, constant electrical properties, and this insulator is in turn surrounded by a carefully made braid. The center wire is itself the axis of a cross-section of the cable, and the insulator and braid, sharing the same axis, are said to be co-axial. The whole cable is covered with an external insulating material, which also protects it from abrasion and weather.

Co-axial cable is specified by an RG-number, which assures required characteristics, regardless of manufacturer. The characteristics we are concerned with are cable impedance and diameter. Only a cable of specified impedance will transfer the picture with full contrast and minimum ghosting. (Specified impedance is found in instruction books, or by checking the RG number of cable supplied originally by the manufacturer.) The most commonly encountered impedance is 72 or 75 ohms.

Diameter of the cable is important to assure proper fit in the plugs we intend to use (and they are almost always plugs ... a cable socket is just about never seen. When longer cables are needed, either longer cables are made up, or double female adapters are used between two plugs.) Only properly matched cables and connectors have any hope at all of lasting, and make-shift splicing, adapting, etc. is very poor video practice. Of all the electronic signals discussed in this book, the video signal is the most complex and the most vulnerable to interference; the one where any signal irregularity becomes instantly obvious and annoying. Most of the video equipment does a remarkably fine job when properly maintained, and we don't want to mess that up with sloppy cable work.

Standard practice at this time (1978) seems to be the use of small diameter, RG-59U cable, with UHF PL-259 connectors, using a UG-176U reducer to fit the cable to the connector. The key to successful co-axial cable making is careful measurement. If you are addicted to numbers, you can measure the whole thing once, make up a small chart, and work from it. If you are more casual, or don't intend to make all that many cables, use the connector as a measuring device.

First, slide the threaded attaching collar over the cable, insert the cable through the reducer and pull the reducer far enough onto the cable to be out of your way.

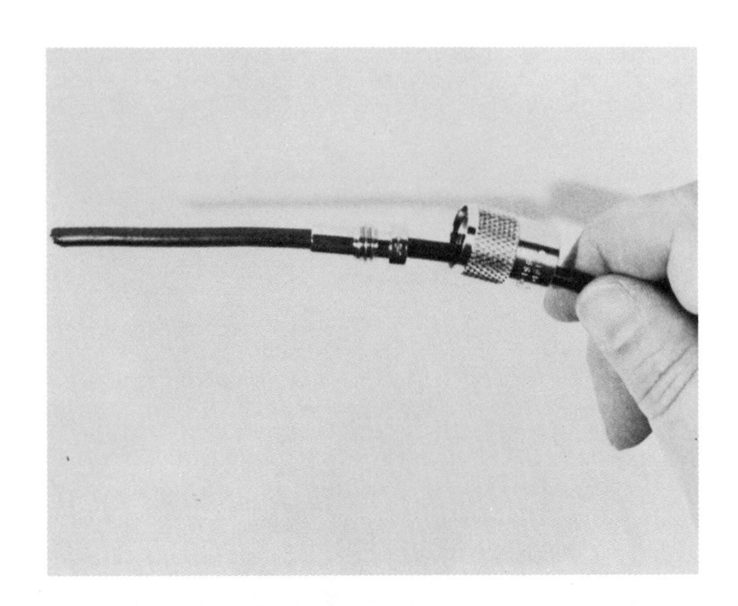

Gently roll the outer cover under a knife blade, 5/8" back from the end of the cable. Strip away the outer cover.

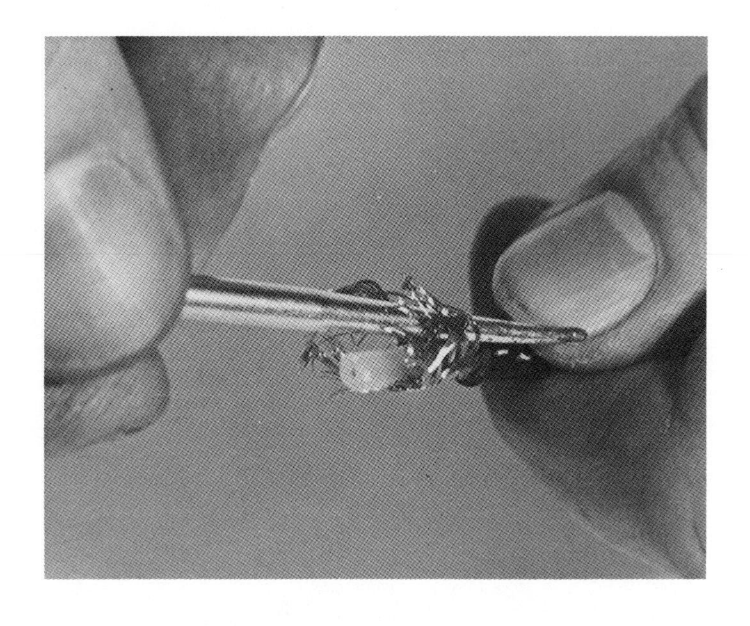

Unbraid the outer shield/conductor and cut all strands to about 1/2" from the center insulator. Bring the reducer to the end of the outer insulation and fold the shield/conductor strands back over it.

Gently cut and strip the center insulator, making the cut about 1/16" from the folded-back strands. Scrape the center conductor lightly.

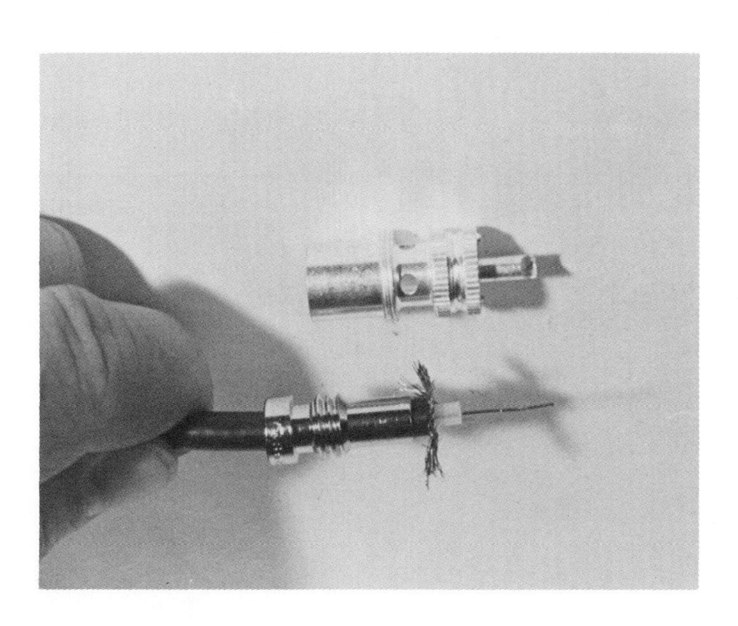

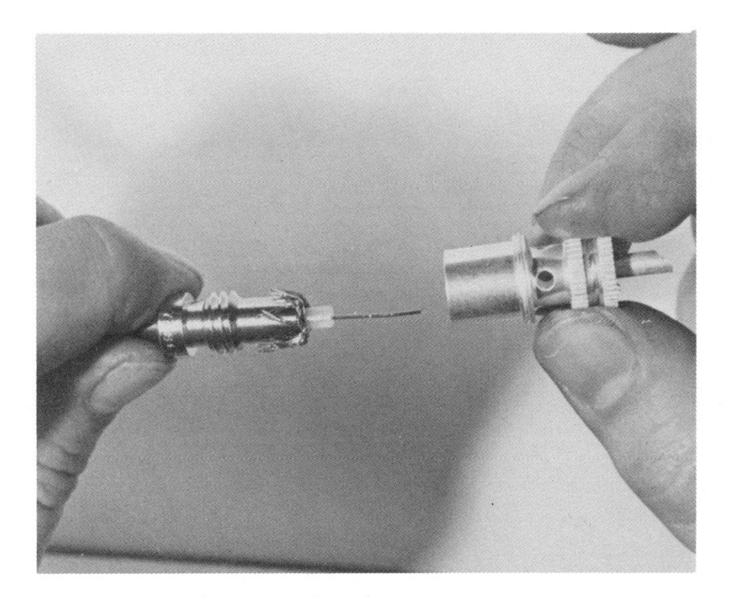

Align the center conductor with the cable by bending slightly, if necessary, and insert the reducer into the plug, being sure the wire is going into the plug prong and threading the reducer into the plug. Be sure the reducer is fully seated in the plug, using pliers on the collar if you must.

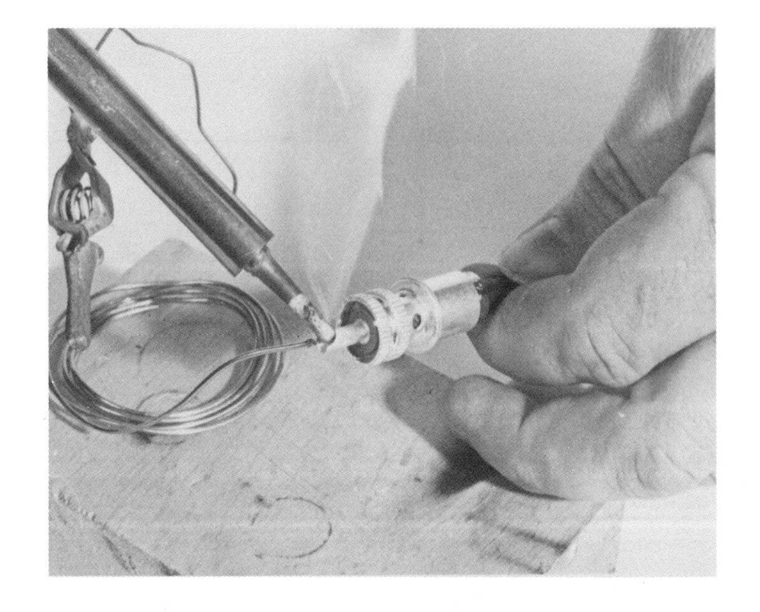

Push some solder into the plug prong and heat, adding solder until the prong is full. When the solder has cooled, cut off any center wire extending beyond the prong. It may also be necessary to clean off the outside of the prong, either by wiping with a hot soldering iron, or cutting/scraping off excess solder with a knife.

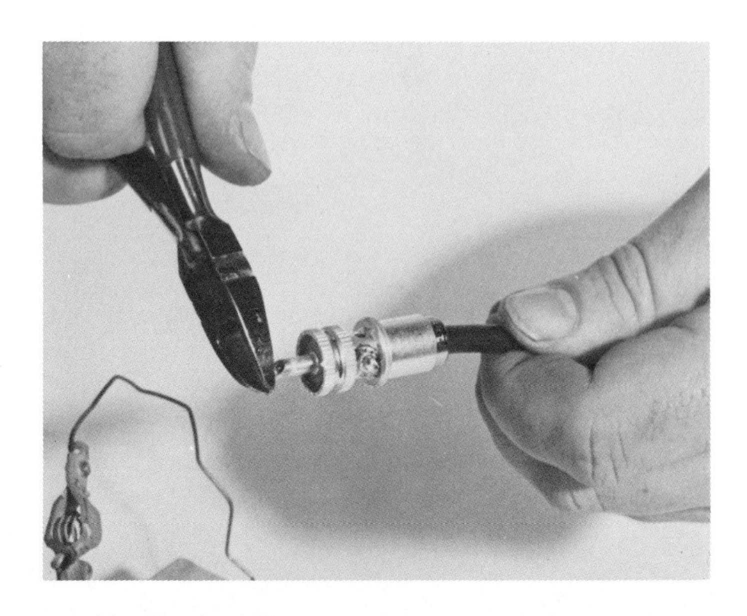

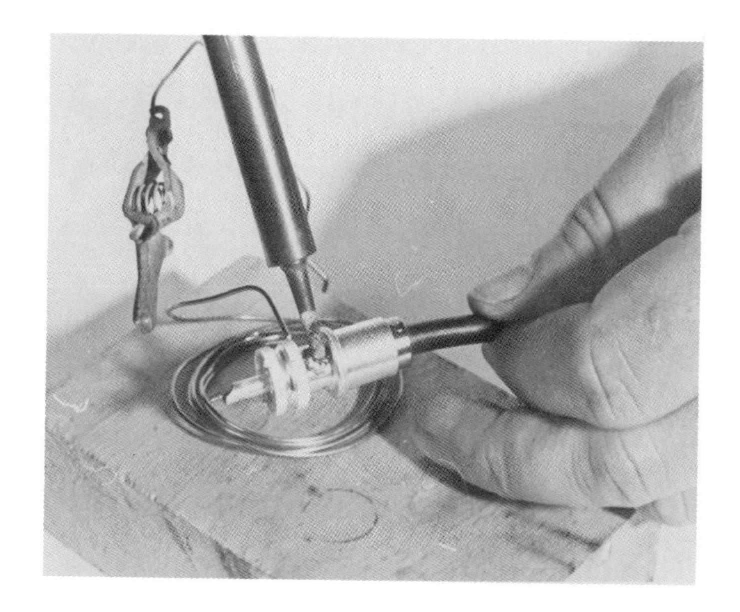

Now flow solder through at least one of the holes in the plug shell, soldering the shield wires to the shell. One hole is enough, two are better, but all four make future repair a tough job. It takes a lot of heat to get a good flow of solder onto the plug shell and wires. It takes skill to get enough heat, but not too much, to avoid melting all the plastic outer and center insulation.

Thread the attaching collar over the outside of the plug. This completes one end of the cable. Most video cables will have the same kind of plug on the other end.

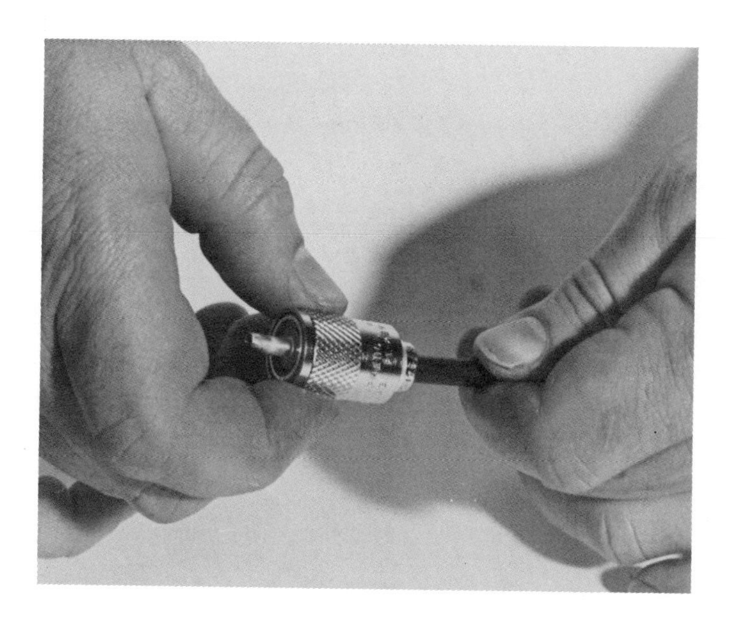

Repair of this kind of cable is necessary when the video signal becomes intermittent, and wiggling or twisting the cable at a connector restores image, however briefly. The problem is most commonly broken shield wires which have come loose because of strain or twisting of the cable in the connector.

Melt the solder in the center prong of the connector and pull the wire out of the connector. Run the threaded collar back off the plug. Hold the knurled section of the plug shell with one pair of pliers, grip the end of the reducer with a second pair of pliers, and remove the reducer from the plug.

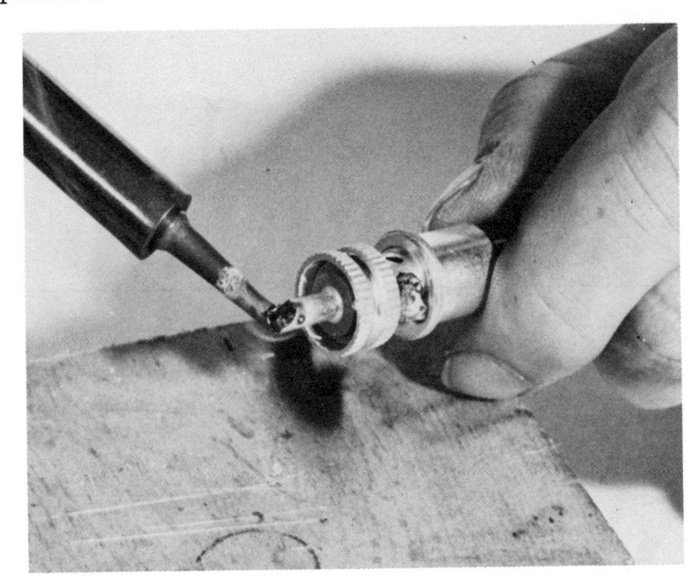

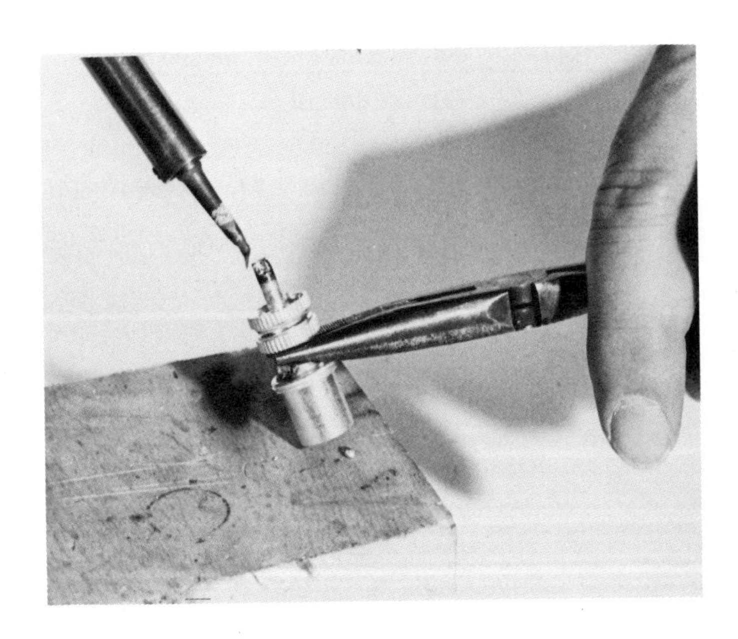

Still holding the plug shell heat the center prong to melt any remaining solder and bang the shell on the table-top to dislodge any solder in the prong. You should be able to look through it when it is properly cleared.

Now shift the pliers to the plug prong and heat the shell at any solder-filled holes. Again bang the shell on the table-top to shake out any solder or bits of wire. These operations must be done rapidly to get solder out before it re-solidifies. When you are satisfied that the shell is about as clean as a

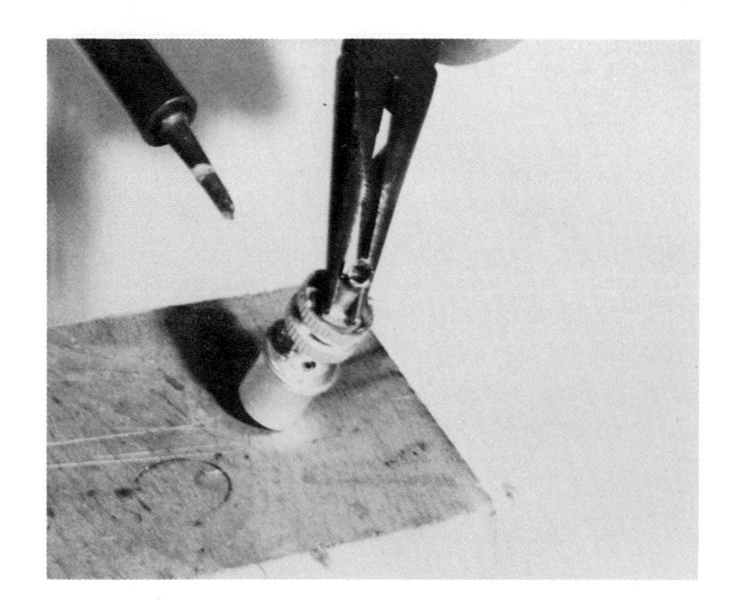

new one, cut off the frayed end of the wire and start the whole procedure as described above for a new connector.

If you have the time, patience and skill, it's not a bad idea to go ahead and re-do the connector on the other end of the cable, since wear on one end is likely to be symptomatic of similar wear on the other end.

Some older video equipment uses the smaller BNC type UG26OU connectors. The cable is still RG-59U. Replacement of these connectors, or making up cables with new connectors, is more delicate work than the larger PL259 plugs. Once again, measurement is the key.

To attach a UG26OU plug, begin by sliding onto the end of the cable the threaded compression collar and the flat metal washer. Push these back several inches to get them out of the way.

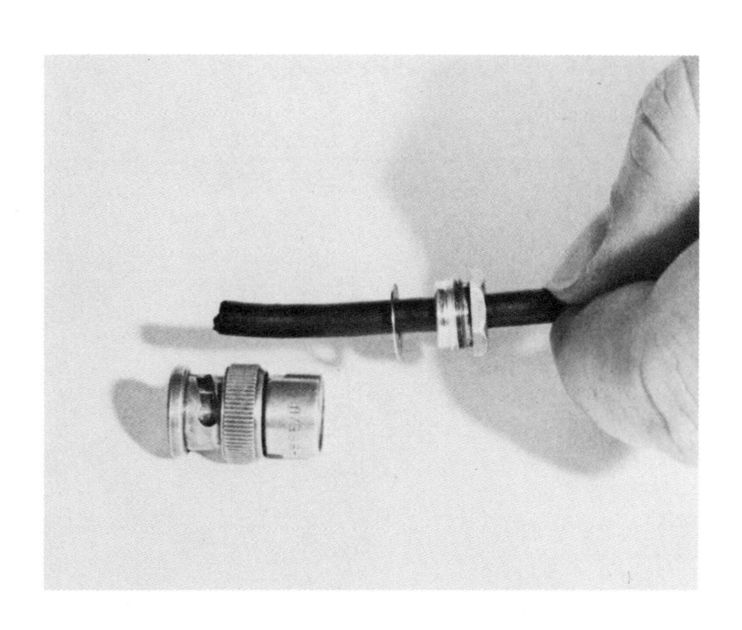

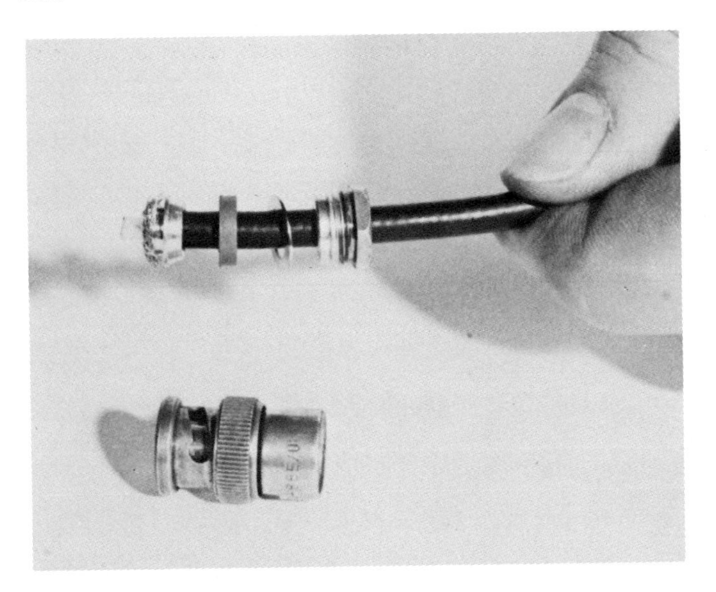

Make a circumferential cut in the outside jacket, 3/16" from the end, and strip away the jacket. Slide the rubber washer and the tapered or shoulder washer over the shield. Unbraid the shield, fold it out from the cable, and clip all strands 1/8" from the center insulation of the cable. Bend the strands of shield back over the tapered washer.

Cut and remove 1/8" of the center insulation. Scrape and tin the center wire, then solder it into the center pin. No solder can extend around the center pin or the pin will not fit into the connector. Wipe and/or shave any external solder from the pin.

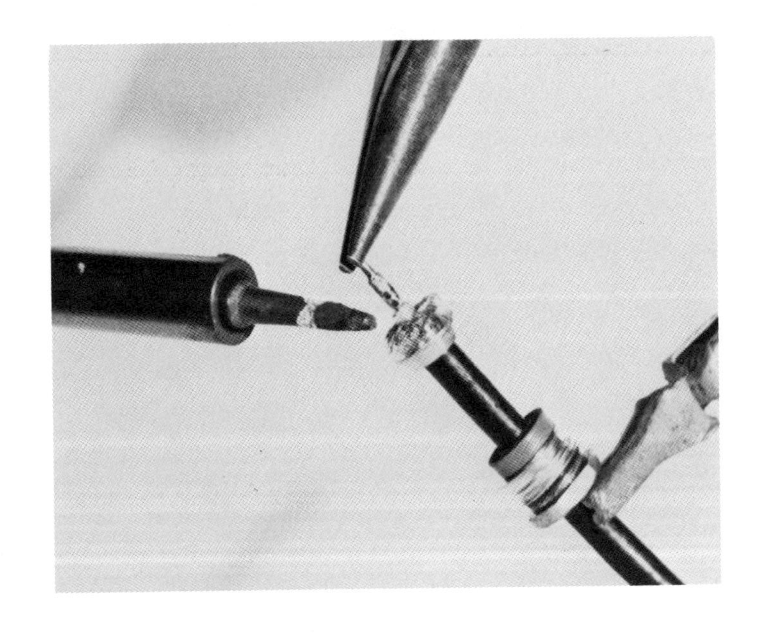

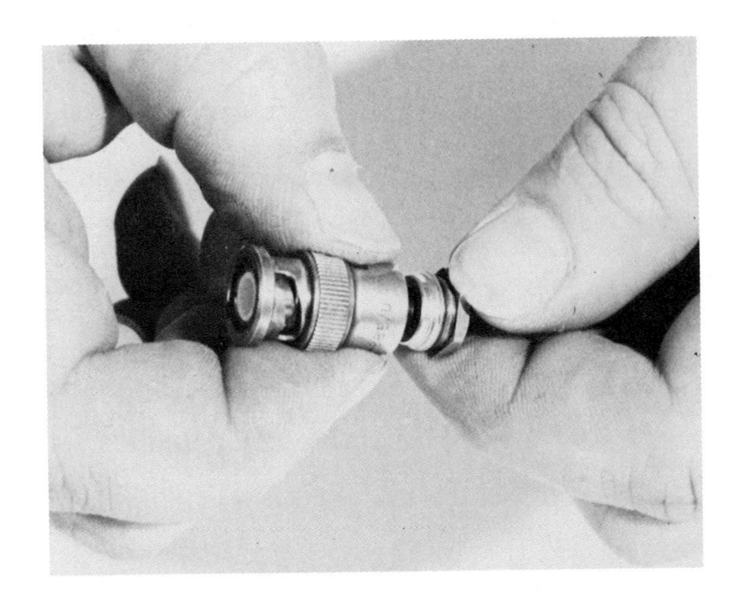

Push the pin and cable into the connector body. Slide the threaded compression collar and washer into the connector body and tighten the collar into the connector body. This completes assembly of the plug.

While the 300-ohm twin-lead used in home TV antenna installations is connected under terminal screws, the 75-ohm antenna distribution systems used institutionally require another type of connector.

Recent installations are using "Motorola" type connectors at the wall outlet. These are the plugs used with auto radio antennas. Once again, the cable is RG-59U.

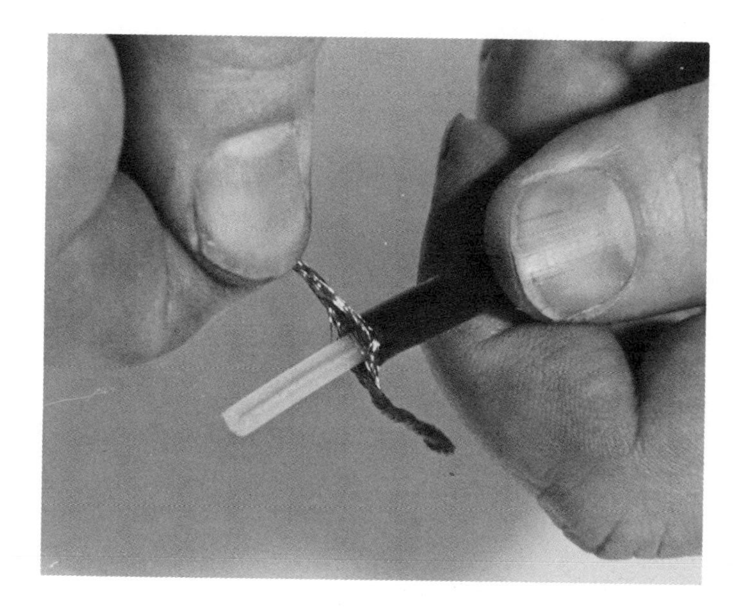

These plugs can be attached by cutting the insulation back about 1". Unbraid the shield and divide the strands into two equal clusters. Twist each cluster to keep the strands together.

Cut the center insulation back about 3/4", scrape and tin the wire.

Push the wire into the plug as far as it will go and solder the wire into the prong, heating from the outside of the pin while feeding solder into the end hole.

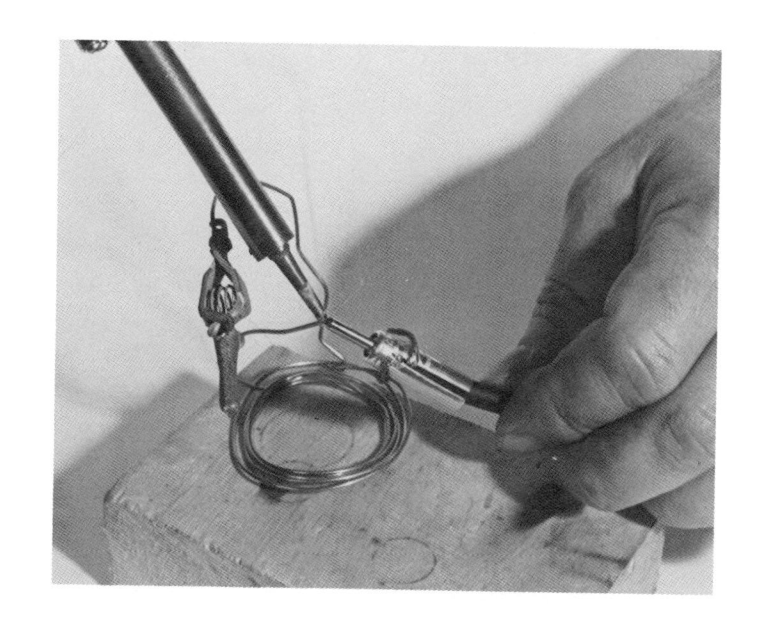

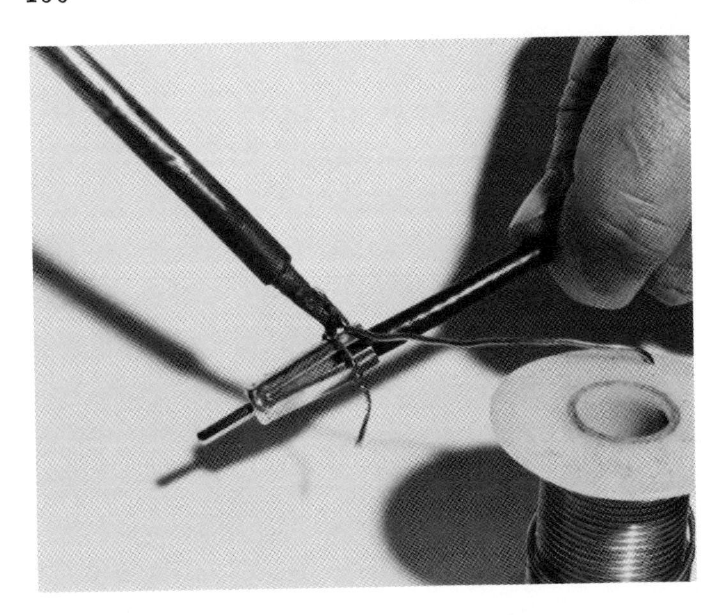

Pull the twisted strands of shield into the side slots and solder near the back of the connector (shield wires must not increase diameter of the plug or full insertion into the outlet will not be possible).

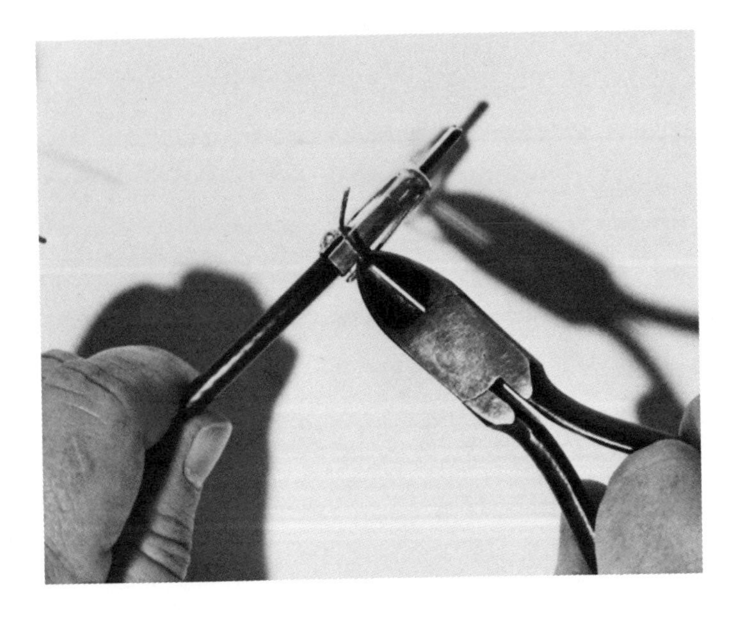

Older distribution systems and most television receivers will require an "F"-type fitting for the 75-ohm connection.

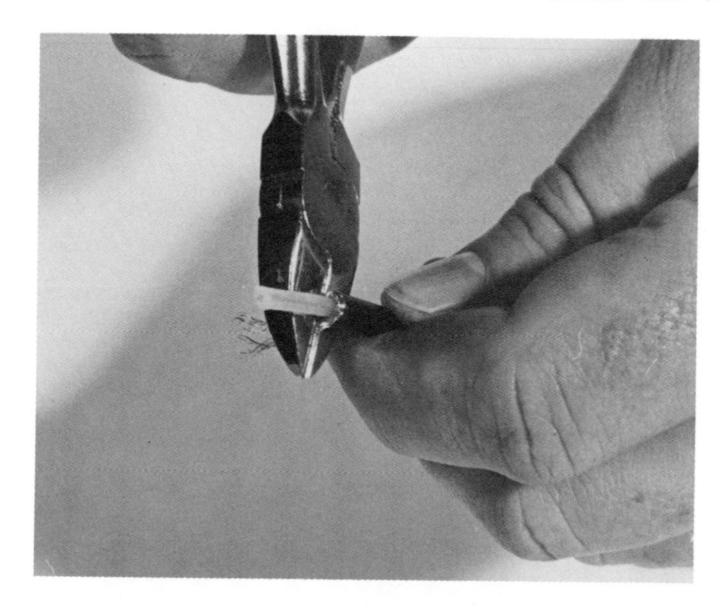

F-type connectors do not require solder. The outer jacket and shield are cut about 5/8" from the end. Cut the center insulation 1/16" from the first cut and remove the insulation.

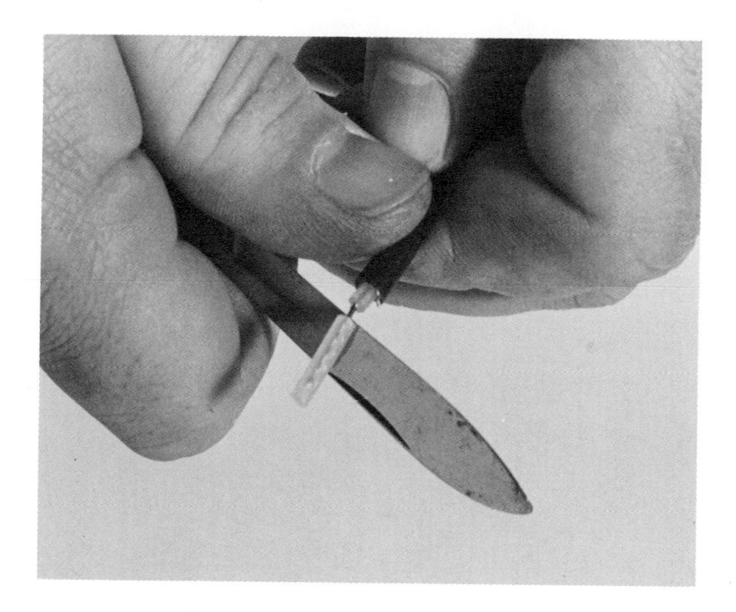

Put the small metal ring that comes with the connector over the cable. Slide the bare center wire through

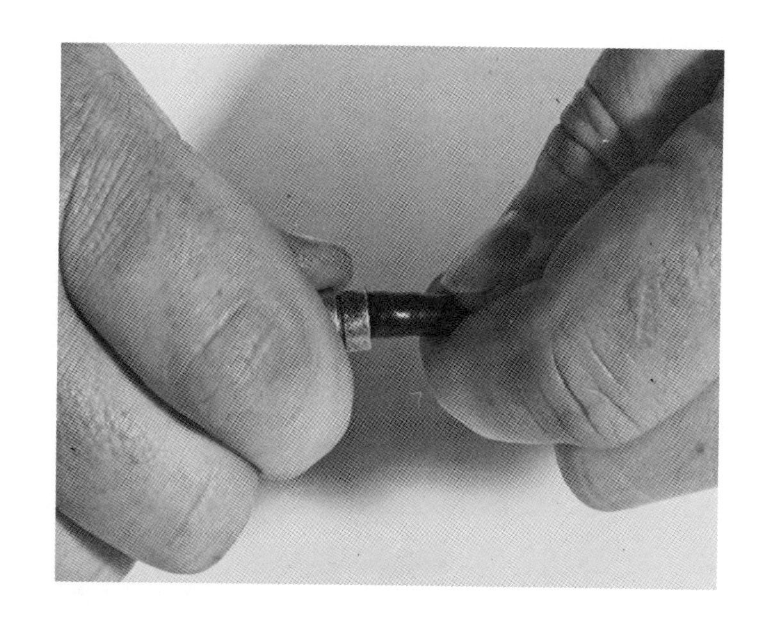

the connector body and, with considerable force, push the connector under the shield as far as you can. Pull the ring over the enlarged cable at the connector, and crimp the ring with a pair of pliers. Do not over-crimp the ring and break it.

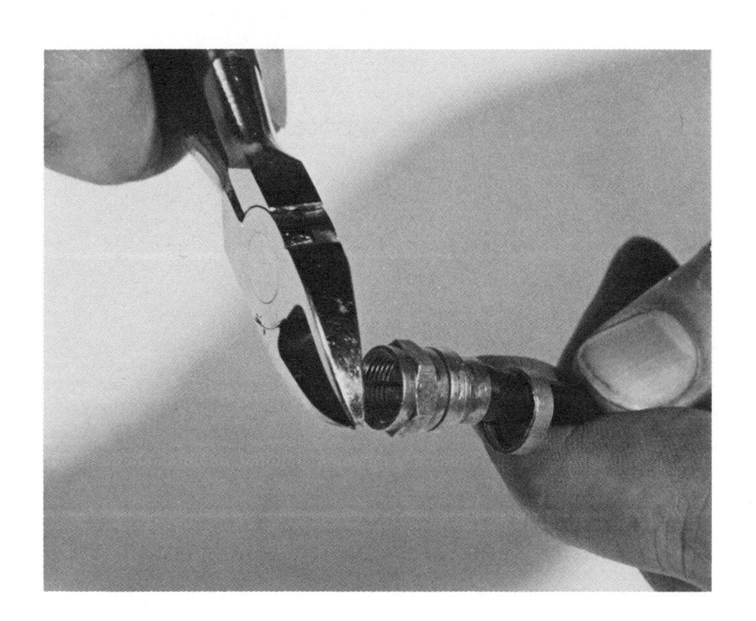

Cable Adapters and Impedance Matching Devices

The impossible dream of any large audiovisual operation is standardized connectors and impedances, assuring that any source can be plugged into any recorder or amplifier with the sure knowledge that grounds are maintained and that all components of systems are fully interchangeable to meet any contingency.

For countless reasons, including divided administration, design changes over the years, and the natural perversity of technical things, we usually find it necessary to acquire an array of adapters.

Probably the most common adapter is the one that converts the now almost standard 3-prong power plug to a 2-prong receptacle. These adapters are always found dangling on the cords, often adding so much bulk as to prevent storage of the cord in the bin provided. Some users, in frustration at never being able to find an adapter, wrap tape around both plug and adapter in a misguided effort to keep them together.

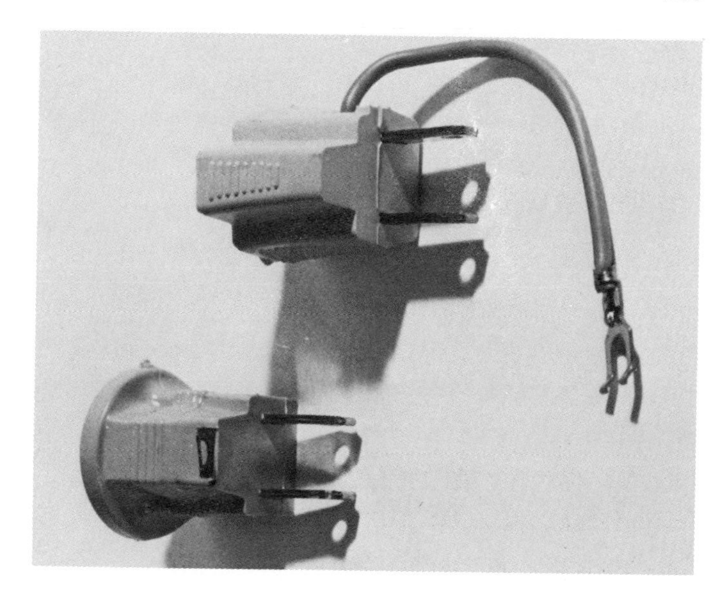

If you must use these adapters (they are a poor substitute for a properly grounded 3-contact receptacle), buy several boxes of them and install them permanently in the two contact outlets, attaching the green ground wire or ground lug to the screw in the center of the cover plate.

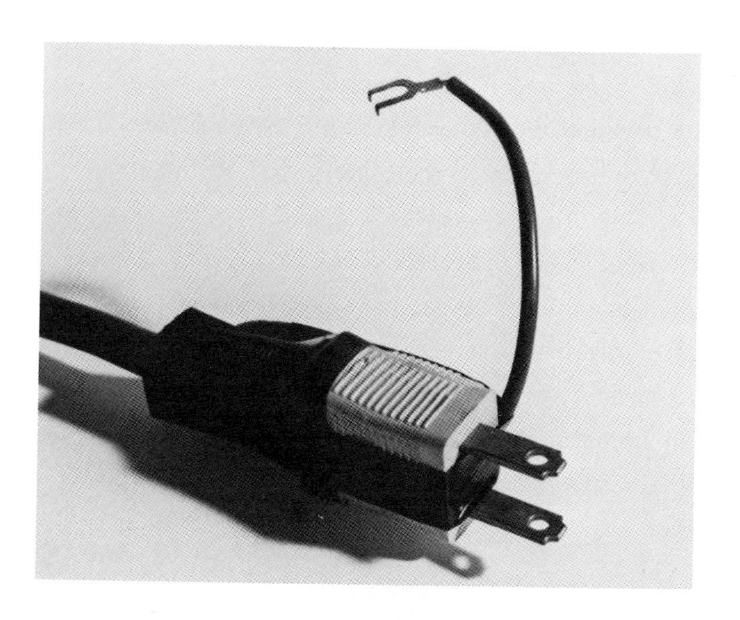

Adding to the complication is the adapter with one wide prong. Most sockets also have one wide slot. When properly wired in the building, this is part of a safety system used primarily with AC-DC devices. Lug-type adapters can be grounded to the center screw when plugged into one of the wall outlets, but not the other. Worst of all, wiring to the center screw is no real guarantee of safety because only a full conduit-encased wiring system has any chance of the boxes into which the screw threads being at ground potential.

Remember, power adapters are a great convenience and enable us to use 3-wire devices with older 2-wire wiring systems. But they defeat a very elaborate safety system designed to protect all of us from possibly fatal electrical shock. Ultimately, there is no substitute for a properly wired building with grounded 3-contact outlets.

AUDIO ADAPTERS generally change one size plug to another, allowing use of a 1/8" plug with a 1/4" jack, or converting an RCA pin plug to a 1/8" or 1/4" plug. There are also what might be called "gender reversing" adapters used with 3-wire microphone connectors. Most PA systems use a 3-pin male fitting in the stage apron, requiring a female connector on the microphone cord. Conversely, most actual recording equipment and the PA amplifiers themselves will have a female connector on the chassis, requiring a male plug on the microphone cable. To use the same microphones with both systems requires a male-to-male adapter or a female-to-female adapter. These are fairly expensive adapters, but a few of them on hand in a drawer can save a lot of time when you need to exchange microphones between systems in a hurry, or to meet some special multi-microphone need.

Another good practice is to keep a spool of double conductor microphone cable on hand and a small assortment of all the audio plugs and jacks. They are always useful for replacement, and short adapters can be made up with 6" of cord between plugs, as needed. This system takes more time than countless adapters, but sometimes the variety is so great that this is the most adaptable method in the long run.

Audio impedance matching can not be taken for granted, but it is a lot less critical with solid-state devices than it was with vacuum tubes. The most common indication of a mismatch is distortion of the sound, or inability to transfer the power that you expect. Sometimes impedance-matching transformers are made up similar to adapters, permitting insertion in an audio line without soldering or splicing. If you think you have an impedance-matching problem, it would be best to consult a PA system installer. They encounter and solve more of these problems than anyone else in the business, and they have, or have sources of, the special transformers.

TELEVISION AND VIDEO ADAPTERS usually involve getting from some kind of coaxial plug to another, or to the spade lugs that attach to the antenna screws. There are also double male and double female adapters for PL-259 type connectors. These permit extending coaxial camera cables and video distribution lines. Again, do not just assume that this can be done because an adapter is available. There are such things as line loss and un-tuned lengths that cause picture deterioration and ghosting. It's always worth a try, but the tries don't always succeed.

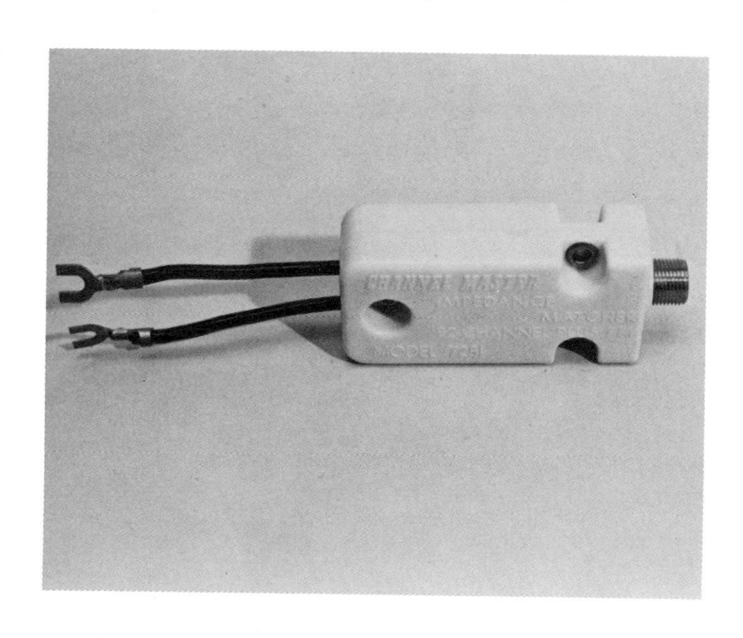

Institutional antenna systems present some unusual impedance-matching problems. The system is almost always 75-ohm, requiring RG-59U cable. But not all television receivers have a 75-ohm connector socket on the back. If you have to use the screw terminals, these are normally 300-ohm, and a 75-ohm to 300-ohm impedance-matching and connector to spade-lug device must be used. Nor is this the end of it.

Large building distribution systems in combination VHF/UHF broadcast areas will down-convert selected UHF channels to VHF channels for distribution in the building. All programs are thus available on the VHF channels from the 75-ohm cable. But where a complete system like this is not used, or where no building system is available and rabbit-ear antennas, UHF loop antennas, and other overwhelming space-age receiver-top designs are used, things often just don't match up. One popular video cassette recorder uses a coax socket for the VHF and screw terminals for the UHF antenna terminals. This is a design consistent with the kind of installation with which the VCR is intended to be used. But the user who expects to use a small combination VHF/UHF indoor antenna with 4-spade lugs at the end of the wire (all 300-ohm) will have to find a 300-ohm to 75-ohm spade lug to F-59 adapter in order to properly accomplish this otherwise simple connection.

Once again, outside help is recommended. Most companies selling this kind of equipment have similar problems with apartment house distribution systems (many of them install these too). If you get into one of these "nothing goes with anything" mix-ups, it is worth the price of a service call and the adapters and matching transformers they will sell you, just to get the whole thing working without all the trial and error those of us not in the business have to go through.

BIBLIOGRAPHY

Most manufacturers publish and sell very detailed maintenance manuals covering their equipment. Most of this information is far beyond the level of this book. The operators' and owners' manuals that come with the equipment often give excellent maintenance advice and have the advantage of direct applicability to the piece of equipment you actually have. These books should be filed carefully, and "only" copies should never be loaned. They should be available on a reference basis only.

A very good book of advice in the evaluation of audiovisual equipment is:

A-V Buyer's Guide: A User's Look at the Audio Visual World, by Dugan Laird. 2nd ed., 1974.

available from

National Audio-Visual Assn., Inc.,
3150 Spring St.,
Fairfax, VA 22030.

Cords, connectors, tools and other items of interest for audiovisual repair are shown in catalogs from:

Burstein-Applebee,
3199 Mercier St.,
Kansas City, MO 64111.

Media Masters, Inc.,
RD #5, Box 342,
East Stroudsburg, PA 18301.

These catalogs are free upon request. Do try to accumulate worthwhile orders (about $20) to minimize handling costs, both in your own organization and that of the supplier.

Both General Electric and GTE Sylvania publish exhaustive and up-to-date projection lamp replacement guides. Write and request a guide from:

General Electric Co.,
Lamp Business Div.,
Nela Park,
Cleveland, OH 44112.

or

GTE Sylvania,
Photolamp Marketing Headquarters,
100 Endicott St.,
Danvers, MA 01923.

A book of 150 pieces of copyright-free line drawings related to the audiovisual field and useful for handouts and bulletins is:

Media Clip Art.

available from

Visual Magic,
1223 S. 28th St.,
LaCrosse, WI 54601.

The line art headings for most of the sections of Part II of this book are from Media Clip Art and are used by permission.

A quick test of motion picture projector operation for effectiveness of repair or for purchase evaluation is the SMPTE Jiffy Test Film, P16-PP. Relatively inexpensive (write for current price), it is available from:

Society of Motion Picture & Television Engineers,
862 Scarsdale Ave.,
Scarsdale, NY 10683.

Most neoprene recorder and projector belts, plus replacement record player idler wheels and tires (write for catalog and measuring device) are available from:

Projector-Recorder Belt Corp.,
Box 176,
Whitewater, WI 53190.

ABOUT THE AUTHORS

GARY LARE holds the position of Director, Curriculum Resources Center and assistant professor of education at the University of Cincinnati. Dr. Lare has taught in the public schools and has been involved in educational media, in both teaching and administrative capacities, at various universities. He holds both a master's and a Ph. D. degree in educational media from Kent State University.

DON SCHROEDER is an Instructional Consultant (Media) with the Cincinnati Public Schools. He began his involvement with instructional media as a classroom projectionist in the St. Louis Public Schools, gained invaluable training and experience as a U. S. Navy aviation electronicsman, taught at the high school level, and completed a master's degree in Education (Instructional Technology) at Syracuse University. He has frequently taught the basic audiovisual media course at colleges and universities in the Cincinnati area.

INDEX